The Battle of Munda (45 BC)

The Battle of Munda (45 BC)

Pompey, Labienus and Caesar's Final Battle of the Third Roman Civil War

Gareth C. Sampson

Pen & Sword
MILITARY

First published in Great Britain in 2025 by
Pen & Sword Military
An imprint of Pen & Sword Books Limited
Yorkshire – Philadelphia

Copyright © Gareth C. Sampson 2025

ISBN 978 1 52679 370 6

The right of Gareth C. Sampson to be identified as
Author of this Work has been asserted by him in accordance
with the Copyright, Designs and Patents Act 1988.

A CIP catalogue record for this book is
available from the British Library.

All rights reserved. No part of this book may be reproduced, transmitted, downloaded, decompiled or reverse engineered in any form or by any means, electronic or mechanical including photocopying, recording or by any information storage and retrieval system, without permission from the Publisher in writing. No part of this book may be used or reproduced in any manner for the purpose of training artificial intelligence technologies or systems.

Typeset by Mac Style
Printed in the UK by CPI Group (UK) Ltd, Croydon, CR0 4YY.

The Publisher's authorised representative in the EU for product safety is Authorised Rep Compliance Ltd., Ground Floor, 71 Lower Baggot Street, Dublin D02 P593, Ireland.
www.arccompliance.com

For a complete list of Pen & Sword titles please contact

PEN & SWORD BOOKS LIMITED
47 Church Street, Barnsley, South Yorkshire, S70 2AS, England
E-mail: enquiries@pen-and-sword.co.uk
Website: www.pen-and-sword.co.uk
or
PEN AND SWORD BOOKS
1950 Lawrence Road, Havertown, PA 19083, USA
E-mail: uspen-and-sword@casematepublishers.com
Website: www.penandswordbooks.com

In loving memory of Geoff Sampson (1947–2019)

Contents

Acknowledgements ix
List of Illustrations x
Maps xi
Introduction: The Battle of Munda – Caesar's Last Battle and a Sense of Deja Vu xiv
Timeline xvii
Notes on Roman Names xxiv

Section I: The Third Civil War (49–46 BC)   1

Chapter 1   A Clash of Titans: The Battles of Dyrrhachium and Pharsalus (49–48 BC)   3

Chapter 2   Distraction, Recovery and Defeat in the Desert   18

Section II: Civil War Renewed – The Second Spanish Campaign   39

Chapter 3   The Never Ending War – Caesar and the New Pompeius   41

Chapter 4   The Renewed Civil War in Spain (46–45 BC)   63

Chapter 5   The Battle of Munda – Caesar's Final Battle (45 BC)   80

Section III: Rising from Defeat – The Pompeian Revival (45–44 BC)   99

Chapter 6   The Rise of Sextus Pompeius and the Pompeian Victories in Spain and Africa (45–44 BC)   101

Chapter 7   The Civil War in Syria and the Parthian Intervention (45–44 BC)   120

Section IV: Caesar The Great (Failure)?   129

Chapter 8   Caesar: The Five Month King   131

viii   The Battle of Munda (45 BC)

Appendix I: Civil War and Empire – The Illyrian Campaigns (45–44 BC)   153
Appendix II: Who's Who in the Third Roman Civil War (45 BC)   156
Appendix III: How Many Civil Wars?   167
Notes   173
Bibliography   180
Index   187

Acknowledgements

As always, the first and greatest acknowledgement must go out to my wonderful wife Alex, without whose support and understanding none of this would be possible. Next must come Thomas and Caitlin, who are a constant source of joy and anxiety.

Special thanks go out to my parents who always encouraged a love of books and learning (even if they did regret the house being filled with books). My father Geoff is no longer with us, and his loss is still felt by us all.

There are a number of individuals who through the years have inspired the love of Roman history in me and mentored me along the way; Michael Gracey at William Hulme, the late David Shotter at Lancaster, and Tim Cornell at Manchester. My heartfelt thanks go out to them all.

A shout goes out to the remaining members of the Manchester diaspora: Gary, Ian, Jason, Sam. Those were good days; we will not see their like again.

As always, my thanks go out to my editor Phil Sidnell, for his patience and understanding.

It must also be said that as an Independent Academic, the job of researching these works is being made easier by the internet, so Alumnus access to JSTOR (Manchester and Lancaster) and Academia.edu must get a round of thanks also.

List of Illustrations

Bust of Cn. Pompeius Magnus.
Bust of C. Iulius Caesar.
Bust of M. Tullius Cicero.
Bust of M. Antonius.
Bust of M. Porcius Cato.
Bust of Sextus Pompeius.
Coin of Metellus Scipio.
Coin issued by Caesar – Dictator for Life.
Coin issued by the Anti-Caesarian faction.
Coin of Octavius.
Bust of C. Octavius, as Augustus.
Theatre of Pompeius.

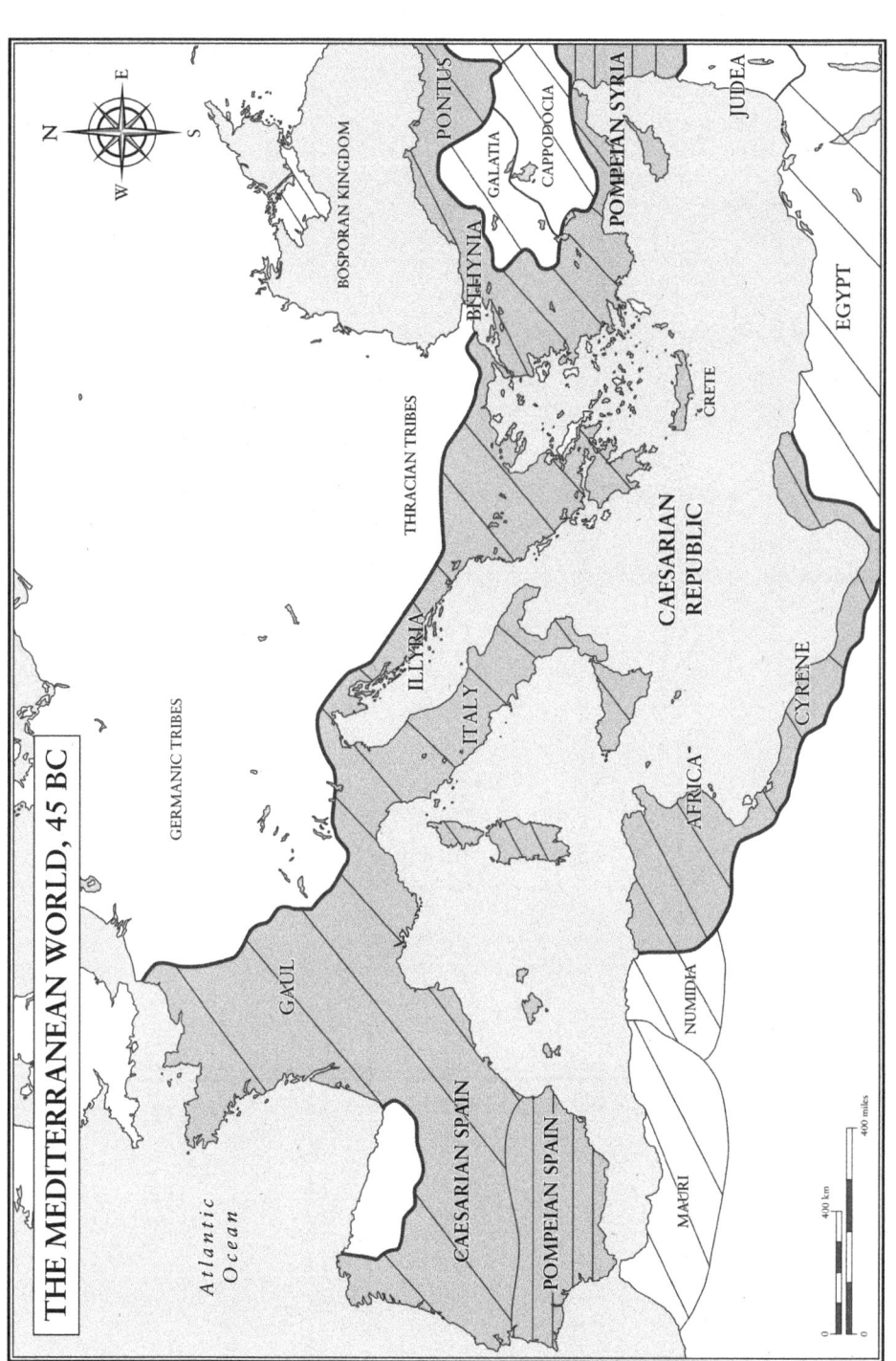

The Mediterranean World in 45 BC

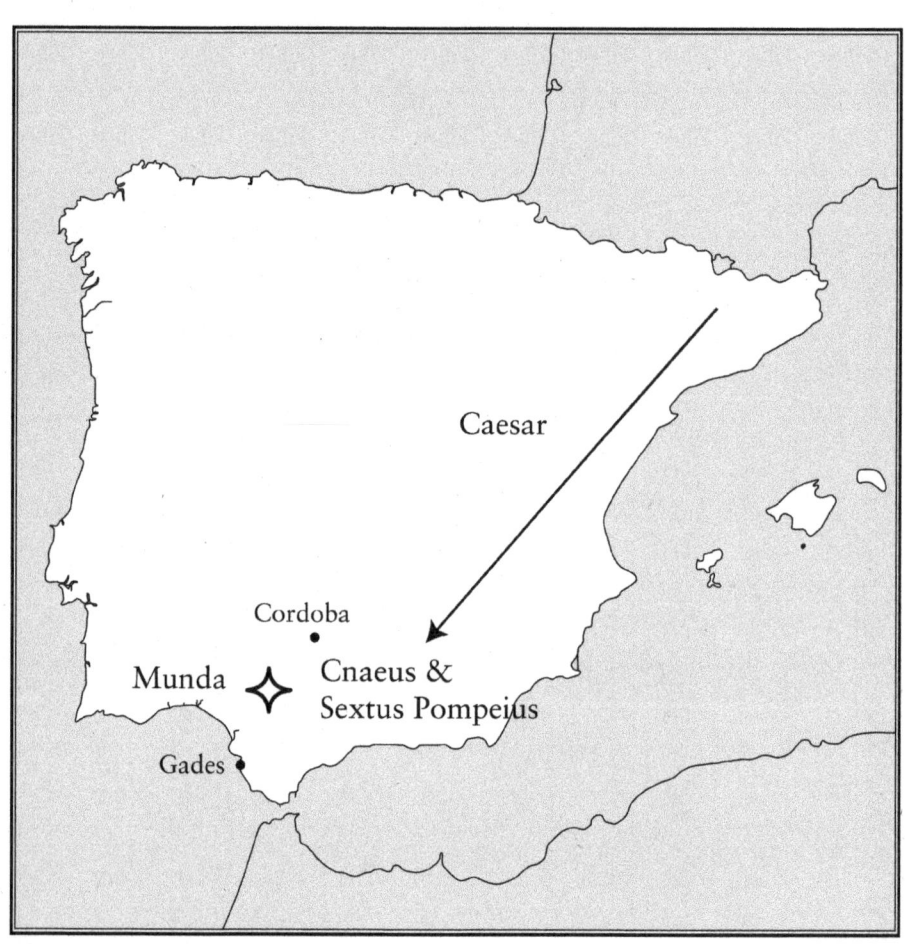

The Spanish Campaigns (45 BC)

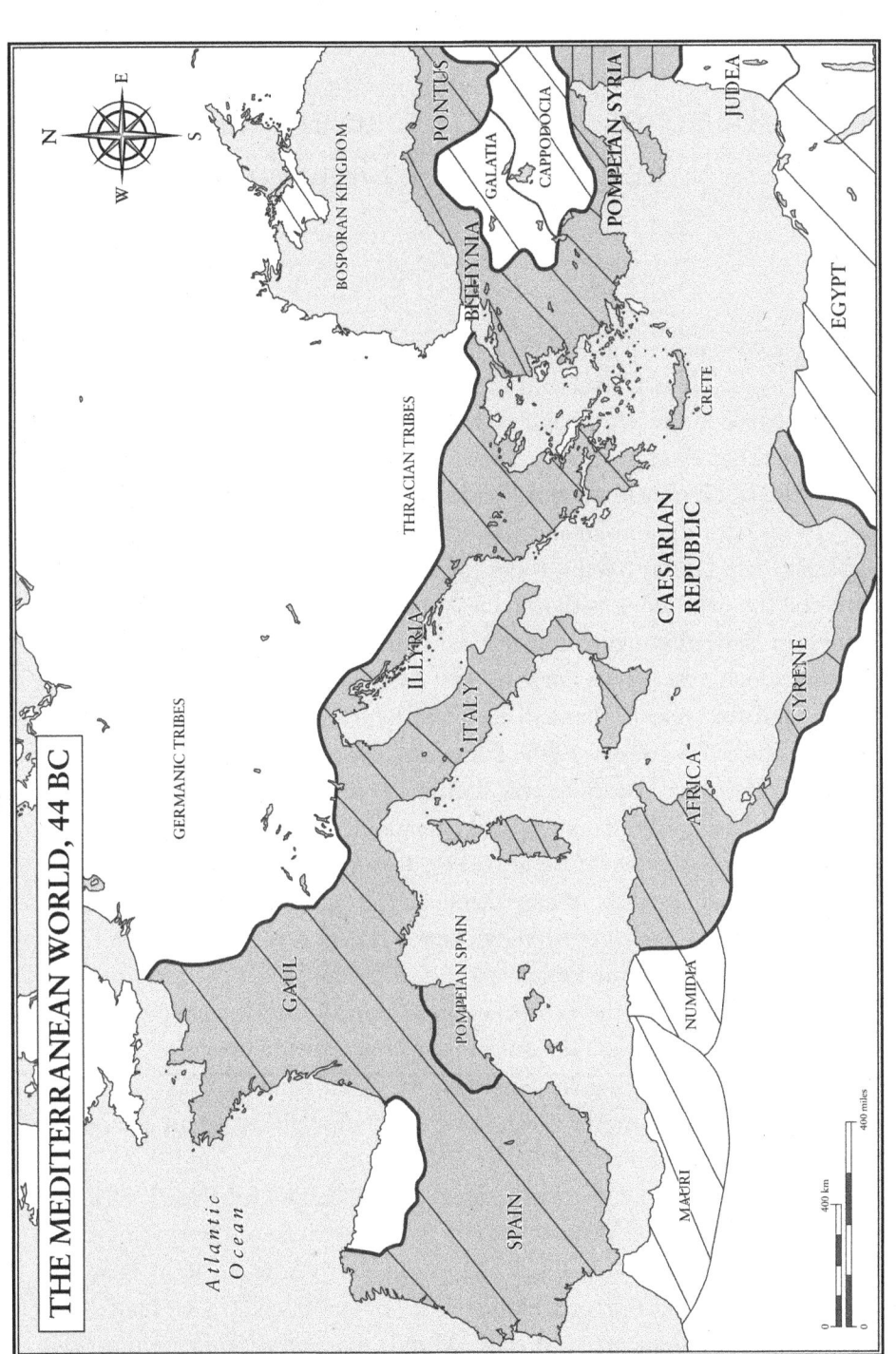

The Mediterranean World in 44 BC

Introduction

The Battle of Munda – Caesar's Last Battle and a Sense of Deja Vu

O n what now equates to 17 March 45 BC, two Roman armies, commanded by C. Iulius Caesar and Cn. Pompeius Magnus met on the field of battle in the fifth major battle of this latest Roman civil war. On the face of it, this may seem strange as two commanders of that name clashed at the Battles of Dyrrhachium and Pharsalus in Greece in 48 BC. Pompeius won the first and lost the second and was murdered shortly afterwards.

Yet the man Caesar faced was not the legendary Cn. Pompeius Magnus but his eldest son, who along with the title Magnus had inherited command of the Pompeian faction's struggle against Caesar, now into its fifth year. For Caesar this was a double case of déjà vu as his first civil war campaign was also fought in Spain, some four years earlier and ended with his victory at the Battle of Ilerda and the subsequent collapse of the Pompeian forces in the region. The fact that four years after that victory he was fighting to subdue Pompeian Spain again and facing the son of the man he had defeated three years previously attested to the lack of progress that Caesar had made in winning this Third Civil War.

This was made even more remarkable by the fact that this battle came less than a year after Caesar's crushing victory at Thapsus in North Africa (April 46 BC), which had seen the Pompeian armies destroyed and the majority of its leadership killed. Truly, the Pompeian opponents of Caesar were persistent to say the least. Thus, Caesar's dreams of following in the footsteps of Alexander the Great and conquering the East (the Parthian Empire in this case) had to be put on hold for another year, as he faced a fourth campaign against the renewed Pompeian threat.

The Battle of Munda forms the fourth great battle of the early period of this Third Roman Civil War (49–44 BC), following those of Dyrrhachium and Pharsalus in Greece (in 48 BC), and Thapsus in North Africa in 46 BC. It was the first clash between the next generation of the Pompeians and Caesar himself and most notably it was also the last clash. Munda marks the last battle that these two commanders fought, with Pompeius mirroring his more famous father and being murdered in the aftermath of the battle, whilst Caesar had just under a

The Battle of Munda – Caesar's Last Battle and a Sense of Deja Vu

year left before his fateful appointment in the Theatre of Pompeius in Rome on the Ides of March. Thus Munda was also C. Iulius Caesar's final battle.

If we are to believe Caesar himself, he considered this battle to be the closest he had come to defeat (conveniently overlooking the disastrous defeat at Dyrrhachium in 48 BC). This alone should raise the status of this battle from the obscurity that it has lain in; most commonly being dismissed as merely a mopping up operation against the last of the Pompeians. Yet as this series of works on the key battles of the Third Civil War has shown, modern historiography is still being stifled by the pro-Caesarian narrative that Caesar himself did much to foster. Fallacies such as this being 'Caesar's Civil War' or that it was won at Pharsalus, with Thapsus and Munda being nothing more than mopping-up operations, distort Roman history into the way that Caesar would have liked it to be viewed, not how it was.

As we have seen, it can be argued that Caesar was manipulated into starting the war by Pompeius, purely playing the role of a puppet being manipulated to secure the elevation of Pompeius to his long-desired role as Princeps of the Republic. That the puppet cut the strings with his victory at Pharsalus is undeniable, but this act was considered to be a shock to all but Caesar himself, and we must cast aside any notions that Caesar was obviously going to win. Any analysis of the campaign up to the defeat at Dyrrhachium shows both the strengths and the deficiencies of Caesar's military ability.

Likewise, any detailed analysis of the aftermath of Pharsalus shows that one battle did not bring Caesar victory in the Civil War, as shown by the Thapsan campaign, which again highlighted both his strengths and weaknesses. The very fact that the Pompeians came back for a third time in Spain in 45 BC, needing Caesar himself to take to the field, shows that Caesar could not convert battlefield victories into anything more than temporary dominance of the Republic.

It was perfectly possible for Caesar to have been defeated in either North Africa in 46 BC or Spain in 45 BC, and the close run nature of the latter should give modern spectators pause for thought. As will be demonstrated, even victory at Munda (Caesar's third of the major conflicts) did not bring him victory in the Civil War, with the Pompeian threat re-emerging yet again, arguably stronger than it had been before Caesar arrived in Spain in 45 BC. As Caesar arrived for his fateful meeting in the Theatre of Pompeius on 15 March 44 BC, Pompeian armies still controlled large parts of Spain and all of Syria. To say the Civil War ended at Munda is to buy into the Caesarian narrative, which could be seen to be nothing more than wishful thinking to those in Rome at the time.

Thus the Battle of Munda and its aftermath encapsulates the whole of Caesar's civil war career to date; another 'rabbit out of the hat' victory that brought him no closer to winning the overall war.

This present volume will seek to understand the continued revival of the Pompeian faction under the next generation, and the inability of Caesar to prevent it. It will analyse the campaigns in Spain that led to the battle, as well as the course of the battle itself, which even Caesar had to admit came close to ending his life and career. This work will seek to throw light on the brief, but near stellar career of Cn. Pompeius Magnus, the son of Caesar's old rival, who seemingly came closer than his father to defeating Caesar and 'restoring the Republic', and on the parallels to Caesar's own eventual successor: the first permanent Princeps of the Republic, Caesar Augustus.

This work will also seek to bring the spotlight onto the key military genius of Caesar's old lieutenant T. Labienus, who had done so much to try to defeat Caesar, first in the deserts of North Africa and finally in Spain itself. On both occasions his cautious hit and run tactics were eventually abandoned in favour of a supposedly more 'noble' set piece battle, with Munda proving to be the final one, bringing an end to the career that had latterly been so dedicated to defeating Caesar. Yet though defeated and killed, Labienus' tactical genius survived his demise and seemingly influenced the surviving Pompeian brother, Sextus, who emerged from the Mundan campaign as the new face of the Pompeian resistance, and one determined to learn the lessons of Munda.

Finally, this work will examine how Caesar wasted yet another victory in his chaotic five month rule in Rome, which brought about the rise of a new Anti-Caesarian faction, in the heart of Rome itself. Composed of both ex-Pompeians and disaffected Caesarians, on the Ides of March they accomplished what no Pompeian army had been able to do to date and brought the rebellion of Caesar to an end, ensuring he joined his former colleague and co-author of this latest civil war (Pompeius Magnus) in an untimely and ignominious death, both men being consumed by the forces they had unleashed.

Timeline

Timeline – Pre-Third Civil War (70–49 BC)

91–70: The First Roman Civil War
- 72   Pompeius victorious in Spain against Perperna
- 71   Crassus victorious in Italy against Spartacus
  Formation of the Duumvirate between Pompeius and Crassus
- 70   Consulship of Pompeius and Crassus - Constitutional Reforms Enacted
- 68   Pompeius is appointed to command the war against the Mediterranean Pirates
- 67   Pompeius is appointed to command the Eastern War against Armenia and Pontus
- 65   Crassus as Censor tries to annex Egypt
- 64   Pompeius annexes the remnants of the Seleucid Empire

63–62: The Second Civil War
- 62   Pompeius returns to Italy
- 60   Reformation of the Duumvirate between Pompeius and Crassus
- 59   Consulship of Caesar – passes Duumvirates' legislation
  Marriage of Pompeius to Caesar's daughter
- 58   Tribunate of Clodius – street violence in Rome
  Caesar launches the Romano-Gallic War
- 57   Tribunate of Milo – street violence escalates
- 56   Pompeius is appointed to take charge of Rome's grain supply
  Conference at Luca – Reformation of the Duumvirate
- 55   Consulships of Pompeius and Crassus
- 54   Crassus take command of the First Romano-Parthian War
- 53   Battle of Carrhae – Crassus defeated by the Parthian Surenas: killed in the retreat
  Violence in Rome prevents Curule elections
- 52   Murder of Clodius, burning of the Senate House
  Pompeius appointed Sole Consul, conducts judicial purge
- 50   Breakdown of the Relationship between Pompeius and Caesar

xviii The Battle of Munda (45 BC)

49   The Senate pass the *senatus consultum ultimum* against Caesar
        Caesar commits treason by invading Italy across the River Rubicon

Timeline - The Early Years of the Third Roman Civil War (49 BC)

49   **Italian Campaign**
        Caesar invades Italy
        Battle of Corfinium
        Pompeius withdraws to Brundisium
        Battle of Brundisium
        Pompeius withdraws across the Adriatic to Dyrrhachium
        Caesar seizes Rome

        Gallic Campaign
        Caesarian forces lay siege to Massilia
        Pompeian-Massilian fleet defeated twice off Massilia
        Massilia surrenders to Caesar after the Fall of Spain

        Spanish Campaign
        Caesarian forces cross Pyrenees and invade Pompeian Spain
        Battles of Ilerda – Caesar trapped in a deteriorating position
        Caesar convinces more Spanish Tribes to back him
        Pompeian forces decide to retreat and are routed by Caesar
        Caesar wins over the Pompeian army and allies in Southern Spain

        Western Mediterranean Campaigns
        Pompeian forces evacuate Sardinia after a local revolt, Caesarian forces occupy island
        Caesarian forces invade Sicily, Cato withdraws without a fight
        Caesarian forces invade Roman Africa
        Siege of Pompeian held Utica
        Caesarian victory at the Battle of Utica
        Caesarian army destroyed at the Battle of Bagradas River by Numidian forces
        Africa held by the Pompeians

        Adriatic and Illyrian Campaign
        Pompeian fleet defeat Caesarian fleet and ensure control of the Adriatic
        Caesarian army starved into surrender; Illyria conquered by Pompeians

Timeline – The Early Years of the Third Roman Civil War (48 BC)

48 **Epirote / Illyrian Campaign**
Caesar crosses the Adriatic and lands in Epirus, Pompeius moves to intercept
Pompeian Fleet cuts Caesar off; skirmishes between Pompeius and Caesar
Pompeian attack on Brundisium
Political disorder in Italy
Antonius crosses the Adriatic with Caesarian reinforcements
Caesar marches on the city of Dyrrhachium, Pompeius follows

Caesar lays siege to Pompeius' army in the Bay of Dyrrhachium
Failed Caesarian attack on the city of Dyrrhachium
Failed Pompeian attack on Caesar's siege lines
Pompeius breaks through Caesar's sieges lines to the south of the Bay
Caesar launches a counterattack on the Pompeian bridgehead
Pompeius launches a counterattack on Caesar
Caesarian army is routed, with thousands of casualties
Caesar regroups his army, breaks off the siege and marches inland to Macedonia, to join up with his other forces and face Metellus Scipio
Pompeius harasses Caesar's army south and then breaks off and marches inland

Greek/Macedonian/Thessalian campaigns
Metellus Scipio crosses into Thessaly from Asia Minor
Caesarian forces spread into Greece, Thessaly, and Macedonia
Metellus Scipio defeats Caesarian forces in Thessaly but is slowed down
Caesarian forces defeated in Macedonia by Faustus Sulla
Caesarian forces secure Aetolia and Acarnania
Pompeian forces fall back to the Isthmus of Corinth

Two Pompeian and two Caesarian armies converge on each other
Domitius' army avoids marching into Pompeian trap and turns southward
The two Caesarian armies unite
Metellus Scipio's army marches to Larissa and is joined by Pompeius
The two Pompeian armies unite
Caesar marches towards Pompeius and offers battle on the plain of Pharsalus

Battle of Pharsalus – Pompeius is defeated
Pompeius retreats eastwards by ship, followed by Caesar on land

xx   The Battle of Munda (45 BC)

   The bulk of the Pompeians retreat to Dyrrhachium and Corcyra and then try to hold the Peloponnese before retreating across the Mediterranean to Cyrene
   Cassius and his fleet fail to attack Caesar at the Bosphorus and defect, giving Caesar the ability to chase Pompeius effectively
   Pompeius chooses to land in Ptolemaic Egypt and is murdered on the beach
   Caesar becomes entangled in a Ptolemaic Civil War
   The Pompeians retreat to Roman Africa to regroup
   Pharnaces II invades Roman Asia Minor

Timeline - The Third Roman Civil War (47 BC)

47   **Epirote/Illyrian Campaign**
   Octavius continues Pompeian resistance
   Battle of Sunodium – Gabinius Defeated, later dies
   Vatinius crosses from Brundisium
   Battle of Tauris – Vatinius defeats Octavius

   Greek Campaign
   Possible continued Caesarian action against Megara

   Spanish Campaign
   Caesarian armies tied down by continued unrest

   Sardinian Campaign
   Pompeian fleet based in Sardinia raids Sicily

   Rome
   Armed clashes between the supporters of warring Tribunes
   Battle of the Forum – Roman army sent in to suppress violence

Timeline - The Third Roman Civil War (46 BC)

46   **North African Campaign – East**
   Caesar invade North Africa, fails to take Hadrumetum
   Battle of Ruspina – Pompeian victory
   Sieges of Leptis and Acylla
   Second Battle of Ruspina – Caesarian victory
   Battle of Uzitta – Pompeian victory

Battles of Leptis and Hadrumetum – Caesarian naval victory
Caesarian retreat to Aggar
Battle of Zeta – stalemate
Battle of Sarsura – Caesarian victory
Battle of Tegea – Caesarian victory
Battle of Thapsus – Total Caesarian victory

Numidian cavalry sack Utica
Afranius and Faustus Sulla retreat westwards towards the Mauri
Metellus Scipio take ship from Utica, Cato commits suicide
Pompeians surrender Utica
Battle of Hippo Regius – Metellus Scipio commits suicide
Juba and Petreius commit suicide
Numidia surrenders to Caesar, becomes a Roman province
L. Iulius Caesar is murdered by unknown assassins
Caesar returns to Rome and is appointed Dictator for ten years

North African Campaign – West
Pompeius Magnus leads an attack on the Mauri
Battle of Ascurum – Pompeius defeated
Maurian invasion of Numidia led by Sittius
Gaetulian Revolt
Sittius defeats Numidian army of Saburra
Sittius defeats Sulla and Afranius, who are subsequently murdered

Spanish Campaign
Pompeius Magnus leads a Pompeian expedition to Spain
Pompeius seizes the Balearic Islands
Pompeians inspire revolt in Farther Spain, Caesarian Governor driven out
Survivors from North Africa arrive
Pompeius invades Southern Spain, raising a new Pompeian army
Caesar sends general to reinforce Northern Spain
Caesar leaves Rome for Spain (again)

Syrian Campaign
Sex. Iulius Caesar is murdered by his own men in a Pompeian-inspired revolt
Caecilius Bassus seizes Syria and its legions in the name of Metellus Scipio

Timeline - The Third Roman Civil War (45 BC)

45 **Spanish Campaign**
Caesar arrives in Spain and links up with Fabius and Pedius
Didius defeats Attius Varus at sea in the Battle of Carteia
Battles of Corduba – Caesar attacks Sex. Pompeius, Cn. Pompeius relieves Corduba
Skirmishes between Cn. Pompeius and Caesar
Caesarian Siege of Ategua, city falls when inhabitants rise up
Battle of Soricaria – Caesarians defeat a Pompeian attack on their siege lines
Battle of Munda – a close run battle but Caesar emerged victorious
Survivors retreat to city of Munda – Caesarian siege
Caesar captures the Pompeian capital of Corduba – Suicide of Scapula
Caesar subdues Baetica
Cn. Pompeius' fleet is intercepted by Didius and destroyed, with Pompeius stranded
Pompeius killed in battle with Caesarian pursuers
Didius killed in battle with the Lusitanians
Munda falls to the Caesarians
Caesar leaves the province to return to Rome
Sextus Pompeius begin his renewed rebellion and captures much of Spain

Syrian Campaign
Caesarian forces from Asia Minor invade Pompeian Syria and besieges Bassus in Apamea
A Parthian force invades Syria and breaks the Caesarian siege

Timeline - The Third Roman Civil War (44 BC)

44 **Spanish Campaign**
Caesar appoints Asinius Pollio to the command against Sex. Pompeius
Pollio defeated in battle by Sex. Pompeius
Following Caesar's assassination, the Senate recall and pardon Sex. Pompeius

Syrian Campaign
Anti-Caesarian faction commanders arrive in Asia to take charge of the Caesarian forces, who attack the Pompeians
Bassus defeats the Caesarian/Anti-Caesarian forces

North African Campaign
Pompeian sponsored invasion of North Africa by Arabio, a Numidian Prince – both Bocchus and Sittius defeated and expelled from occupied Numidian territory

Notes on Roman Names

All Roman names in the following text will be given in their traditional form, including the abbreviated first name. Below is a list of the Roman first names referred to in the text and their abbreviations.

A.	Aulus.
Ap.	Appius
C.	Caius
Cn.	Cnaeus
D.	Decimus
F.	Faustus
K.	Kaeso
L.	Lucius
M.	Marcus
Mam.	Mamercus
P.	Publius
Q.	Quintus
Ser.	Servius
Sex.	Sextus
Sp.	Spurius
T.	Titus
Ti.	Tiberius

Section I

The Third Civil War (49–46 BC)

Chapter One

A Clash of Titans: The Battles of Dyrrhachium and Pharsalus (49–48 BC)

The Doomed Architects of the Third Civil War

In what equates now to January 49 BC, the Roman general C. Iulius Caesar marched one legion of his army across the now lost River Rubicon, the boundary between his province of Cisalpine Gaul and Roman Italy. It was a symbolic act which signified that Caesar had committed treason and crossed from his duly assigned province into Roman Italy under arms. Caesar was openly declaring himself an enemy of the Republic, and this act plunged the Republic into its Third Civil War (all within fifty years – see Appendix Three).

Whilst we are all aware of what Caesar did, there will never be agreement as to why he did it (and that can only be a good thing). There are in general two schools of thought on this. One is that he seized the initiative, with a characteristically bold move, wrong footing his political enemies in Rome, who were trying to end his political and military career. Feeling that his enemies, and in particular Cn. Pompeius Magnus, would not brook a political compromise, Caesar resorted to force of arms (as his then more famous uncle C. Marius had done during the First Civil War) to either force a political compromise or seize control of the Republic.

The other school of thought however has just the opposite; namely that Caesar, whose political acumen had always lagged behind his military ability, was just a pawn in the game of a master manipulator and that he had been forced into taking this risky action by someone who had left him with no choice and knew very well how he would react, and was not only ready for it, but banking on it. That someone, naturally, was Cn. Pompeius Magnus, a man who had been at the heart of the post-First Civil War Republic for over thirty years. For all that time he had been trying to occupy the position envisaged by his late mentor, L. Cornelius Sulla, namely Guardian, or Princeps, of the Republic. For the majority of those thirty years Pompeius had been thwarted, either by the combined efforts of the rest of the Senatorial oligarchy, or his long time rivalry with the only man in Rome who rivalled his political power; namely M. Licinius Crassus.

4 The Battle of Munda (45 BC)

Yet by 49 BC Crassus was dead, killed in Mesopotamia during the retreat from the disastrous (from the Roman point of view anyway) defeat at the Battle of Carrhae (in 53 BC). It was no coincidence that less than a year later, Pompeius was named sole Consul of Rome by the Senatorial oligarchy and asked to 'save the Republic', partially from events that he himself had caused (an irony lost on none of his contemporaries). Having shown the ruthless efficiency he was noted for, Pompeius did just that and had to either lay down this temporary role as Princeps or undo all the work he had accomplished to date.

Yet, as the First Civil War had shown (to both Pompeius and Caesar), if a temporary crisis brought about temporary sole rule, then a greater crisis would surely lead to a longer rule. To those ends, Pompeius, if we subscribe to this school of thought (as the current author does), engineered a political crisis that forced Caesar to either be humiliated politically and see the glory for his Gallic conquests stolen by another or be forced to act and become the 'enemy of the Republic' that Pompeius needed to defeat in order to secure him permanent elevation as the Princeps of the Republic.

As we know, ironically, Pompeius was the first man to be consumed by the chaos he (and Caesar) had unleashed, murdered on an Egyptian beach, following his defeat at the Battle of Pharsalus (in 48 BC), mirroring in death the man whose career he had for so long mirrored in life; his old sometime partner/sometime adversary, M. Licinius Crassus. Though the first notable victim of the forces he had done so much to unleash he was hardly the last.

Caesar was next man to seize his mantle, unwilling, or unable, to relinquish the role of Princeps that his military victories had brought. Yet despite this elevation and a string of battlefield victories across Spain, Greece, Egypt, Asia Minor and Africa, Caesar was unable to bring an end to the civil war which he had unleashed in January 49 BC, with each victory seemingly taking him further away from the peace that he wanted to restore, which in turn would allow him to concentrate on his dreams of 'Alexandrian' conquest in the East. Each victory reduced the strength of his enemies, but not their will to continue their opposition. A crushing victory over the combined factions that comprised the Pompeian alliance in the deserts of North Africa at the Battle of Thapsus in 46 BC, and its bloody aftermath, saw the opposition recover and carve out a new stronghold in Spain, which had fallen to Caesar in 49 BC, in less than a year.

Thus the scene was set for Caesar to fight a fourth civil war campaign, which saw him fight what was to be his last battle, against the son of Pompeius and his old lieutenant Labienus, at Munda in Spain in 45 BC, in the hope (doomed as it turned out to be) that he could bring the civil war to an end and concentrate on his plans for the future. Yet his career too ended in fatal disappointment, with another battlefield victory again not only failing to bring the civil war to an end,

A Clash of Titans: The Battles of Dyrrhachium and Pharsalus (49–48 BC)

but in turn leading to the Ides of March in 44 BC, when Caesar joined his fellow civil war architect (and former son in law) Pompeius, in being unexpectedly murdered by men he considered to be his allies. The civil war that these two men unleashed, not only consumed both men, but raged for nearly another two decades until Caesar's adopted son was the last man standing and learnt the lesson of both men's fates, to create the position that they both aspired to: a secure Principate over the Republic.

The First Year – Civil War by Proxy

In order to understand what turned out to be Caesar's final civil war campaign in Spain and his final battle at Munda, the reader needs a grounding in the campaigns and events that preceded it. These have naturally been covered in detail elsewhere,[1] but a refresher will be of benefit.

The Italian Campaigns (49 BC)

Having been forced to invade Italy, Caesar needed to make sure that it was a short campaign and a quick victory. Holding only Gaul and Illyria, Caesar needed to stop Pompeius from being able to tap into the resources of the wider Republic, especially in Spain and the Near and Middle East. Likewise, Pompeius knew that Caesar needed a short sharp victory, and took steps to ensure that he was denied one. As discussed, Pompeius' plan to be established as Rome's permanent Princeps required a grave crisis and one that was not over too quickly. If Caesar was expecting Pompeius to face him in Italy and stop him marching on Rome, then he was sorely mistaken, as were the Senate.

Instead, Pompeius made only token efforts at slowing Caesar down before evacuating his legions and supporters to Greece. There are two schools of thought as to this tactic, determined by how one views Pompeius: as a political genius or as a bungler. If we were to take the view that Pompeius did not realise that Caesar would invade Italy, then he was clearly taken by surprise and did not have enough time to march north to meet him, with the only legionary forces available in Italy being two legions in the south, which had been sent to him by Caesar anyway and whose loyalty was therefore suspect.

However, if we accept that Pompeius manipulated Caesar into attacking Italy, then he wasn't taken by surprise and deliberately failed to defend Rome. If Caesar was able to march on Rome, then images of the brutal sack of 87 BC (undertaken by Caesar's uncle Marius) would be conjured up and the Senatorial oligarchy, who were neither pro-Caesar, nor pro-Pompeius (which would have been the majority of them), would be forced to come off the fence and choose a side, with the majority likely to side with the 'defender of the Republic' rather than its attacker.

Crossing the Rubicon has far more impact today than it would have in 49 BC, and the situation could have been defused by negotiations, again which Pompeius only indulged in a tokenistic effort. Yet if Caesar took Rome, then there would be no turning back. Thus Pompeius sacrificed Rome to Caesar but got the backing of the majority of the Senate, who came with him.

Thus Pompeius slowly organised the evacuation of Italy, to ensure it did not look like flight, a task which was easily done given his naval control of the Adriatic. There were two minor battles fought in Italy; the first came at Corfinium between the forces of Caesar and those of L. Domitius Ahenobarbus (Cos. 54 BC), the man the Senate had appointed to replace Caesar as commander in Gaul. With only a scratch force Ahenobarbus was able to slow Caesar down, but when Pompeius refused to send reinforcements (as it did not suit his masterplan), his army revolted and turned to Caesar.

The second battle came at Brundisium, the embarkation point for travel to Greece and Illyria. When hearing of Pompeius' plan, Caesar naturally ignored the undefended Rome and headed directly to Brundisium to try and stop his enemies from escaping and thus ensuring a long civil war. Again Pompeius could have evacuated the city in time, but chose to wait until Caesar arrived, showing his defence of the Republic and there was a brief siege, with Pompeius theatrically ensuring he was one of the last to leave.

Thus again Caesar was gifted control of another city, theoretically the embarkation point to Greece, but in reality, faced a Pompeian-controlled Adriatic, preventing him from giving chase. Even though Caesar theoretically had command of Illyria on the far side of the Adriatic, the Pompeian navy held sway between the two. Thus Caesar had control of Rome and what was left of the Senate and the Assemblies to give him tokenistic legitimacy. However, with the bulk of the Roman world controlled by Pompeius and the Original Senate sitting in Thessalonica, Caesar was still a rebel.

Having failed to bring the war to a swift conclusion, Caesar now faced a tactical quandary, and one which was to be repeated in the years which followed; namely which direction to campaign in. His forces only controlled Gaul (recently conquered) to the North and Italy itself. To the West lay the two Spanish provinces, a Pompeian heartland, along with seven legions threatening his flank. To the south lay Sicily and North Africa, Pompeian controlled provinces which were the perfect springboard to launch naval assaults on Italy. To the East lay the main prize, Pompeius himself, who would need time to assemble a large army to fight Caesar. Once assembled he could then either re-invade Italy or let Caesar cross to Greece and use that as a battleground, and thus inflict less damage on Italy (as had happened in the First Civil War, which took decades to recover from).

Though Caesar had a toehold in Greece, in the shape of the province of Illyria, he did not have the ability to cross the Adriatic unchallenged and his revolt could have ended in such a crossing. The land route to Illyria was not under Roman control and would involve fighting the native tribes of the region first. Thus Caesar faced a dilemma: either a quick bold dash across the Adriatic and challenge Pompeius before he had the chance to build his army, or consolidate his position in the Western Republic. Atypically, on this occasion Caesar chose consolidation, hoping that Caesarian-controlled Illyria could hold out in his absence, whilst eliminated the Pompeian threats to the West and South. Naturally Caesar chose the grander campaign for himself, to defeat the Pompeian threat from Spain, leaving subordinates to handle the southern campaigns in Sicily and North Africa.

The Sardinian and Sicilian Campaigns

Initially, the Caesarian force met with success. The inhabitants of Sardinia having no wish to become a battlefield, revolted against the Pompeian garrison and thus it was evacuated. Sicily should have been a tougher proposition, with heavily defended cities such as Syracuse, sufficient Pompeian forces and a good food supply, all supported by the Pompeian fleets. Unfortunately for the Pompeians, overall command fell to M. Porcius Cato, whose military ability was of questionable quality and whose Republican 'virtues' apparently did not extend to actually fighting his opponents in a civil war.

Thus Cato ordered the evacuation of Sicily without a shot being fired and retreated to Greece, gifting Caesar a major strategic asset, costing the Pompeians an important base from which to threaten Italy and opening up a Caesarian attack on North Africa. Such an act quite rightly appalled his Pompeian allies, and unsurprisingly Cato saw no further active fighting in the civil war campaigns and can usually be found in charge of garrisoning cities (Dyrrhachium and then Utica).

The North African Campaign

With the swift capture of Sicily, the way was now open for the Caesarians to invade North Africa, with its one Roman province (the coastal region that had been the rump of the Carthaginian Empire), the bulk of North Africa being the Kingdom of Numidia, a long-standing Roman ally (and occasional enemy). The initial Caesarian assault looked like it too would have been a quick success, with the Caesarians defeating the small Pompeian garrison at the Battle of Utica and besieging the capital city.

Unfortunately for the Caesarians, command of the Pompeian garrison had been seized by P. Attius Varus, who had commanded the province before. He used his contacts at the royal Numidian court to convince the Numidian King (Juba I) to intervene on the side of the 'legitimate' Roman government. For a variety of reasons – personal dislike of Caesar, long standing ties with Pompeius dating back to the First Civil War, and an ambition to be on the winning side – Juba threw the weight of the Numidian Kingdom behind Varus and sent a relief army to the Pompeians.

Massively outnumbered, a fact that the Caesarian commander C. Scribonius Curio did not immediately realise, the Caesarians broke off from the siege of Utica to fight the arriving Numidian relief army but fell for a feint (a retreating Numidian advance guard) and blundered straight into the whole Numidian army with a predictable outcome, a Caesarian massacre. With only a handful of Caesarian survivors reaching their ships to sail away from Africa, the Pompeians had their first victory and Caesar his first defeat.

Though a small victory at the time, the importance of this victory only became apparent after the defeats in Greece in 48 BC, allowing the Pompeians not only a safe haven, but one supported by one of the richest kingdoms in the Mediterranean, providing them with the chance to rebuild (see Chapter Two). In the meantime, Attius Varus and Juba ruled North Africa in a Romano-Numidian alliance, with quasi-independence from both warring parties.

The Spanish Campaign

The bulk of the Pompeian forces in the Western Republic however lay in Spain, a noted Pompeian stronghold. Not only had Pompeius re-conquered the region during the First Civil War (in the 70s BC), but he had seized military control of the two Roman provinces in 55 BC with a five-year military command and the right to govern through legates. Thus the Pompeians had had five years to prepare for any forthcoming civil war. The two main Pompeian commanders were both experienced military men, L. Afranius (Cos. 60 BC), a long standing Pompeian deputy, and M. Petreius, and between them they had seven legions.

When Pompeius learnt that Caesar had marched on Spain, he would have been delighted as he would have believed that this move would bring him the time he needed to assemble his grand army, drawing on all the resources of the Eastern Republic. Thus Afranius and Petreius would have had orders to tie Caesar down in Spain for the rest of the year and into the subsequent one, buying Pompeius the time he needed.

A Clash of Titans: The Battles of Dyrrhachium and Pharsalus (49–48 BC)

Initially Afranius and Petreius successfully followed this strategy, with the fighting between the two armies consisting of skirmishes and ambushes, centred on the city of Ilerda. At one point they even seemed to have Caesar ripe for defeat, but failed to press home their advantage, no doubt aware that their master reserved the right to defeat Caesar for himself rather than having the civil war ending prematurely in Spain. It was a failure that would come back to haunt them, and Caesar used this respite to dig himself out of the situation which his rashness had got him into (another theme that repeats itself over the course of the subsequent campaigns).

With Caesar's position at Ilerda strengthening, Afranius and Petreius made what was to be a disastrous decision to abandon their position and retreat further into the Spanish interior, and thus winter down and drag the campaign into its desired second year. Unfortunately (for them anyway), whilst this plan looked good on paper (papyrus), they failed to account for the fact that Caesar needed the campaign wrapped up that year and would not simply allow them the luxury of a staged withdrawal. Thus the Caesarian army chased down the retreating Pompeian one and an orderly retreat became a rout, with a harried and starving Pompeian army being forced to surrender.

Thus, in just one summer season of campaigning, Caesar had defeated the Pompeian forces in Spain and removed them as a threat (temporarily at least – another recurring theme). Though again, seen as a prelude to the main event in Greece the following year, this defeat proved to be a hammer blow to the overall Pompeian strategy, as it freed Caesar up to return to Italy that year and then storm a crossing into Greece to challenge Pompeius before he had had sufficient time to assemble and train his grand army. This was a key factor behind the subsequent loss at Pharsalus the following year.

Yet Caesar's victory in Spain also came back to haunt him, as defeating the Pompeian army was not the same as securing the Roman provinces in Spain to the Caesarian cause. Naturally, with no active Pompeian forces, the cities and tribes of the region paid homage to Caesar, which they promptly cast aside when he left for Italy. As we will see, Pompeian revolts in Spain in 48 BC and again in 46–44 BC had a major impact on Caesar's strategies and the course of the civil war, which would see Caesar repeating this campaign in 45 BC.

The Gallic Campaign

A side show to the Spanish campaign came in the form of the Gallic campaign, which was nothing more than the siege of Massilia, the oldest and most powerful Greek city in Gaul. Key to the route from Italy to Spain, and a long standing Roman ally, Massilia chose to buck the trend of remaining neutral when faced with a Roman army and declared for Pompeius and the (Original) Senate. Unwilling to leave an active opponent cutting off his supply and communication route from Italy, Caesar had no choice but to have his commanders lay siege to the city.

The subsequent siege continued throughout Caesar's Spanish campaigns and even saw Pompeian naval reinforcements being sent from Greece, though they were subsequently defeated by the Caesarians. The siege only ended when news reached the Massiliotes that the Pompeian armies in Spain had surrendered, and thus with no hope of Pompeian relief they agreed to a negotiated surrender, giving Caesar nominal control of the whole Western Republic (aside from North Africa).

The Illyrian Campaigns

Yet for Pompeius the campaigns in the Western Republic were a side show, one which would hopefully slow Caesar down, but which were not worth investing any more forces in, hence the scant reinforcements sent west (just a few ships to Massilia). For Pompeius the key strategic objective was the Roman province of Illyria, which was nominally controlled by Caesarian forces, forming a Caesarian bridgehead on the eastern shore of the Adriatic, and thus clearly needed to be eliminated. It is often overlooked that Caesar's military commands were not just the two Gallic provinces (Cisalpine and Transalpine), but also Illyria. This gave him a crucial bridgehead in the Pompeian East and one which, if he could overcome the Pompeian navy in-between, would act as a staging post for an invasion of the East.

Thus it was critical for Pompeius' plans that this bridgehead be eliminated before Caesar returned from Spain. This marked the Illyrian campaign as Pompeius' chief concern for 49 BC and the one that saw the bulk of the fighting for the Eastern Pompeian forces. It is worth noting that there are no details of this campaign in Caesar's own commentary of the civil war (for obvious reasons). Whilst the defeat in North Africa receives a full account, particularly drawing attention to the role of the 'perfidious' Numidians (justifying their later annexation), there is no such account of the Illyrian campaigns.

This is clearly thanks to it being the wrong type of defeat. Africa was a sideshow, and a 'brave' Roman army was wiped out by the 'treacherous' actions of a foreign army, and thus became a heroic defeat. The losses the Caesarians suffered in Illyria, however, were to the Pompeians themselves and were a significant setback to Caesar's plans.

Details are few and have to be compiled from the other surviving sources, but the result was clear; a total Pompeian victory, with the Caesarian land forces under C. Antonius (brother of Marcus) being captured and the only Caesarian fleet in the Adriatic, commanded by P. Cornelius Dolabella, being driven out into the Mediterranean. This gave Pompeius uncontested control of the Adriatic and removed the platform for a Caesarian crossing, thus fitting into Pompeius' masterplan for buying time to assemble and train his new grand army.

Thus, on the face of it, the year ended in a stalemate, with Caesarian victories in Sicily and Spain and Pompeian ones in Africa and Illyria. Caesar had nominal control of the bulk of the Western Republic, Pompeius solid control of the Eastern one, each with a fully functioning Roman Senate, electing magistratures and issuing commands to the wider Mediterranean world in the name of Rome. Caesar returned to Rome at the end of 49 BC, and had the choice of forcing a crossing to Greece or defending Italy. Pompeius spent the winter waiting for his eastern reinforcements under Metellus Scipio (his father-in-law), which were wintering in Asia Minor, waiting to cross the Bosphorus into Thrace.

The Second Year (48 BC) – The Clash of Titans

The Illyrian/Epirote Campaigns

Caesar too would have spent the winter pondering the problem of Metellus Scipio and his eastern army. Once they reached Pompeius and were integrated with his other legions, then Pompeius would have a formidable army and would put his own battle plan into action. Therefore, until they did so there was a window of opportunity. Caesar's victories in Spain had brought him the time to exploit this opportunity, but it involved a considerable risk. Between him and Pompeius lay the Adriatic, which was now completely controlled by the Pompeians since the elimination of his garrison in Illyria. Even if he could force his way past or evade the Pompeian navy, there was the considerable risk that he would be trapped in Epirus/Illyria, facing two large Pompeian armies ahead of him and only the Pompeian controlled Adriatic behind him.

However, equally there was the danger of waiting too long, as Caesar was well aware that time was against him and the longer Pompeius had to receive his eastern reinforcements, then the greater the chances were that Caesar would be defeated. With that in mind, Caesar launched a risky dash across the Adriatic, evaded the Pompeian fleet and successfully landed on the Illyrian coastline. Pompeius naturally reacted by raising his forces from their winter quarters and set off to pin Caesar down before he broke out of his bridgehead. At the same time, the Pompeian navy received orders to attack Brundisium and, at all costs, prevent any further Caesarian reinforcements from crossing to relieve Caesar.

In this, they failed quite spectacularly as M. Antonius was able to cross with Caesarian reinforcements and relieve the pressure on Caesar. Skirmishes between

12   The Battle of Munda (45 BC)

Caesar and Pompeius followed, but Pompeius stuck to a strategy of avoiding a set piece battle until he had the eastern army of Metellus Scipio to support him.

The Battle of Dyrrhachium – Caesar Defeated

Caesar clearly needed to force Pompeius out of these 'Fabian tactics',[2] and in an effort to do so moved to attack the Pompeian regional capital of Dyrrhachium (now Durres in Albania). Not only was this city the largest port on the eastern Adriatic, but it was the Pompeian supply base for Epirus and the start of the Via Egnatia, the Roman road that cut across Greece and Macedonia and connected to the Bosphorus, and thus the road that Metellus Scipio would be taking.

Clearly Pompeius could not allow such a prize to fall into Caesar's hands, but not only did he not fall into Caesar's trap (and give battle) but he reached the city first, leaving Caesar to face both the city (with its garrison) and Pompeius' army. Not being able to force a battle, and having dispatched a force to slow down Metellus, Caesar then made a tactical error and sacrificed his speed and mobility by trying to lay siege to both the city and, more importantly, Pompeius' army now trapped in the bay.

What followed was one of the oddest 'battles' in Roman history, with two Roman armies engaging in what can only be described as several months' worth (April to July) of trench warfare in the hills that surrounded the bay. Each side fought for the high ground, laid down fortifications and strong points, and launched sallies against the opposition's defences. Pompeius' forces were technically trapped by the Caesarian army, but they held the city and the bay itself and, more importantly, had total naval control of the Adriatic, meaning that they could be resupplied by sea. Pompeius, waiting for Scipio's eastern army, could afford to wait, but Caesar could not.

Several Caesarian attempts were made to end the stalemate, the most notable being when Caesar launched a sneak attack on the city of Dyrrhachium itself aided by 'sympathisers' within the city. However, these sympathisers were nothing of the sort and Caesar walked into a trap, which he barely escaped from with his life. A Pompeian counterattack on the Caesarian lines of defence was then barely repulsed.

The end came, not with the arrival of Metellus Scipio, whose advance had been delayed by the blocking Caesarian force, but by a successful Pompeian assault on the southernmost point of Caesar's line of defences. A successful Pompeian bridgehead was established, and Caesar rushed to counterattack it with his usual boldness. On this occasion however, the tactic backfired, as Pompeius reacted swiftly and counterattacked himself, cutting Caesar off from his main army. Overwhelmed, Caesar's forces broke, with several thousand casualties and Caesar was forced to retreat.

The outcome of the battle was clear (despite later Caesarian attempts to play it down): Caesar had been defeated, both on the day and in the wider battle. The loss of the south meant that his siege lines had been broken and were now pointless, and Caesar was forced to retreat towards Macedonia, shaking off the Pompeian pursuit to link up with his second army and try to defeat Metellus before he could link up with Pompeius.

The Battle of Pharsalus – Pompeius Defeated

Thus the focus spread into Macedonia and Greece proper, with four different armies searching for each other: Pompeius and Caesar heading eastwards, and Metellus Scipio and the second Caesarian army marching westwards. It was a strangely balletic period, with four armies looking for their counterparts whilst simultaneously trying to avoid the opposition. In the end and with some excellent scouting on the part of all four armies, the two Pompeian and two Caesarian armies avoided their opponents and met up with their counterparts, making the possible scenarios and outcomes far simpler.

Having failed to prevent the two Pompeian armies from combining (another tactical failure) and being stuck in what was ostensibly Pompeian held territory and facing a far larger Pompeian army, Caesar's options had been reduced to two: fight or flight. Again Caesar chose to gamble and went on the offensive, judging that Pompeius would now have to give battle, in front of all the Senate and his eastern allies; the moment he had been waiting for, for over a year.

Yet Caesar's gamble was based on three solid foundations. Firstly, the two Pompeian armies had only just joined together and had not had time to integrate, being of multi-ethic composition with a huge variety of fighting styles: from legionaries to eastern cavalry, archers, and slingers. This meant that Pompeius would have to rely on sheer weight of numbers and his two clear advantages, cavalry and range weaponry.

Secondly, Caesar had been training a specialist element of his army in a new anti-cavalry fighting style, by combining his own legionaries with cavalry in a mixed unit, designed to combat Pompeian cavalry. These tactics had been used on several occasions against Pompeius' advance guard and had met with success. The only gamble was whether these tactics would work on a far larger scale?

The third factor was location, and Caesar chose his ground well, anchoring his left wing against a large river (Enipeus), meaning Pompeius could only utilise his cavalry on one wing in a flanking move, not both, and thus Caesar could focus his efforts on just that one wing; his right, Pompeius' left.

14　The Battle of Munda (45 BC)

The subsequent battle did indeed turn on that right wing, and Pompeius followed the logical tactic of deploying his massive cavalry advantage on that one wing. Caesar, however, had not deployed in the usual three battle lines, but had created a fourth line: his specialist anti-cavalry force. When his wing inevitably buckled under the weight of the Pompeian cavalry onslaught, he unleashed this surprise force on the Pompeian cavalry and on that point the battle turned.

It was not inevitable that the Pompeian cavalry would be defeated, given their weight of numbers, but they were turned, and they did subsequently break. With Caesar victorious on the wing and the Pompeians having lost their decisive advantage and the momentum, overall victory would go to the general who was able to react the quickest to these new circumstances. With the smaller and more homogeneous army, and expecting his tactic to work, it was Caesar who was able to react the quickest and disrupt the Pompeian army from that wing. Victory took several hours, but the Pompeian army, though fighting hard, inevitably began to turn and finally break up. Caesar had his victory and the whole course of the civil war was turned on its head.

The Pompeian Withdrawal

Caesar had his victory on the day, but not in the war; for that he would need to kill or capture the leading Pompeians, especially Pompeius himself. Pompeian casualties in the battle were not heavy, principally falling on the eastern allied contingents, and none of the leading Pompeians were killed or captured in the battle. Furthermore, despite his victory, the Pompeians still held the bulk of the surrounding region, including its eastern capital at Thessalonica and western capital at Dyrrhachium, not to mention the island of Corcyra, its main naval base.

Furthermore, the Pompeians still had naval control of the seas around Greece. All this helped the Pompeian faction leaders to escape Caesar and regroup. Key to this retreat was its dual nature, with Pompeius himself heading to Thessalonica before moving eastwards to his powerbase in the Near and Middle East, which he had conquered for Rome, and which had supplied him with his large army. The rest of the Pompeian leadership, though, headed west to Dyrrhachium and Corcyra.

Caesar had two key problems, despite his unexpected victory. Firstly, he could only focus his attentions in one direction and naturally he had to chase down Pompeius himself, which allowed the rest of the Pompeian leadership to slip away and regroup: first on the Adriatic coast and then the Peloponnese, before eventually evacuating Greece for Cyrene on the North African coast. Secondly, though Caesar was victorious on land with no Pompeian forces to stand up to him, he did not have a meaningful fleet, meaning he would have to chase

A Clash of Titans: The Battles of Dyrrhachium and Pharsalus (49–48 BC)

Pompeius, who had taken to the seas, on land and thus march to the Middle East, giving Pompeius a considerable head start.

Cassius, Caesar and the Bosphorus

The turning point of this chase came at the Bosphorus, when a Pompeian fleet commanded by C. Cassius Longinus arrived to find Caesar crossing undefended. Had they attacked there and then they could have at the very least stopped him from crossing, or perhaps even killed him. In the event they did neither and actually turned themselves over to him. Thus, not only did Caesar avoid defeat, but he now had a fleet with which to chase down Pompeius. The tortoise had become the hare.

There is considerable debate about why the fleet turned to Caesar when it had him trapped, and especially given who the commander was. Appian is clear that the commander was none other than C. Cassius, who later famously co-authored the conspiracy that led to Caesar's assassination on the Ides of March. This ties in with earlier evidence that Cassius was in command of a Pompeian fleet off Sicily, who then received orders after Pharsalus to go to the Black Sea and the court of the Pontic King of the Bosporan Kingdom (Crimea) – Pharnaces II. Modern academia disagrees[3] and states that it must have been another (hitherto unknown Cassius, along with a hitherto unknown fleet) rather than C. Cassius himself, based on a handful of other surviving fragments that have Cassius in the east subsequently seeking Caesar's pardon.

Thus despite all sources pointing to Cassius being in the East after Pharsalus and thus perfectly capable of being the commander, many feel the need to deny him the role and subsequent understanding of his later actions. These other sources do not preclude Cassius being the commander, but can be understood if we argue that Cassius did not surrender to Caesar but was mutinied on by his fleet who threw in their lot with Caesar, as happened to other Pompeian fleets after Pharsalus. If Cassius opposed this, then he may well have been the one to flee rather than go over to Caesar himself, only to have to backtrack and eat his words when faced with the news of Pompeius' murder, and only then see the need to reconcile with Caesar.

Murder in Egypt

Regardless of the identity of the commander, the outcome was clear; not only was Caesar not stopped, but he now had a fleet to transport his legions in pursuit of Pompeius. With his options closing down and many in the east wary of antagonising Caesar and his advancing legions, Pompeius found that past loyalties counted for little when faced with this harsh new reality, and therefore unsurprisingly he found no welcome in the Middle East. The obvious line of retreat would have been to link up with the rest of the Pompeian army that had been evacuated from Greece and were making for Cyrene, sandwiched between Pompeian North Africa and Ptolemaic Egypt (see Map One).

Pompeius however was not willing to give up, and realised that fresh forces and monies were needed and so decided to call upon the loyalty of the Ptolemaic dynasty of Egypt. However, whilst the previous Pharaoh (Ptolemy XII) had been a Pompeian client and had been placed back on the Egyptian throne by Roman soldiers (in 55 BC), he had died recently (51 BC) and the current Egyptian Pharaoh was his young son Ptolemy XIII (co-ruling, somewhat acrimoniously with his sister, Cleopatra VII). Pompeius should have realised that the boy's loyalty to his father's patron was never going to trump his own fears (Caesar's army) or ambitions (sole rule) and so in an attempt to curry favour with Caesar (and totally misreading the Roman character) he arranged for Pompeius to be murdered (by a former Roman legionary) on the beach he landed at.

Thus the Pompeian alliance was robbed of its charismatic and talented leader and Caesar was robbed of the chance of a negotiated settlement to end the civil war, whilst the Republic gained the first (of many) 'martyrs'.

Summary – A Shock Result

Pharsalus was the culmination of the year-and-a-half-long civil war campaigns; the long awaited decisive clash between the two architects of this Third Civil War. The result naturally turned the narrative of the war to date on its head. The favourite and current Princeps of the Republic, Rome's greatest living general, was comprehensively defeated by the rebel and outsider Caesar, who from a position of desperation now found himself the new front runner and Princeps of the Republic. Nowadays it is difficult to understand the shock that this result would have caused throughout the Roman and wider world.

Pompeius was expected to win and crush the upstart rebel, relegating Caesar to a footnote in history; a failed rebel, similar to the status occupied by the elder Lepidus and his failed rebellion in 77 BC. Caesar's defeat at Dyrrhachium in mid-48 BC seemed to confirm this probability. Yet by advanced planning (his anti-cavalry tactics), good choice of battlefield (anchoring one side on a river) and forcing the pace (before Pompeius could integrate the two disparate elements of his army), Caesar turning the whole campaign on its head, and emerged as the new front runner.

Yet, though Pharsalus has often been judged by historians as the clear turning point, in this phase of the war and in the Republic's history, the overall result was less clear cut than it now seems. Caesar certainly had temporary military control of the Republic, but not the political backing that Pompeius had. He only had his own small faction to support him, alongside a number of neutrals, both within the ruling elites of Rome, their provinces, and allies, all of whom would sway with the prevailing wind.

Winning a battle was one thing, winning the war was a task of a different magnitude, and as Pompeius' fate had shown, turning temporary dominance into a lasting one was more difficult than it seemed and fortunes could turn in the space of an afternoon, as Caesar himself ultimately found out on the Ides of March.

Chapter Two

Distraction, Recovery and Defeat in the Desert

The Renewed Civil War to Thapsus (47–46 BC)

Wasting a Victory?

Thus in the space of a few weeks, the course of this Third Civil War had been turned on its head. Pompeius, Rome's greatest general and the man who had instigated this war for his own personal advancement (or as he would have put it, for the good of the Republic), had been defeated and then murdered. The outsider, Caesar, was now the favourite and the new (albeit temporary) Princeps.

Yet, paradoxically, the murder of Pompeius on an Egyptian beach did more harm to Caesar's cause than good, for two reasons. Firstly, it meant that there would be no agreed settlement between the two old partners and that the two major Pompeian factions of the alliance (Pompeians and Anti-Caesarians) would continue to fight on, though for different reasons. For the adherents of Pompeius himself, it was now a matter of vengeance. For the Anti-Caesarians, there was relief that Pompeius was dead, as they could now fight to defeat Caesar without the risk of installing Pompeius in his place; a dead martyr, rather than a live threat.

The second reason is that the murder led to Caesar becoming entangled in the Ptolemaic Civil War in Egypt, which aside from the very real threat to his own life,[1] meant that he spent months entangled in Egyptian affairs, rather than pursuing and mopping up the retreating Pompeians. By the time that Caesar had settled matters in Egypt and then was forced to fight the Fourth Romano-Pontic War against an invading Pharnaces II, the Pompeian factions had recovered, regrouped and were ready to face Caesar once more.

The Recovery of the Pompeian Alliance

Whilst Caesar was so distracted, the same could not be said of his enemies in the civil war, the Pompeian alliance. In point of fact, their purpose was now crystal clear and not hampered by any external distractions; recover from the physical and psychological blows that the previous year had brought, notably Pharsalus and the subsequent murder of Pompeius. However, this recovery was aided by three factors: leadership, time, and space.

The first of these (leadership) was the most important. Despite the rhetoric of later sources, the casualty rate at Pharsalus was remarkably light, with the bulk of the Pompeian casualties coming from the Eastern allied forces. What was most remarkable however was not the casualties suffered by the troops themselves, but the lack of casualties suffered by the leadership of the Pompeian alliance. Whilst fresh troops could always be raised, fresh leaders could not. What is often overlooked in the rhetoric of Caesar's victory at Pharsalus is the absence of noble casualties, with none being killed in the battle itself and only one (L. Domitius Ahenobarbus, Cos. 54 BC) killed in the aftermath – and even then, we get the feeling that this was more down to his own incompetence. Every other Pompeian commander made it safely from the battlefield and reached Pompeian territory.

There were several reasons for this. Firstly, the battle itself was not the overwhelming rout that later sources liked to portray it as. As has been detailed in depth elsewhere,[2] the Pompeian army was overwhelmed on the far wing, but then fought a long rearguard action to stave off the inevitable; clearly it did not suddenly collapse, thus giving the leaders time to make their escape. Secondly, Caesar's pursuit of the survivors seems to have been half-hearted at best, and Caesar appears to have continued to pursue his policy of deliberate clemency to avoid affirming the Pompeian propaganda of being a bloodthirsty tyrant.

Thus, in sparing his enemies he hoped to end the civil war and not create the enmity that followed the First Civil War, which had seen his own Marian relations comprehensively wiped out. The third reason was due to the fact that the battle took place in Pompeian-controlled territory, in mainland Greece, with the Pompeians controlling the Illyrian and Epirote coastlines, the Peloponnese, and Macedon. Thus the survivors had a range of nearby secure locations to retreat to.

Consequently, all of the key Pompeian leadership (with the notable exception of Pompeius himself) survived to fight on. What Caesar must have been hoping for was that, although they had survived physically, they would have been wounded psychologically and would not continue the fight. At best this must have been a vain hope, especially concerning the 'Anti-Caesarian' faction. Any chance of coming to terms with the hard-core Pompeian faction disappeared on that Egyptian beach, with the murder of Pompeius again posing another of ancient history's great 'what ifs'.

As has been stated before, it is notable that none of the major figures of the Pompeian alliance sought terms with Caesar. The only ones to do so were from the lesser members of the oligarchy, the most notable of which were three men whose reputations are far greater today than they were at the time, namely Cicero, Brutus and Cassius. Of those it was Cassius' defection that had the greatest impact on the course of the war, as, even though he was a lesser Pompeian commander, his fleet could have destroyed Caesar when he was crossing the Bosphorus and thus either ended the civil war (with Caesar dead) or, if Caesar had survived, then ended Caesar's pursuit of Pompeius and thus negated Pompeius' need to land in Egypt without his army. Nevertheless, by the end of 48 BC/beginning of 47 BC, the leadership of the Pompeian alliance remained intact and determined to fight on.

Yet their survival alone would not have meant anything if they had not been given time to regroup. Whether by design or by chance, the Pompeian alliance split in the aftermath of Pharsalus, with Pompeius going eastwards and the other leaders westwards, naturally giving Caesar a choice and a dilemma. Understandably he chose to follow Pompeius eastwards as he was the most dangerous. Far less understandable is Caesar's decision in late 48 BC not to immediately move on the remnants of the Pompeian alliance who had travelled from Greece to Cyrene (and thus neighbouring Egypt) to meet up with Pompeius. It was this decision more than anything that allowed the Pompeian alliance time to group and rebuild.

Ultimately, we will never know why Caesar chose this course of action. It certainly can't have been how few forces he had, as that had never stopped him acting swiftly in the past when his opponents were in disarray. We are left with three options; firstly, he took an arrogant view and considered them to be no longer a threat (a risky strategy which backfired); secondly is the opposite view and is a Machiavellian one, namely that he wanted his opponents to recover and thus justify the ongoing crisis and his ongoing supreme power (the Dictatorship). However, this required a level of political forethought that Caesar seemed to lack. The third is that, having gone to Egypt, the resting place of Alexander the Great, a long time idol of his, he became enamoured with the idea of carving out an Egyptian powerbase for himself, which had been a long standing aim of both Pompeius and Crassus (his former patrons/partners).

Whatever the motivation, the key outcome was that by ignoring the Pompeians in Cyrene, and focusing on the east, Caesar gave them the time they needed to regroup. Yet time is nothing without the means, and here the third factor came into play; namely location. As Pompeius himself had found to his ultimate cost, there were few provinces or kingdoms in the Mediterranean that wanted to be seen supporting the losing side, hence the defection of the Pompeian Eastern Republic to nominally supporting Caesar, but actually wanting to be left alone by both sides.

Distraction, Recovery and Defeat in the Desert   21

With the east ruled out, and Caesarian forces in Greece, Italy and Spain, there was only one logical destination: Roman North Africa, and again we seen the failings of Caesar in this choice of destination. As detailed earlier (see Chapter One), Roman North Africa was a Pompeian stronghold due to the failure of the Caesarian-sponsored expedition of 49 BC. Furthermore, he had deliberately chosen to leave it on his southern flank in his eagerness to attack Pompeius in 48 BC. A further Caesarian scheme to attack Pompeian Africa from Spain using the Maurian Kingdom in 48 BC failed when elements of Caesarian Spain rebelled and actually needed Maurian forces to invade Spain to quell it.

Pompeian North Africa (see Map One) was two-fold; the Roman province of North Africa (formerly the rump of the Carthaginian Empire) and the Kingdom of Numidia, the superpower of the region. Though reduced from its heights of the Second Century, after being defeated by Rome in the Romano-Numidian War (by none other than Caesar's uncle Marius),[3] Numidia was still a superpower in its own right, with significant armed forces, treasury, and food production. In short Numidia was the perfect base to support a faction in the civil war.

The kingdom was ruled by King Juba I, who stands out in this period as a native ruler who bucked the trend of blowing with the wind and not only firmly came out for Pompeius, when he was on top, but continued to oppose Caesar when he became the front runner; an act which was to ultimately cost him both his life and his kingdom's independence. Thus the Pompeian stronghold of North Africa gave the Pompeians both the space and resources they needed to rebuild, and thus attracted the bulk of the Pompeian forces, leaders, and supporters in late-48/early-47 BC, aside from those under Octavius who continued to fight in Illyria (see below).

The New Leadership of the Pompeian Alliance

Without the unifying figure of Pompeius, the two leading factions (Pompeian adherents and Anti-Caesarians) needed to coalesce around a new central leader. The figure that emerged was Q. Caecilius Metellus Pius Scipio Nasica, a Scipio by birth and a Metellus by adoption, thus embodying two of the Middle/Late Republic's leading oligarchic families.[4] Being Pompeius' father in law and his former consular colleague of 52 BC, combined with his ancestry, made him acceptable to both factions within the alliance, especially given the youth and inexperience of Pompeius' two sons (Cnaeus and Sextus).

Supporting Metellus Scipio was the leader of the other major faction (the Anti-Caesarians) M. Porcius Cato, who had led the bulk of the surviving Pompeian forces from Greece, first to Cyrene and then to North Africa. Yet far greater support, both militarily and financial, came from the third faction of the Pompeian alliance: the Romano-Numidians, centred on the figures of King Juba and his Roman ally, P. Attius Varus. Thus the Pompeian alliance was effectively ruled by a new Triumvirate of Metellus Scipio, Cato, and Attius Varus (supported by King Juba).

In addition, supporting Metellus militarily were a host of Pompeian generals, most notably the former Caesarian lieutenant T. Labienus, along with L. Afranius and M. Petreius. This ruling cabal was rounded off by three young men: the brothers Cn. and Sex. Pompeius, and Pompeius' son-in-law, the son of the ex-Dictator, F. Cornelius Sulla.

The Rise of the Three Hundred – Economic Power and the Pompeians

The detail held within the Caesarian account of the civil war in Africa allows us an insight into a much-overlooked aspect of support for the Pompeian alliance and its recovery in Africa, namely economic support. Though the details only emerge at the end of the *de bello africo*, the account refers to a group of Pompeian supporters known as the Three Hundred.[5]

This group receives several mentions at the end of this work, and this is the only detailed account of them.[6] As far as we can tell they were an organised cartel of Roman bankers and businessmen (equestrians) who bankrolled the Pompeian alliance. As was later demonstrated, the size of their wealth can be seen by the fine of two hundred million sesterces they were forced to pay to secure their freedom.

The implications are interesting, as we do not often have an insight into the role of the businessmen and traders during a civil war, unless when they are suffering the economic consequences. This is different however, and we can clearly see a substantial cartel backing a Roman faction with large sums of money and basing themselves in North Africa, lending their economic and financial support to the Pompeian alliance. Again, aside from the immediate injection of cash into the Pompeians, its shows the depth of support that they had amongst the business community, seemingly far more than Caesar could muster.

The Caesarian Faction without Caesar – The Vacuum

Much as the Pompeian faction had to regroup without its leader, ironically the Caesarian faction too faced the same issue. At first this may seem strange, as unlike Pompeius, Caesar was still alive and well. Yet in terms of fighting the civil war, Caesar was just as absent as Pompeius was in 47 BC, and we need to understand not only why this occurred, but what the impact was. Caesar was effectively absent from the civil war between September 48 BC, when he reached Egypt in pursuit of Pompeius, and September 47 BC, when he returned to Rome to shore up his faltering political and military position. Throughout this period he remained in the Eastern Mediterranean, firstly in Egypt and then in Asia Minor. Though, after being rescued from being trapped in Alexandria, he was able to send orders to his subordinates throughout the Republic's territories, effectively he was an absentee leader.

As has already been mentioned, his constitutional position was unique as he was an absentee Dictator. Throughout the First Civil War there had been several men who had occupied the dominant political position that Caesar now occupied, most notably his uncle Marius, his father in law Cinna, and their opponent Sulla. It had been Sulla who had revived the Dictatorship and made it into a supreme post without specific time limit, but he did so whilst occupying Rome itself and using the Senate as a rubber stamp. Caesar was the first to use the Dictatorship as an overseas command, leaving a vacuum in Roman politics, with no Consuls elected and M. Antonius as his Master of the Horse (the official deputy of a Dictator) trying to wield power in Rome.

Despite being the victor of Pharsalus and with his main opponent dead, Caesar faced a catalogue of political and military problems, many of which were contradictory, and the choices he made were revealing. As stated before, despite his victory at Pharsalus, the civil war was clearly not over, with potential campaigns in Africa and Illyria, yet there were also two potential military campaigns in the east, against Ptolemy XIII and Pharnaces II.

Despite being Dictator, with theoretically unlimited power, his control of the Republic was actually quite weak in practice, with few actual enthusiastic supporters and most (both Roman and native) offering only tokenistic support, based on his (temporary) military superiority. The Senate and Rome's ruling oligarchy was composed of three sections: his own supporters, neutrals, and pardoned Pompeians, and the latter two factions would not take kindly to being ruled from overseas or by a Caesarian governor (Antonius).

Despite having nominal control of the Roman world, aside from North Africa, in the west his grip on Spain and Gaul was tenuous at best, with both regions on the edge of revolt, whilst in the mid-Mediterranean his control of Illyria was being contested by the Pompeians (see below) and in the east he was losing Asia Minor (to Pharnaces II) and had the Parthian Empire poised to resume the Romano-Parthian War which had petered out in 52/51 BC.

At the heart of Caesar's problem, lay two factors. Firstly, he had seized control of the Republic by military victory and was now the new front runner, but despite this he actually had a very narrow powerbase: his army, elements of the Roman oligarchy and popularity with the People; everyone else simply tolerated him.

24 The Battle of Munda (45 BC)

The second was that the Caesarian faction was built around him and suffered from a cult of personality that required him to be present. When he was absent, his presence (and the implied threat) was removed, and the spell was broken.

That Caesar chose to ignore the rest of the Roman world and the ongoing civil war to focus on the east is telling. His (typically) Roman obsession with Alexander the Great[7] was well-known and can only have been enflamed by his stay in Alexandria and his encounter with the resting place of the legendary king. The campaigns he chose to focus on were seizing control of Egypt (via a pliant proxy), an essential step for any eastern campaign. and defeating the renewed Pontic threat of Pharnaces II (son of another legendary king, Mithridates VI).

One gets the feeling that his return to Rome in September 47 BC was an annoyance and that he would rather have continued to stay in the east and renew the Romano-Parthian War that he had helped (along with his Triumviral colleagues) to foster, leading to an Alexandrian style conquest of the east. It seems that for Caesar himself, the civil war, and politics in Rome (which had never been his forte) were matters that were distractions from his dreams of becoming the new Alexander. Thus the Caesarian faction had to do without its charismatic leader and driving force for the next year, with predictable results.

The Civil War in Illyria (47 BC)

Naturally enough, the surviving sources we have focus on Caesar, first in Egypt and then in Asia Minor. Yet despite their neglect of events in other parts of the Roman world, fragments of narrative do survive. With the present state of our fragmentary sources we will never know to what extent armed clashes between the two factions continued to take place, but what we do know for certain is that civil war campaigns continued in Illyria, formerly the heartland of the Pompeian alliance, centred on the island of Corcyra (Corfu).

We have been told that, after Pharsalus, the surviving Pompeian land forces evacuated Illyria, first for the Peloponnese and then for the North African province of Cyrene, in an aborted attempt to link up with Pompeius. Yet the sources are silent on the remaining Pompeian navy, which had been heavily diminished in the aftermath of Pharsalus by defections (of allied contingents). Nevertheless, despite these defections, the Pompeian navy was still a force to be reckoned with. Most crucially we are not told whether the Pompeians abandoned their naval headquarters of Corcyra when they evacuated the coastal cities.

Nevertheless, we are informed of at least one Pompeian commander whose fleet remained in Illyrian waters to challenge Caesarian control of the region: namely M. Octavius. Octavius had been the Pompeian commander who had secured the region for Pompeius in 49 BC, defeating the Caesarian forces in Illyria, a major victory which denied Caesar a bridgehead in the region.[8] Thus he was an experienced commander in fighting in that region and its particular topography.

Initially he was faced by the experienced Caesarian commander (and noted former Pompeian) A. Gabinius. Unfortunately for Gabinius (and Caesar), he was ambushed by the native tribes, who had used the ongoing civil war as an opportunity to divest themselves of Roman control, who proceeded to trap his army in a gorge and annihilate it, during the winter of 48/47 BC (the Battle of Sunodium).[9]

It is interesting to note that, coming in the midst of a civil war (and after Pharsalus), this total destruction of a Roman army by native tribes, complete with the loss of legionary standards, attracts so little attention. The scale of the defeat can be seen by the fact that the author of the pseudo-Caesarian Alexandrian Wars had to acknowledge it,[10] though downplays the number of casualties. Appian's number of just under 7,000 foot and 3,000 cavalry far outstrips the 2,000 soldiers in the 'Caesarian' account.[11]

Given Octavius' experience and knowledge of the region, and a later statement by the 'Caesarian' account (see below) that Octavius conducted treaties with various native tribes, it is tempting to speculate on whether Octavius had been the architect of this Caesarian defeat. Whatever the cause, the effect was that the largest Caesarian military force in Illyria had been removed and that once again we find Pompeian commanders working with native allies (as in Africa and Spain) to face the Caesarians. This would have suited Octavius' strategy, with the Pompeians operating from the sea with their fleet and using the native forces to compensate for a lack of Pompeian land forces.

With the death of Gabinius, command of the Caesarian forces in Illyria fell to Q. Cornificius (Pr. 45 BC), who from the Caesarian accounts was clearly out of his depth.[12] Thus we can see that Octavius was engaging in a process of eliminating the various coastal garrisons that the Caesarians had placed in the Illyrian/Epirote cities and trying to secure the eastern flank of the Adriatic for the Pompeians once more. Realising the danger, this forced the Caesarian commander of Brundisium (P. Vatinius) to create a scratch force from both Caesarian reserve naval and land forces and lead his own expedition, without orders from either Caesar or Antonius. Having learnt of this new arrival, Octavius committed to destroying it.

Yet, despite the edge of experience and the element of surprise, Octavius was defeated by Vatinius and in one battle his whole campaign was ended, nominally securing the province for the Caesarians once more. Naturally, this account overlooks the fact that the various native tribes were still in revolt (see Appendix One), but the province was lost to the Pompeians, as was the threat to the vital shipping route from Brundisium to the east.

26 The Battle of Munda (45 BC)

Of the two commanders, Caesar clearly recognised the major contribution that Vatinius had played in the civil war campaigns and awarded him with the Consulship later in the year. Octavius by contrast, never reached such heights again: he clearly escaped to Pompeian Africa, where the following year he is to be found once again commanding a naval squadron. However, from that point onwards he disappears from our (fragmentary) records.

The Civil War in Greece (47 BC)

By contrast we have no explicit testimony from our surviving sources on events in Greece and Macedon. The Pompeian forces had all withdrawn, first to the Peloponnese and then been evacuated from Greece altogether. We have previously been told that late in 48 BC, the Caesarian commander in Greece, Q. Fufius Calenus, was campaigning against the key cities of Athens and Megara, who had declared for Pompeius.[13]

Thus the majority of the Greek cities all surrendered to Calenus after the news of Pharsalus reached them. The notable exception was the city of Megara which still held out. The translation of Dio can be 'a considerably later date', which may well infer that the siege lasted throughout late 48 and into 47 BC. We are certainly aware that Calenus was still the Caesarian commander in Greece throughout 47 BC, until he was recalled by Caesar on his return to Italy to become Consul (along with Vatinius – see above). All we can surmise is that, apart from the siege of Megara, there was no other fighting in Greece or Macedonia and that Calenus ensured that each Pompeian city now swore allegiance to the Caesarian cause (however half-hearted it was).

The Civil War in Spain and North Africa (47 BC)

There is a similar silence from the sources concerning matters in the two Roman provinces of Spain and North Africa, and this in itself is most interesting. Spain had been secured to the Caesarian cause in 49 BC by Caesar himself, in a lightning campaign against the Pompeian generals (see Chapter One). Yet, as we have been told,[14] Caesar, in 48 BC, intended to use Spain as a launch pad for an invasion of North Africa, crossing the Straits and using the pro-Caesarian Kingdom of the Mauri (see Map One) to attack Numidia on its western flank. As we have also seen, in point of fact the situation was reversed when the Mauri had to cross into Caesarian Spain to assist Caesar's governors in putting down a rebellion, which seems to have been organic, but then claimed they were supporting the Pompeian cause. Using both military force and negotiations the rebellion was quashed and the governor who did much to create the rebellion

(Q. Cassius Longinus) was replaced and suspiciously died of drowning when his ship went down on the journey home.

Of the two governors of the Spanish provinces, the most notable was M. Aemilius Lepidus, himself the son of a notorious First Civil War general, who had marched his army against Rome (77 BC) and who was a key Caesarian lieutenant. He had been appointed Governor of Nearer Spain in 48 BC and remained there throughout 47 BC. His colleague was the newly-appointed Governor of Farther Spain, C. Trebonius, another key Caesarian supporter, who had served (with mixed success) as the commander of the Caesarian siege of Massilia in 49 BC and who was the Caesarian Praetor in 48 BC, who had opposed his colleague M. Caelius Rufus.

In theory, with the rebellion dealt with, these two commanders, along with the two Maurian kings (Bocchus II and Bogud), should have resurrected their plans to cross to North Africa and engage the Pompeian-supporting Numidia on its western flank. Yet all we do know is that this never happened; critically we do not know why. In strategic terns, with Caesar unable (or unwilling) to engage with the Pompeians from the east, it was imperative that the Caesarians applied pressure from other quarters, and without control of the Mediterranean, this meant from the west and the Maurian Kingdom.

Dio conflates the events of 47 and 46 BC into a few sentences and more importantly into a 'few days'.[15] Yet, despite his inaccuracies in terms of timescale, Dio seems to identify a key factor when he indicated that Spain was not in a fit state to be left without Caesarian legions due to its instability. Though the rebellion of 48 BC had been suppressed and battles had been fought (Corduba and Alia), key protagonists (such as the Questor M. Claudius Marcellus Aeserninus) had been pardoned. Thus it may well have been the case that the two governors judged that Spain was barely pacified and that if they did transfer the bulk of their legions to North Africa then the region would rise up again and they would be cut off from the Caesarian-controlled areas of the Western Republic.

This caution may well have been fuelled by the lack of instructions from Caesar himself, and we have no way of knowing whether he sent instructions to them or received news of the rebellion and had to rely on their judgement as to the wisdom of invading North Africa. Unlike Vatinius in Illyria (see above), there were seemingly no Caesarian commanders willing to take the initiative and persecute the war in this region. Such inertia would cost them the following year.

Whatever the cause, the outcome was clear. There was no Caesarian invasion of North Africa from Spain and no pressure applied to the Pompeians' recovery in Numidia/Roman North Africa, giving them more time to regain the initiative.

The Civil War in Sicily and Sardinia (47 BC)

Both the strategic islands of Sicily and Sardinia had fallen to the Caesarians in 49 BC without a fight, yet Sicily in particular had suffered from Pompeian naval attacks in 48 BC in a campaign parallel to that on land, campaigns which came to an abrupt halt when the news of Pharsalus spread.[16] Yet the Pompeians still had significant naval resources to contest control of the Western Mediterranean, and Sicily was the closest Caesarian-controlled region to Pompeian North Africa and so would be the key staging post to any invasion of Italy and thus the Pompeians most logical target. Again, we must rely on passing references, the first from Dio, which, as usual, has no due concern to precise timings and a second from the *de bello africo*.[17]

From these we can see that the Pompeians had a fleet based on Sardinia, despite being evicted from there in 49 BC by the Caesarians. The fleet, commanded by L. Nasidius, had at some point in 47 BC returned to the island and made their base at Caralis, the capital of Sardinia, aided by the locals. Again, a passing reference in a surviving source reveals that the ongoing civil war was of a far larger scope than the main accounts preserve. Furthermore, despite declaring for Caesar in 49 BC and Caesar's victory in 48 BC, the locals turned to the Pompeians once more, yet another example of the 'wafer thin' nature of Caesar's control of the Republic.

With bases in North Africa and Sardinia, the entire Italian and Sicilian coastlines would have been vulnerable to the raids of the Pompeian ships and this indicates that, with Caesar in the east, the Pompeians held a degree of naval superiority over the Caesarians.

The Planned Pompeian Offensive

The school of Caesarian history would like to paint the Pompeians in 47 BC as being a defeated band of survivors hiding in North Africa, waiting for the imperious Caesar to find the time in his busy schedule to put them out of their misery. As the reader will have noticed, this is not a school that this present study adheres to. As we have seen above, the Pompeians used the absence of Caesar and the inaction of his lieutenants to rebuild their strength and plan their next moves.

Whilst Caesar had spent the year 47 BC gaining control of the Eastern Republic and its allies, as we have seen above, his control of the Western Republic was fragmenting. Although the Caesarians had finally driven the Pompeians out of Illyria, their control of Spain and Italy was loosening, and Sardinia and Sicily were subject to Pompeian raids. Having secured the East, it was clear that

Caesar intended to invade Pompeian North Africa, but it was equally clear that the renewed Pompeian alliance had no desire to be passive and simply wait for Caesar, but went on the offensive, with a plan detailed by Dio involving an invasion of Spain, who's loyalty to the Caesarian cause was weak.[18]

Whilst the Pompeian invasion of Spain did not take place until after Caesar had invaded Africa in January 46 BC, it is clear that the Pompeians had clearly laid plans to exploit the chaos in Spain and open up a second front. Thus the scene was set for the renewal of the civil war in earnest for the coming year, with a Pompeian invasion of Spain and a Caesarian invasion of Africa.

The Caesarian Invasion of North Africa

Having returned to Rome in late-47 BC, Caesar first needed to regain control of both the political and military chaos he found there. In his absence (and as had happened in 49 and 48 BC) political clashes had broken out in Rome, leading to bloodshed, on this occasion Caesarian veterans battling in the Forum.[19] The key clash was between M. Antonius (ruling in Caesar's name as his Master of the Horse) and the Tribune P. Cornelius Dolabella. Once that clash had been settled and temporary political and social reforms enacted, Caesar then had to restore control of his mutinous legions, many of whom were ex-Pompeians, and most of whom were angry at missing out on the lucrative eastern campaigns. The situation had escalated to such a degree that the mutinous legions had murdered two Roman Senators and marched on the Campus Martius, on the outskirts of Rome itself. Nevertheless, Caesar was able to defuse the situation in person.[20]

Thus, upon his return to Italy, Caesar had managed to (temporarily) quell the political and military chaos that had broken out in his absence and could plan for his next move: to crush the Pompeian threat once and for all, restore his control over the Western Republic, and plan for life (and campaigns) after the civil war. Naturally his opponents planned on it being his last civil war campaign as well, and the one that would see his rebellion crushed and the 'true' Republic restored.

Never one to stand idle, especially when it meant him having to engage in the daily grind of Roman politics, Caesar planned on an immediate attack on North Africa, even though it was winter. Aside from his natural impatience, the political and military situation in the Caesarian Western Republic was not secure enough for him to be sat idle over the winter months. If he had, then the recently-calmed army would have been given time to stew on their situation and the Pompeian naval attacks would have increased, as would the instability in Spain.

Without control of the Mediterranean and with Pompeian fleets an ever present danger, Caesar opted for the shortest route possible, so transferred his army from Italy to Sicily and then marched across Sicily to the embarkation point of the city of Lilybaeum (modern Marsala), following the ancient Carthaginian route between North Africa and Sicily.

According to the *de bello africo*, Caesar reached Lilybaeum on 17 December 47 BC, with just one legion. Over the next week a total of six legions (roughly 30,000 men) had been mustered and embarked, along with 6,000 cavalry. We are also told that it was 25 December when Caesar's invasion fleet left Sicily and crossed to Africa, taking three days. Unfortunately for him, the fleet was scattered by the winter winds disputing their crossing.

Though the Pompeians knew that Caesar was coming, the exact point of his landfall was unknown to them, so all they could do was to adopt a flexible defensive position, fortifying the obvious ports and harbours and having cavalry cover the coastline. The largest city on the Roman North African coast at the time was that of Utica, the capital of the Roman province (with Carthage still being a ruin).

It seems that it was here that the Pompeian alliance made its official headquarters, including hosting the Pompeian Original Senate which had previously been convened in Greece, and the Three Hundred (see above). The city had been the target of the Caesarians' first, and ultimately disastrous, invasion of 49 BC and the city was commanded by M. Porcius Cato, probably more due to the need to keep him away from any major land engagements than any other considerations. Thus Utica would have been the most heavily defended of all the North African coastal cities.

The Battle of Hadrumetum (46 BC)

That being the case, Caesar chose a lesser port as his target and thus chose the city of Hadrumetum, further to the south on the African coastline. As he had done with his bold invasion of Epirus in 48 BC, Caesar needed to deploy his army quickly and secure the port as a base before the Pompeians could deploy in sufficient numbers to drive him back into the sea. The *de bello africo* tells us that the town had a Pompeian garrison, which when combined with the locals, amounted to the equivalent of two legions,[21] commanded by a C. Considius Longus. This was supplemented by a force of 3,000 Numidian cavalry commanded by Cn. Calpurnius Piso Frugi, who had been patrolling the coast.

The Pompeians chose not to contest Caesar landing a portion of his army by the city (some 3,000 infantry and 150 cavalry, according to the *de bello africo*[22]) and establishing a bridgehead. Again, we will never know why they allowed him to do so, perhaps having orders to let Caesar land and thus trap him on African soil. With the bulk of his army still at sea, Caesar fell back on his usual tactic, namely trying to suborn either the garrison, the populace, or their commander, a tactic that had worked so well upon his initial landings in Epirus in 48 BC. However, unlike Epirus, the cities of Roman North Africa had had over two years of being governed by the Pompeian faction and were initially not for turning (especially with Numidian contingents so close). Considius himself too proved to be immune to Caesar's persuasion.

Thus, with insufficient forces to attack the city (the bulk still being at sea) and with the city proving immune to his charms, Caesar was left with the usual three choices; wait, retreat, or march inland. Of the three, waiting would have allowed him the chance to contact and muster the rest of his army, but would equally allow Metellus and the Pompeians the chance to muster against him. Retreat was not only against his nature but would have undermined the shaky morale of his army. Thus Caesar was left with one option (his favourite), that of striking camp and marching against his opponents at speed, so disrupting their plans, as had proved so successful in Greece in 48 BC. The *de bello africo* states that he waited only 'a day and a night' before doing so.[23]

It was when he struck camp however, presumably to march southwards, that Considius and Piso saw their chance and attacked. Though on paper Considius had the greater number of soldiers, we do not know how many of the aforementioned two legions were actually Roman legionaries and how many were local auxiliaries, but we must suspect there were very few actual legionaries in his force. Thus Caesar had the greater number of Roman legionaries. What evened the balance was Piso's 3,000 Numidian cavalry, which compared to Caesar's 150.[24] Furthermore, Caesar's force was on the march and had just struck camp and were not in battle formation. The clash which followed was little more than a skirmish, but given how vulnerable Caesar's position was could have ended his campaign there and then.

Nevertheless, Caesar was able to beat off both the initial attack and subsequent sorties by the Numidian cavalry. The whole clash is resonant of the ones that took place following Caesar's landing in Illyria when he was pursued by a Pompeian vanguard who were also beaten off by his specialist force of mixed cavalry and infantry that had been trained at countering cavalry and that proved to be so influential at Pharsalus itself.

The Caesarian Recovery

Yet, whilst Caesar had been able to extricate himself from Hadrumetum, as was common his invasion plans were already running out of steam. The bulk of his army was still at sea, he had been driven from his initial landing zone, and the Pompeians now knew where he was and could direct their forces accordingly. However, if we are to believe the *de bello africo*, there were other coastal towns who did throw open their doors to Caesar, including Ruspina and Leptis (Minor), further to the south and further away from the control of Utica.

However, whilst Caesar now had a safe port from which he could properly organise his invasion fleet, the Numidians controlled the local watering holes and were keeping Caesar bottled up in the city whilst the Pompeians mustered their forces. With access to local resources denied him, Caesar took steps to secure his supply route from overseas (the islands of Sardinia and Sicily) from the Pompeian fleet. Having done this, he then advanced on the city of Ruspina, another apparently friendly city, garrisoning both it and Leptis. The *de bello africo* provides an excellent summary of Caesar's restlessness, rushing hither and thither, whilst the rest of his fleet slowly assembled at Ruspina and Leptis and disembarked his main army.[25]

Naturally, the clear danger of using a source like the *de bello africo* is that it presents a one-sided view of affairs, and we can only view the Pompeian response through the eyes of Caesar or one of his officers. Having been given prior warning of the imminent departure of Caesar from Sicily, and having a strategy that required Caesar to land and then be defeated, Metellus Scipio and the Pompeians needed to muster their forces inland and prepare for Caesar's arrival at the unknown point.

Thus they garrisoned the major ports (Utica, Hadrumetum) and had Numidian cavalry patrol the coastline in between. Once Caesar's landing point had been identified then word would have been sent to Metellus so that he could start organising a counter attack, whilst the cavalry harried Caesar and denied him an uncontested bridgehead. Then sources state that Metellus went to King Juba to discuss a joint action.

Therefore, within the week, the Pompeian initial response force was sent towards Ruspina, commanded by none other than T. Labienus himself, Caesar's old colleague from the Gallic War, who had famously defected to the Pompeian cause upon Caesar crossing the Rubicon. Though Labienus had been present at the Battles of Dyrrhachium and Pharsalus, this was the first time he had faced Caesar one-on-one. Following behind Labienus and his force were reinforcements, led by M. Petreius, one of the Pompeian commanders Caesar had faced in Spain in 49 BC, and Cn. Calpurnius Piso Frugi.

Thus the Pompeians swiftly launched a sizeable counter attack, under some of their best commanders, determined to either defeat Caesar in battle or blockade him in a port before he had had the chance to fully deploy his army on African soil. Inevitably, Caesar was out on manoeuvres with a force when the Pompeian army was sighted approaching Ruspina. Equally inevitably he chose to face it rather than retreat to the city. Caesar faced Labienus with a substantial force of 15,000 legionaries, along with cavalry and archers. The *de bello africo* provides an excellent summary of the composition of Labienus' forces, which included Roman legionaries, Numidian cavalry, and German and Gallic cavalry from the Pompeian 'grand army' of 48 BC.[26]

Labienus' army was composed of at least 20,000 men, with 12,000 legionaries, 8,000 Numidian cavalry, not to mention the German and Gallic cavalry, alongside African war elephants. Aside from the size of this force, the aspect which immediately strikes us is the multi-racial composition of the army, blending Roman, African Gallic and German forces. This immediately draws a parallels between Labienus' army of 46 BC and that of Pompeius at Pharsalus in 48 BC which too was a multi-ethnic one, combining a core of Roman legionaries with cavalry and ballistic forces from the eastern territories. On this occasion, for Pompeius' Eastern forces we can read Labienus' African contingents.

The major difference between the army of Pompeius and that of Labienus however, aside from the size, was that Labienus had had more time to integrate the various elements of his hybrid army and forge them into a new fighting style. Time for training and integration was the one major factor that Caesar had denied Pompeius in 48 BC and which contributed to his defeat at Pharsalus. The resulting clash between the two forces, the first of the African campaign, was the Battle of Ruspina, fought on what now equates to 4 January 46 BC.

The Battle of Ruspina (46 BC) – Echoes of Pharsalus and Carrhae

In many ways this description owes much to the Battle of Carrhae (53 BC), when Crassus' superior infantry forces were pinned down by range weapons and cavalry attacks. Labienus, it seems, had learnt from the Roman defeats at Carrhae and Pharsalus and, like his former mentor before him, had crafted a force created to deny Caesar his strengths (infantry power) and play to his forces' own speciality, speed, and distance.

According to the *de bello africo*, sensing the danger, and having recalled the experience of Pharsalus, Caesar gave orders to his army to change their formation to avoid encirclement and annihilation.[27] Thus Caesar was able to break the encirclement and begin an orderly retreat, only to find the arrival of the Pompeian reinforcements gave his opponents fresh impetus. Caesar was therefore forced to break off his retreat and launch a counter attack to drive off this renewed onslaught. If we are to believe the *de bello africo*, then this battle ended in a stalemate, with Caesar able to fight off the two waves of Pompeian attacks and retreat safely to his camp at the end of the day.

Nevertheless, in the other sources, Ruspina is presented as a Caesarian defeat, only saved when Labienus was carried from the field and Petreius retired, though the *de bello africo* has Petreius carried wounded from the battle.[28] None of these sources provide casualty figures for either side. As always, the truth will lie somewhere in-between. If Ruspina was a stalemate, then Caesar certainly came off the worst, unable to defeat Labienus' army and forced to retire from the battlefield. The result left him pinned down at the city of Ruspina.

Thus within just six days, the Pompeians had been able to counter the momentum of Caesar's invasion and bottle him up in a coastal city, and had proved the effectiveness of their new hybrid armies and damaged the reputation of Caesar's military invincibility. They now awaited the arrival of two more armies to bolster their forces further and see if they could deliver the 'knock out' blow to Caesar.

Stalemate in the Desert

However this 'knock out' blow never came, which was due to Caesar successfully extricating his army from that perilous position. What followed was a subsequent three-month campaign of cat-and-mouse tactics in the desert between the Pompeians (masterminded by Labienus) and Caesarians, with move and counter move. Despite coming off worst in some of the subsequent clashes (Uzitta, Zeta), the Pompeians were able to keep Caesar pinned down in the Numidian interior, avoiding a full set piece battle, slowing grinding him down, much as they had done in Greece in 48 BC. Thus we can see the Labienan tactics.

However, just as in 48 BC, Caesar, realising that he was playing to his opponents' strengths, made another bold move and thrust towards the coastal city of Thapsus, held by a Pompeian garrison, which he intended to place under siege. This move left the Pompeians with a dilemma: give chase to Caesar but change their successful tactics or take the pressure off Caesar and let him invest and potentially capture a valuable bridgehead. Thus Metellus Scipio abandoned the Labienan tactics of hit and run and moved after Caesar. It is unclear whether Labienus agreed with him or even accompanied him.

The Battle of Thapsus (46 BC)

The battle itself has naturally been covered in depth elsewhere,[29] but the key to this clash lay in the Pompeians abandoning their hit-and-run tactics in the desert and choosing to invest Caesar as he began to lay siege to the Pompeian-held port of Thapsus. Key to the battle was the geography of the city and its environs, with a vast marsh to the city's west, resulting in only one narrow approach in the north and one to the south. Metellus Scipio clearly envisioned a repeat of the Battle of Dyrrhachium (48 BC) with Caesar trapped against a Pompeian-held city and cut off by siege works.

This tactic may well have worked in the long term but, as at Pharsalus, Caesar did not allow him the time, but waited for Metellus to split his army (to cover both the northern and southern approaches to Thapsus) and then attacked him whilst he was building his fortifications. Metellus had been banking on using the narrowness of the approach to Thapsus (between marshes and sea) to bottle Caesar up. In actual fact it had the opposite effect and bottled up Metellus' army, negating his advantages in terms of cavalry and elephants and evening the odds, if not favouring Caesar's superior quality of infantry.

Thapsus was in fact three battles in one. The first and greatest was between Metellus Scipio and Caesar on the Northern Approach. As stated, the geography bottled up Metellus superior cavalry and elephants and the Caesarian attack overwhelmed an unprepared Pompeian army, forcing it to rout. Again, as with Pharsalus, Caesar attacked the stronger Metellan wings (where their elephants were stationed) and turned them back onto the centre.

The second battle was far smaller but just as important, and came when the Pompeian garrison in Thapsus saw what was happening and attacked Caesar's rear, hoping to trap him between the two Pompeian forces. Unfortunately for them Caesar had left a substantial rear-guard which fought them off, buying Caesar the time he needed to overwhelm Metellus.

The third and final battle is the one we are told least about, when Caesar turned south to attack the Pompeian army guarding the southern approach, commanded by King Juba and L. Afranius. For this attack, Caesar used the shorter route between the marshes and the city, whilst the retreating Metellans had to take the longer route around the marshes. Again, we have few details but the Pompeian/Numidian armies under Juba were routed, giving Caesar total victory, and scattering the Pompeian/Numidian army.

The Bloody Aftermath

Again, as with Pharsalus, Pompeian elite casualties in the battle were few, but unlike with Pharsalus, on this occasion Caesar was ruthless in tracking down his enemies in the aftermath. In fact, the only major Pompeian leaders who escaped from North Africa were T. Labienus and P. Attius Varus. Of the two, Varus was already at sea, commanding a naval contingent at the time of the defeat, making easier his escape to the Balearic Islands, where Cn. Pompeius was.

In terms of Labienus, he was the only major Pompeian figure in command on land that escaped North Africa, also turning up in Spain. This has led to speculation that he was not actually present at the battle itself (no source specifically places him there), which saw the Pompeians abandon his cautious hit-and-run tactics, leading to questions over whether he and Metellus Scipio had fallen out over the change in tactics. Whatever the cause he was the only major figure to escape North Africa.

Of the others, Metellus Scipio escaped Thapsus and made for the Roman capital of Utica, where he took ship, bound for Spain. Unfortunately, he was intercepted by the Maurian navy and committed suicide, after a spirited defence, rather than be captured. Behind him in Utica, a similar situation was playing out as the figurehead of the Anti-Caesarian faction, M. Porcius Cato, who had been left out of the fighting (due to lack of ability and his cowardice in Sicily in 49 BC – see Chapter One), also chose to end his own life, again without lifting a sword other than the one that took his own life. Of the two men, Cato, who had never risen to the top of the Senatorial Oligarchy, entered Roman and later Western consciousness as a Republican martyr, whilst Metellus Scipio, and his jaded past, faded from memory.

Suicide was also the method chosen by the Numidian King Juba, who fled into the Numidian interior with the Roman commander M. Petrius. Finding that his own people were turning on him, naturally enough given the presence of the victorious Caesarian army and being pursued closely by them, he and Petrius ended their lives in a suicide pact. To the far West this choice was denied to the other two notable Pompeian commanders, L. Afranius and F. Cornelius Sulla, who had chosen to flee to Spain by land, along the North Africa coast, but were intercepted by the Maurian army, allies of Caesar and both discretely murdered to save Caesar the inconvenience of having to do so himself.

Thus the ranks of the Pompeian leadership had been greatly thinned out, and though Labienus and Attius Varus survived and had the military acumen, neither man had the *auctoritas* to revive the Pompeian cause. Fortunately for them, there were two men who did: the two sons of Pompeius, Cnaeus and Sextus, the eldest of whom could now inherit the mantle of his father and rally the Pompeian and Republican cause once more, safe in Spain and actively stirring up rebellion in the region.

Summary – History Repeating

Thus we can see a similar pattern to the campaign of 48 BC, a bold/rash advance by Caesar across the seas, landing in enemy territory, initially getting himself into trouble and suffering a reversal/defeat (first Dyrrhachium, then Ruspina), before finally making a bold move which forced the Pompeian army into battle on ground unfavourable to it and at a time not of its choosing, resulting in an overwhelming victory.

For Caesar it was a second crushing victory and for the Pompeians a second crushing defeat. As we have seen, however, the key difference came in the aftermath, with the bulk of the Pompeian alliance leadership killed off, either by their own hands or those of Caesarians. Yet, as we have also seen, not all of the Pompeian alliance leaders had been killed, with a mix of youth (the Pompeian brothers) and experience (Labienus and Attius Varus) surviving. Furthermore, as in 48 BC, the Pompeians had a new, easy-to-reach base of operations to retreat to: Spain.

Section II

Civil War Renewed – The Second Spanish Campaign

Chapter Three

The Never Ending War – Caesar and the New Pompeius

Caesar and the Illusion of Victory

In late 46 BC (August or September by modern dating) Caesar staged the most magnificent display of his marital prowess by staging four consecutive Triumphs for his many victories, an unprecedented and unrepeated feat.[1] In order of precedence (and munificence) they were for his victories in Gaul (58–50 BC), Egypt (48–47 BC), Pontus (47 BC) and Africa (46 BC). Clearly in Caesar's mind these were a fitting celebration of his unprecedented martial prowess, which marked him as the greatest ever Roman general and well on the way to emulating his great idol, Alexander the Great. To be fair there would have been many in Rome, both amongst his more enthusiastic supporters and the populace of Rome, who agreed with this self-analysis.

Yet, as always when you look at the details of these campaigns, the lustre of this achievement begins to fade. The Gallic campaigns were an unprecedented feat. The Roman conquest of the whole of Gaul to the north of the Rhone and west of the Rhine, finally removed the tribal threat to Rome that as recently as Caesar's uncle's day (C. Marius, some sixty-years earlier) had nearly destroyed Rome. It would not be churlish however to point out that Caesar had the full support from Rome's two leading men (the Duumvirate of Pompeius and Crassus) and an unprecedented ten-year command, thus both the time and the resources. Furthermore, as late as 52 BC, the depth of this 'conquest' proved to be surface deep only, with massive tribal rebellions nearly unravelling the whole campaign. Certainly with Caesar having left Gaul we do hear of further low-level rebellions. Nevertheless, it was a major military achievement.

Next came the Triumph over Egypt, which in reality was an unnecessary entanglement in a Ptolemaic Civil War, and Caesar himself (again) came close to disaster.[2] This was followed by a victory in the Fourth Romano-Pontic War when he defeated the invading Bosporan (Pontic) Kingdom in a short sharp victory at the Battle of Zela and recovered lost Roman territory in the Eastern Republic. Finally came the African campaign and the 'war that dare not speak its name'. Officially this final Triumph was over the Numidian King Juba and was thus a Second Romano-Numidian War that ended with the conquest of Africa's most powerful king, and another piece of unfinished business which he inherited from his uncle, Marius.

In reality however, this last Triumph was the one that was in the poorest taste, as it was not a victory over the Numidians, but over his civil war opponents in the Pompeian faction, with whom Juba and the Numidians were allied. The inclusion of this African Triumph immediately drew attention to the absence of the campaigns of 49- and 48-BC in Spain and Greece respectively, despite the major victories over the Pompeians at Ilerda and Pharsalus. If Caesar had enough good taste and good sense not to draw attention to these, then why did he choose to do so with the victory at Thapsus?

In many ways, it must have chafed Caesar that he could not publicly celebrate victories over his greatest rivals, especially that of Pharsalus over Pompeius, due to the delicacies of Roman oligarchic and popular opinion. Pompeius had previously been Rome's greatest living general, the new Roman Alexander, and had added huge territories to Rome's empire in the East, which in the educated Roman mind always trumped those of the 'barbarian west'. This was an insecurity that Caesar never lost and one which contributed to his impending downfall.

Furthermore, he needed a public demonstration that the current civil war was over and that this was down to Caesar and no one else. Hence the narrative he chose for this fourth and final Triumph was one of victory over the 'evil' Juba, who had destroyed a Roman army in 49 BC (at the Battle of Bagradas River; an event given prominence in Caesar's own commentaries), and thus was a treacherous Roman ally. Whilst the memory of Pompeius was clearly unimpeachable (in public), those of his successors were not, and thus whilst no Roman captives formed part of this Fourth Triumph, Caesar could not resist his own attempt at *damnatio memoriae* and apparently included images of the deaths of Metellus Scipio, Cato, and Petreius,[3] with the clear message of 'thus perish all those that oppose Caesar'. However as Appian pointed out, each of these three images showed a Republican nobleman dying 'nobly' by his own hand, rather than face rule under Caesar.[4] Of these three Republican martyrdoms, that of Cato still holds sway today (whilst those of Metellus Scipio and Petrius have faded from popular memory).

Thus, whilst Caesar wished to make a very public statement that the civil wars were over and his enemies were dead, all he managed to do was draw attention to the martyrdom of his opponents, who in many minds died to defend the 'freedom of the Republic'. Not that this would have bothered Caesar with his notoriously poor political radar. In his mind he had won and 'saved the Republic' and should be hailed as such and reap the rewards. He was the winner, so he wrote the history (literally in his case).

Naturally, these demonstrations of his military prowess were supported by equally lavish displays of 'bread and circuses' for the people, with outright donations of money to each citizen, larger amounts to his soldiers, public banquets, corn and meat doles to the populace and lavish games. Thus the People of Rome had a clear demonstration of the rewards of the New Golden Age of the Peaceful Republic (under the 'benevolent rule' and 'wise guidance') of the Princeps, C. Iulius Caesar.

There was only one problem with this reality that Caesar had shaped, namely that it wasn't true and within a couple of months, and before the year was out, he had to go back on campaign to face the Pompeian faction one more time (his fourth civil war campaign so far), against opponents who seemingly would not stay defeated for long. Furthermore, Caesar faced Pompeian-held territory in both the West and the East, one challenging his immediate control of the Republic and one challenging his wider control of the Middle East. Ever the practical man, Caesar chose the more immediate (and nearest) threat and set off for Spain once more, this time to confront the son of his old enemy.

Having appointed himself to another Dictatorship and sole Consulship, no other Curule magistrates were elected, leaving Rome ruled by his Master of the Horse, now M. Aemilius Lepidus, rather than Antonius, along with a body of prefects. There would of course be the Plebeian Tribunes and Questors elected, not subject to Caesar's whims. Again, Caesar chose expediency over established Republican practice, a process that not only robbed his opponents of office, but also his expectant supporters.

Cn. Pompeius 'Magnus' and the Pompeian Survival in the West

Whilst the Pompeian elite had survived the disastrous defeat at the Battle of Pharsalus (see Chapters One and Two), the same could not be said in the aftermath of Thapsus. In many ways, Caesar's victory at Thapsus was of far greater practical importance than that of Pharsalus. It was in the aftermath (not on the battlefield) that the political and economic might of the Pompeian factions was destroyed, with the deaths of the majority of the Pompeian leadership, the loss of their African ally, and the desertion of their support from the business community. The Pompeians lost their leader, Q. Caecilius Metellus Pius Scipio Nasica (Pompeius' father-in-law), the talismanic leader of the Anti-Caesarian faction; M. Porcius Cato; the King of Numida, Juba I; and a host of leading Pompeian commanders, including L. Afranius and F. Cornelius Sulla.

The survivors fled North Africa for the nearest safe haven they could find, ironically in Caesarian held Spain. Though Caesar had defeated the Pompeian armies holding Spain in the lightning campaign of 49 BC (see Chapter One), it could not be said that he had conquered Spain or that it was loyal to the Caesarian cause. Despite nearly 180 years of campaigning in Spain, the Roman grip on the region was superficial at best, and the provinces had proved to be a safe haven for rival factions during the First Roman Civil War, when it became the base of the losing Marian-Cinnan faction, led by Q. Sertorius. Ironically it was Pompeius Magnus who had (eventually) defeated Sertorius and restored control from Rome. Yet this left the province with both a spirit of rebellion from control of Rome and a loyalty to the figure of Pompeius Magnus himself, and it was this duality of rejection of control from Rome and loyalty to Pompeius that the survivors of Thapsus exploited.

Spain itself was barely under Caesarian control, despite the absence of any official Pompeian armies. Though Caesar had won his campaign just three years earlier, the bulk of the Pompeian legions surrendered (after tactical ineptitude on the part of their own commanders) and the bulk of the soldiers would have been dispersed back to their homes, ready to fight again. With the Pompeian causes still thriving in nearby Africa, the Spanish provinces rose in revolt against Caesarian control in 47 BC, forcing Caesar to divert valuable resources from an attack on Africa. By mid-46 BC the rebellion had been settled by negotiation rather than force and remained under nominal control. Therefore, the last thing Caesar needed was for a figurehead to escape the slaughter in Africa and stir up fresh rebellion. Unfortunately for him, that figure was none other than Cn. Pompeius Magnus, the eldest son of his old enemy and a man who could rely on the old loyalties to his father whilst raising the prospect of freedom from the control of Rome (for now).

It is clear that Cn. Pompeius had been a peripheral figure until the aftermath of the defeat at Thapsus. It is estimated that he was born in the mid-70s BC, when his father was campaigning in Spain during the First Civil War, which made him around thirty years old at this point. To date he had only received junior commands. During the campaigns of 48 BC in Greece, he was not at his father's side at Pharsalus, but held command of a Romano-Egyptian fleet operating in the Adriatic. Having been deserted by the fleet when news of Pharsalus reached them, he linked up with the other Pompeian commanders and eventually retreated to their powerbase of Numidia in North Africa.

His father's subsequent murder on an Egyptian beach meant that he inherited his father's title of 'Magnus' and became nominal head of the Pompeian family, though the true power lay with his father's father-in-law, Metellus Scipio. Though of considerable name value, his youth prevented him being amongst the ranks of the senior Pompeian commanders who took charge after Pharsalus, this being the triumvirate of Metellus Scipio, Cato and Attius Varus. Either in late-47 BC or early-46 BC, he received his first military command, leading

The Never Ending War – Caesar and the New Pompeius   45

an attack on the Caesarian supporting Kingdom of the Mauri, which was on Numidia's western flank. This was an inauspicious start for the son of Rome's greatest general, leading to a loss at the Battle of Ascurum, and forcing the abandonment of the expedition. Thus the new Magnus retreated from Africa and was dispatched to the Balearic Islands (off the coast of Spain) to stir up trouble in the rebellious Spanish provinces (and it must be admitted, also to keep him out of the way of the serious fighting in Africa).[5]

Therefore, as we can see, this was not an auspicious start to a Pompeian revival; a young man with impeccable credentials but little in the way of military experience. Yet the slaughter of the Pompeian leaders in Africa (many by their own hand) not only propelled him into leadership of the Pompeian faction, but gave him the moral duty to continue the fight. The pantheon of great Republican martyrs was bolstered by the suicides of Cato, Metellus Scipio and Petreius, all who died (in the propaganda of the time) fighting tyranny and defending the Republic. Furthermore, his 'useful exile' to the Balearic Islands gave him the ideal base for survivors of the African slaughter to flock to. Thus fate propelled him into the leadership of the civil war against Caesar.

The Rise of a New Pompeian Triumvirate – T. Labienus

Yet, importantly, the new Pompeius Magnus was not alone in this fight and was bolstered by two other key figures. The first was T. Labienus, a general whose career had been forged fighting with Caesar in his Gallic campaigns.[6] Labienus is an enigmatic figure and one whose reputation and career deserve to be better known. He was perhaps Caesar's finest lieutenant in the Romano-Gallic War, receiving much coverage in Caesar's later memoirs[7] (a feat in itself given his subsequent role in the civil war) and was a specialist in cavalry fighting and tactics – probably Rome's finest at the time.

Yet despite this long term service and friendship, when Caesar crossed the Rubicon in early-49 BC, having been manipulated into doing so by Pompeius, Labienus demonstrably refused to accompany his commander and defected to the Senatorial (Pompeian) side, the only notable Caesarian officer to do so.[8] Not only did he bring a wealth of his own military experience, but he brought invaluable military experience of Caesar and the fighting style he had developed in Gaul. Yet, despite this, one gets the feeling that his previous closeness to Caesar meant that he was an outsider amongst the Pompeian elite. His role in the subsequent Greek campaigns is not clear. Caesar himself places Labienus with Pompeius at the Pompeian victory at Dyrrhachium and again at Pharsalus. Plutarch places Labienus in command of the key cavalry contingent on the

Pompeiian left,⁹ who's failure to turn Caesar's flank was the decisive moment of the battle.

Having survived Pharsalus, he retreated to the Pompeian-held cities on the western coast and then eventually to Numidia in North Africa, where he set about creating a new hybrid cavalry force composed of Gallic, German and Numidian cavalry. This force was so effective that Labienus nearly defeated Caesar in the first major clash of the African campaign at the Battle of Ruspina (Jan 46 BC). Following Ruspina, Labienus and his cavalry harried Caesar, pinning him down in the Numidian interior – Labienan tactics.

Labienus' role in the subsequent Battle of Thapsus is an intriguing one. There is no explicit surviving reference that he actually took part in the battle, which would be strange. Furthermore, there is the ease of his escape, when so many of the other commanders were caught, almost as if he wasn't present at all. For the Pompeians' leading general, and a man who had nearly defeated Caesar not to be present would indicate a falling out between him and Metellus Scipio, perhaps over the change of tactics to give Battle at Thapsus and abandon the harrying strategy that had proved so successful. Certainty Valerius Maximus preserves a passing reference to an argument between the two men over rewarding cavalry commanders, which revealed their different personalities.¹⁰ Added to this is the strange reference in Appian which indicates that Labienus accompanied Pompeius Magnus to Spain, which he cannot have done due to the Pseudo-Caesarian commentary detailing his campaigns in Africa against Caesar. This could be reconciled by him falling out with Metellus prior to Thapsus and being dispatched (again in useful exile) to the Balearics Islands.

Without any additional ancient sources turning up, we will never know the truth of the matter. The important issue for the Pompeian cause was that their finest general and the man who had come close to defeating Caesar, had survived the massacre of Pompeian leaders, and made his way to Spain to support the younger Pompeius. Thus the Pompeian leadership now had a figurehead and a military strategist to support him.

The Rise of a New Pompeian Triumvirate – P. Attius Varus

P. Attius Varus was an even more obscure figure, yet he played a key role in the Pompeian faction throughout the civil war campaigns. He rose to prominence in 49 BC when he seized control of the Roman Province of North Africa, ousting a Senatorial appointment. Having previously been a governor of this province (c.53/52 BC) he seemingly had formed a close relationship with the King of Numidia (Juba I), which was the regional power. He used this relationship to convince the king to support the Pompeians, and thus when the Caesarian forces invaded Roman Africa from Sicily in 49 BC, they were annihilated by a Numidian army at the Battle of Bagradas River, a defeat which Caesar devoted a considerable amount of time to in his civil war commentaries and which he seemingly never forgave.

Varus subsequently commanded a Romano-Numidian powerbase, nominally under Pompeius' command but in effect ruled over by himself and King Juba. With Pompeius commanding the whole of Rome's Eastern Republic and its associated allies, this could be overlooked, but Varus came to the fore in the aftermath of Pharsalus, when the Pompeian control over the Eastern Republic evaporated. He now commanded the one stronghold they had left: North Africa. Thus when the two existing Pompeian factions (Pompeius' supports and the Anti-Caesarians) arrived in retreat, they now found a third faction – the Romano-Numidians, who had both the territory and the largest military forces. Thus Varus found himself as the third member of the new Pompeian Triumvirate, albeit there due to the backing of King Juba, who, as a 'foreigner', could not be on a par with the other Roman commanders. To maintain Republican propriety, Varus formerly handed over his African imperium (which he had stolen anyway) to Metellus Scipio.

Perhaps to avoid this embarrassment, or perhaps as it was his speciality, Varus commanded a large Pompeian fleet during the African campaigns of 46 BC, leading the attacks against the Caesarian fleet. This meant he was well placed to retreat from North Africa when news of the defeat at Thapsus reached him. Thus he too turned to the Balearic Islands along with a battle hardened fleet.

Thus the new ruling Triumvirate had its third member, actually the only surviving member of the previous one, and though he no longer had the resources of Numidia to call on, he was an experienced naval commander and had inflicted the most obvious defeat of the civil war on Caesar to date (with Caesar disputing his loss at Dyrrhachium, and it being overshadowed by the subsequent Pharsalus). Thus the Pompeians now had a figurehead, an experienced land commander, and an experienced naval commander.

The Fourth Man – Sex. Pompeius

This new ruling Triumvirate did have a junior member, none other than Pompeius Magnus' own younger brother, Sextus. Sextus had been too young to take an active part in the civil war campaigns, had joined with his father on the latter's retreat from Pharsalus to the East, and had been present (on the boat) when his father was murdered on an Egyptian beach. Also present in Africa, he seemed not to have taken part in the fighting there but was able to escape the aftermath of Thapsus and naturally headed to his brother in the Balearic Islands. Thus both sons of Pompeius were re-united, and he could provide moral support to his brother and was a second, junior figurehead (an heir and a spare).

Cn. Pompeius 'Magnus' and the Pompeian Revival in the West

Yet the key question is how was this loose band of survivors, fleeing defeat in Africa, able to pose so serious a threat to the Caesarian faction's control of the Republic that Caesar himself was forced to take up arms again and fight a second Spanish campaign (rather than focus on the developing crisis in the Eastern Republic – see below). The answer is naturally two-fold, with the right men being in the right place at the right time (the Pompeians) and the inherent weakness of the Caesarian factions' control of the Republic. Fortunately, Dio presents a brief account of what transpired in Spain, which took place in a series of now lost campaigns:

> *The legions in Spain under* [Q. Cassius] *Longinus and Marcellus had rebelled and some of the cities had revolted. When Longinus had been removed and Trebonius had become his successor, they kept quiet for a few days; then, through fear of vengeance on Caesar's part, they secretly sent ambassadors to Scipio, expressing a desire to transfer their allegiance, and he sent to them Cnaeus Pompeius among others.*[11]

The Pompeian Attack on the Balearic Islands

As we have seen in previous volumes, one of the strengths of the Pompeian faction in the early years of this civil war was their control of the seas, with multiple fleets bottling up Caesarian forces. Yet following the defeat at Pharsalus, the bulk of Pompeius' eastern allies deserted him, taking their fleets with them, restoring parity between the two sides. The aftermath of the defeat at Thapsus showed that whilst some Pompeians were able to escape North Africa (Sex. Pompeius, Varus, Labienus) others, most notably Metellus Scipio, were intercepted.

Yet Pompeius' attack on the Balearic Islands seems to have gone undetected and caught the Caesarians on the hop. Again we have no figures for the size of Pompeius' force but given how few men he had for the abortive invasion of the Mauri, it cannot have been a large one. All we have is one line of Dio for this subsequent small, but crucial campaign:

> *Pompeius put in at the Balearic Isles and took these islands without a battle, except Ebusus, which he gained with difficulty; then, falling sick, he tarried there with his troops.*[12]

Thus by what must have been early-46 BC, the Pompeians now had a secure naval base off the coast of Caesarian Spain. This proved to be crucial for three reasons. Firstly, it gave the Pompeians a well-defended safe haven to re-group, and a clear destination to retreat to after Thapsus, rather than surrender. Secondly it gave the Pompeians a base from which to strike out at Caesarian-controlled Spain. Finally, it gave hope to Pompeian supporters that the fight against Caesar was not done. From this small acorn, a large Pompeian oak soon grew.

As has been previously documented, Caesarian Spain suffered a massive rebellion in 48 BC which ran into the following year. Whether it was originated by Pompeians or not, it soon became associated with the Pompeian cause and was not quelled until 47 BC by Caesar's loyal deputy L. Aemilius Lepidus, and even then through negotiation despite the use of military force. The Caesarian commander of the Roman province of Farther Spain was C. Trebonius, who had been the commander of the Caesarian siege of Massilia in 49 BC.

News of Pompeius' victory in the Balearics must have reached Caesar, as Dio reports that he dispatched a legate, C. Didius, there with a small fleet (see below).

The Revolt of Farther Spain

Unfortunately for the Caesarians, Pompeius' victory sparked off a fresh rebellion in southern Spain, as reported by Dio:

As a result of his delay, the soldiers in Spain, who had learned that Scipio was dead and that [C.] Didius was setting sail against them, feared that they would be annihilated before Pompeius could arrive, and so failed to wait for him; but putting at their head Titus Quintius Scapula and Quintus Aponius, both knights, they drove out [C.] Trebonius and led the whole Baetic nation to revolt at the same time.

They had gone thus far when Pompeius, recovering from his illness, sailed across to the mainland opposite. He immediately won over several cities without resistance, for, being vexed at the commands of their rulers and also reposing no little hope in him because of the memory of his father, they readily received him; and [New] Carthage, which was unwilling to come to terms, he besieged. The followers of Scapula, on learning of this, went there and chose him general with full powers, after which they were most devoted to him and showed the greatest zeal, regarding his successes as the successes of each one of them and his disasters as their own. Consequently, their resolution was confirmed by their double purpose of obtaining the successes and avoiding the disasters.

For Pompeius, too, did what all are accustomed to do in the midst of such turbulent conditions, especially after the desertion of some of the Allobroges whom Juba had taken alive in the war against Curio and had given to him: that is, he granted to the rest every possible favour both in word and in deed. Not only these men, therefore, became more zealous in his behalf, but a number of the opposing side, also, particularly all who had once served under Afranius, came over to him.[13]

Thus, we can again see the combination of the two factors of native rebellion against rule from Rome and (paradoxically) support for the Pompeian cause, clearly a case of 'the devil you know'. The role of the Caesarian Governor and forces in Farther Spain is an interesting one. Previously we had been told that much of the rebellion of 48–47 BC had been caused by the actions of Q. Cassius Longinus, the Caesarian Governor, and that his replacement (by C. Trebonius) did much to reduce tension in the province. Yet during this subsequent rebellion in 46 BC, we hear that C. Trebonius was ousted from his province without any reports of fighting.[14] Furthermore, the *de bello hispaniensi* later reports that Pompeius had two Spanish native legions who had rebelled against Trebonius.[15] Thus Trebonius seemingly fared worse than Cassius two years earlier and lost his province without a fight. We are not told where he fled to, either Nearer Spain, or to Caesar in Africa or to Rome itself.

Though he seemingly had no hand in sparking off the fresh rebellion in Spain, Pompeius reacted quickly enough to take advantage of this good fortune and landed in Spain proper (the first time that a Pompeius had been physically in Spain for a generation). Building on his role as the rightful inheritor of his father, he seems to have quickly brought a number of cities to his side and then laid siege to the regional capital of New Carthage.[16] Dio goes on to state that the rebels acclaimed him as their leader and the former troops of Afranius (from the campaign of 49 BC), now rejoined the Pompeian cause. Thus Pompeius found himself in the position held by Q. Sertorius in the First Civil War, commander of a joint native rebellion and Spanish Roman army. Dio presents us with the following, which may well have summed up the heady attitude at the time:

Elated, therefore, by the multitude of his army and by its zeal, he proceeded fearlessly through the country, gaining some cities of their own accord, and others against their will, and seemed to surpass even his father in power.[17]

Pompeian Reinforcements

Furthermore, Dio reports the following:

Then there were those who came to him from Africa, among others his brother Sextus, and Varus, and Labienus with his fleet.[18]

The Never Ending War – Caesar and the New Pompeius

If we follow Dio's rough timeline, then this lightning campaign took place before the Pompeian survivors reached Spain, though that leaves a very narrow window between news of Thapsus (pre-rebellion) and the arrival of the survivors (post-rebellion), so we must conclude that Dio's narrative (as happens all too often) mixes and condenses the events. In any case, the remnants of the Pompeian faction now found they had a mainland province, its resources, and an army. As happened in the aftermath of Pharsalus, they were also given time to entrench their position by relative Caesarian inaction (see below).

We don't know how many men came over from Africa, but clearly the Pompeians' best field commander T. Labienus came with them to add some veteran command experience, and specifically experience in fighting Caesar. This would have given the inexperienced Pompeius a ready-made command staff for his new army. The account of the Pseudo-Caesarian author on the subsequent Spanish campaign shows how quickly the Pompeians were able to create a new field army, putting it at thirteen legions, some 65,000 men (if full strength), which, whilst being the smallest Pompeian army to date, was still a formidable fighting force.

> *He had the eagles and standards of thirteen legions; but among those which he thought afforded him any solid support two were native legions, having deserted from Trebonius; a third had been raised from the local Roman settlers; a fourth was one which was once commanded by Afranius and which Pompeius had brought with him from Africa, while the rest were made up of runaways or auxiliaries. As for light-armed units and cavalry, our troops were in fact far superior both in quality and quantity.*[19]

> [Pompeius] *collected a new army of Spaniards, Celtiberians, and slaves, and made formidable preparations for war. So great were the forces still remaining which Pompeius had prepared, and which Pompeius himself overlooked and ran away from in his infatuation.*
>
> *This great and formidable war had been stirred up by Cnaeus Pompeius, the son of Pompeius Magnus, a young man of great energy in war, and reinforcements flowed in from all parts of the world from among those who still followed his father's great name.*
>
> *The army was composed of soldiers from Pharsalus and Africa itself, who had come hither with their leaders, and of Spaniards and Celtiberians, a strong and warlike race. There was also a great number of emancipated slaves in Pompeius' camp, who had all been under discipline for years and were ready to fight with desperation.*[20]

Thus, we can see that though the force was large in number, it varied in quality, with only four legions (a third of the total) being composed of Roman legionaries or having been in existence prior to this campaign. Nevertheless, the intention was clearly that they would fight in their home territory, and they had a command staff with a mixture of youthful enthusiasm and veteran experience.

The Caesarian Reaction/Inaction

Obviously, we are given no clear timeframe for these Pompeian campaigns in Spain, and it would be interesting to see how they tallied with Caesar's actions. Clearly, we are told that they took place after the Battle of Thapsus, but the key question is whether they were serious enough to warrant Caesar himself breaking off the 'mopping up' campaigns in North Africa or whether Caesar had already left for Rome?

Dio is the only source to provide a summary of the Caesarian reaction:

Meanwhile he [Caesar] was learning in detail all that Pompeius was doing in Spain; but thinking him easy to vanquish, he at first despatched the fleet from Sardinia against him, and later sent on also the armies that had been enrolled, intending to conduct the whole war through others.[21]

Thus C. Didius was dispatched first with the Sardinian fleet to deal with Pompeius' attack on the Balearic Islands. Later, when news of the fall of Farther Spain reached him, possibly brought by Trebonius himself, he dispatched an army of unknown size. We are told the commanders of that force though: Q. Fabius Maximus and Q. Pedius. Of the two, we know more about Pedius the man and more about Fabius' ancestry.

Q. Fabius Maximus was the latest oligarch to bear an illustrious Roman name, that of the Punic War general who had done so much to frustrate Hannibal. The family however had suffered politically in the last seventy years, with 116 BC being their last Consulship and none of them featuring during the First Civil War. The only attested post we have for Fabius is an Aedileship in 57 BC, through if he followed the *cursus honorum* (never a given in this period) then he would have held a Praetorship by 48 BC at the latest. There are no surviving references to him during the civil war prior to this campaign, or for why a man from a long-standing Republican family was following Caesar.

His colleague, Q. Pedius, was by contrast a man from a family which had never seemingly attained high office in the Republic, and probably would not have done so without the patronage of Caesar and the civil wars. The years 58–56 BC saw Pedius as a legate in Caesar's Gallic campaign, service for which he was rewarded when he was made a Praetor in 48 BC in Caesarian-controlled Rome. He took command of the Caesarian forces that crushed the Pompeian-inspired revolt of T. Annius Milo in Italy during that year. References to neither Fabius nor Pedius can be found in the civil war campaigns of 49–46 BC prior to this point.

Thus this pair of mis-matched Praetorians were dispatched to Spain with a force of unknown size (though it must have been smaller than Pompeius' thirteen legions). Given the size of the Pompeian army (as stated above), it is not a surprise that Dio reports that both men failed to engage Pompeius:

For though Caesar also had generals in Spain, namely Quintus Fabius Maximus and Quintus Pedius, yet they did not regard themselves as a match for Pompeius but remained quiet themselves and kept sending urgently for Caesar.[22]

Clearly Caesar sent them to prevent the situation getting worse and at least try to hold onto Nearer Spain and block any route to Italy, until such time as Caesar himself could take to the field. The Governor of Cisalpine Gaul was none other than M. Iunius Brutus, an ex-Pompeian, which may have given Caesar further cause to worry.

Thus, it is clear that the Caesarians ceded the initiative to the Pompeians in Spain, sending only a token force to try to hold onto Northern Spain rather than immediately contest their control of the south, thus allowing the Pompeians to consolidate their position and grow stronger. The clear question is: why did Caesar himself not react more quickly and move directly on Spain?

Again, as we have seen before, there are always questions over Caesar's motives. Whilst he took great pride in celebrating victories over his enemies, he continually needed crises to keep his role as military leader and Dictator, during the period of the emergency. Clearly if there was no emergency then there would be no need for a Dictator. Yet Caesar did not need the crisis in Spain to justify his position, as there was a similar crisis on the East, with a Pompeian-inspired revolt in the province of Syria, which in strategic terms was potentially worse for Rome's control of the East as Syria was the gateway to the Eastern Republic, beyond which lay an aggressive Parthian Empire (see below and Chapter Seven).

Thus the revolt in the East more than justified the current military emergency continuing, and to Caesar would have been the most attractive campaign, especially given his recent sojourn to Egypt and his personal connections there (Cleopatra and Caesarion). Thus there is no need to see Machiavellian politics in play in terms of the Caesarian position in Spain – just the reverse. Whilst Caesar was scoring what he must have hoped would be the final victory in the civil war, crushing the Pompeians and their allies once and for all at Thapsus, Caesarian control of Spain collapsed, reviving the Pompeian faction.

Caesar and the Pyrrhic Paradox

That Caesar chose to return to Rome rather than attack the Pompeians may well highlight the paradoxical weakness of his political position. Though he had won militarily in Africa, the Republic now had a new Pantheon of Martyrs to worship, including their new 'high priest', his old enemy Cato, whose military contributions to the campaign had been disastrous for the Pompeians, but whose death made a far bigger statement. The longer the war went on and the more battles Caesar won, the more martyrs he created and the more men he had to pardon (or be labelled a bloodthirsty tyrant if he chose the expedient position of killing them). The more men he pardoned, the more the Senate filled up with those who had been his enemies, creating three major groupings: his diehard supporters, the neutrals and now the ex-Pompeians.

Thus in many ways Caesar was facing a paradox of Pyrrhic proportions: the more he won, the weaker his political position became. He desperately needed to escape this paradox by stopping the fighting with his fellow Romans and starting the fighting with the enemies of the Republic: in this case that meant the Parthians (given that by 46 BC, they were only seven years from the disaster at Carrhae and five from the last Parthian invasion of Syria). Yet he was once again dragged back into continuing the civil war campaigns and now faced a new threat from a new Pompeius.

For Caesar, the threat from Pompeius was more political than military. Though he had thirteen legions, many of battle-hardened veterans, Pompeius himself was untested in combat and Caesar's legions now had two major victories over the Pompeian forces (Pharsalus and Thapsus) and one defeat (Dyrrhachium) – though Caesar naturally downplayed that.

Though his opponent was too young to officially hold Republican office, it was his very youth that made him so dangerous. Many of the oligarchic ruling class had held their noses when they supported the elder Pompeius, given his role in fanning the very chaos they were now supporting him to clear up. The same could also be said of his successor, Metellus Scipio. Yet they could have none of those issues with the younger Pompeius, who had 'clean hands' in political terms. Here was a young man with an impeccable Roman lineage doing the most Roman thing and upholding the honour of his family and demonstrating clear 'Republican' virtues.

Thus here was a blank slate upon which the opponents of Caesar could paint. The clear threat he represented in political terms can be seen by his 'successor', as it were – Caesar Octavianus, whose lineage and youth was used to create the image of a defender/restorer of the Republic and whose considerable success came despite his own lack of military ability.

Caesar was now playing the role of the old man (he was fifty-four this year), a blood soaked veteran who had attacked his own city and caused the deaths of a number of the great Republican figures (Pompeius, Cato). Thus Caesar's enemies could look to Pompeius as the restorer of the Republic, regardless of whether he would turn out to be as ruthless as his father or grandfather (Cn. Pompeius Strabo, who played a short but notable role in the First Civil War).

Caesar had none of this political capital, and the longer he fought (in civil wars), the worse his position became. What he did have was an aura of military invincibility as the four Triumphs in Rome demonstrated and the support of the army. What Caesar needed was to keep his enemies frightened of that military ability and support, long enough for him to start winning plaudits as the defender of the Republic and wash away the stains left by his civil wars actions.

Thus Caesar returned to Rome to shore up his political position, both with the ruling oligarchy, the People, and the Army, leaving him secure enough to once more march on Spain and this latest Pompeian threat. Having done so he set off as quickly as possible, not even waiting for the New Year, again wanting a quick campaign, so he could finally turn his focus on the East.

Pompeians and Parthians in the East- the Rebellion in Syria

Caesar's problems however were compounded by the fact that Spain was not the only province that had declared for the Pompeians. Just as the Caesarians had lost control of Spain in the west, which had long standing links to the elder Pompeius, a similar occurrence had taken place in the East. The Roman province of Syria had been created by Pompeius less than twenty years earlier (in 63/62 BC) during his Great Eastern War against the various powers of the East, carved out from the rump of Seleucid Empire.[23] As such it was the lynchpin to Roman control of the near-East, being home to the greatest concentration of legionary forces, a rich and prosperous region in its own right with control of the trade routes and just as importantly acted as the gateway to both Asia Minor and Ptolemaic Egypt.

As we have seen, in 49–48 BC the East was the powerbase of Pompeius' civil war campaign, supplying armies, navies, and monies to his cause, all of which deserted him in the aftermath of the defeat at Pharsalus. Caesar's attempt to subdue the region to his control was challenged, not by the Pompeians, but by the outbreak of a Fourth Romano-Pontic War led by King Pharnaces II of the Bosporan Kingdom (Crimea), a former Pompeian client. What is often overlooked in this civil war narrative of the region is the role of the Romano-Parthian War. It is often forgotten that the First Romano-Parthian War (55–51 BC) had taken place less than a decade before and had ended (inconclusively) with a Parthian army invading Syria in 52 BC and being driven off by none other than C. Cassius Longinus. From that time onwards however, a renewed Parthian assault had been consistently expected, especially given that Rome had collapsed into civil war.

Recognising these factors, Caesar left none other than Sex. Iulius Caesar, one of his cousins, and a possible protégé, in command in Syria, with orders to hold it for him, secure from any Parthian attacks. Unfortunately for both Caesars, the threat came from within and not without. Whilst the elder Caesar was campaigning in Africa, a revolt erupted in Roman Syria against the younger Caesar. At the centre of this revolt is the figure of Q. Caecilius Bassus, a man whose background is lost to us, and who remains a shadowy figure in the mould of P. Sittius; a military adventurer who used the chaos of the civil wars to rise to prominence.

Both Appian and Dio have detailed accounts of the revolt and the subsequent civil war campaign, but Appian himself admits that he found contrasting stories about Bassus in the sources he used:

> *The following events took place in Syria and Macedonia about the same time. Caius Caesar, when he passed through Syria, left a legion there, as he was already contemplating an expedition against the Parthians. Caecilius Bassus had charge of it, but the title of commander was held by Sextus Iulius, a young man related to Caesar himself, who was given over to dissipation and who led the legion around everywhere in an indecorous manner. Once, when Bassus reproved him, he replied insultingly, and sometime later, when he called Bassus to him and the latter was slow in obeying, he ordered him to be dragged before him. A tumult and blows ensued. The soldiers would not tolerate the indignity and slew Iulius. This act was followed by repentance and fear of Caesar. Accordingly, they took an oath together that they would defend themselves to the death if they were not pardoned and restored to confidence, and they compelled Bassus to take the same oath. They also enlisted and drilled another legion as associates with themselves.*
>
> *This is one account of Bassus, but Libo says that he belonged to the army of Pompeius and that after the latter's defeat, he became a private citizen in Tyre, where he corrupted certain members of the legion, who slew Sextus and chose Bassus for their leader.*[24]

The question of the timing of this revolt is an interesting one. The *Periochae* of Livy places it before the Battle of Thapsus, which is seemingly confirmed by Dio's version of the Bassan revolt:

The Never Ending War – Caesar and the New Pompeius   57

Moreover, many alarming reports kept coming in from Africa about Caesar, he [Bassus] *was no longer content with the existing state of affairs, but began to stir up a rebellion, his aim being either to help the followers of Scipio and Cato and the Pompeians or to win for himself some political power. But he was discovered by Sextus before he had finished his preparations and explained that he was collecting these troops for the use of Mithridates the Pergamenian in an expedition against Bosporus; his story was believed, and he was released.*

So after this he forged a letter, which he pretended had been sent to him by Scipio, on the basis of which he announced that Caesar had been defeated and had perished in Africa and claimed that the governorship of Syria had been assigned to him. He then seized Tyre with the aid of the forces he had got ready, and from there he advanced against the legions of Sextus but was defeated and wounded while attacking him. After this experience, he did not again make an attempt by force upon Sextus, but sent messages to his soldiers, and in some way or other won some of them to himself to such an extent that they murdered Sextus with their own hands.[25]

Regardless of his origins, the important point was that Sextus was dead and could be of no future use to Caesar (an intriguing point in itself) and Syria had fallen to a rebellion and was now held in the name of the Pompeians. With (initially) only one legion, Bassus clearly did not pose a direct threat to Caesar and his control of the Republic.

Yet, beyond these numbers, the more serious aspect was that this rebellion represented the loss of Syria, Rome's only province in the Middle East and one which had been at the centre of support for the Pompeian cause. Clearly this rebellion could spread throughout the Middle and Near East. Furthermore, Syria was the gateway into the Roman East for the Parthian Empire, who were looking at Rome's perceived weakness for an opportunity to exploit.

An extract from Strabo (below) shows that Bassus was already using the revolt to grow support from amongst allies in the region, all keen to throw off the Roman yoke:

... and he [Bassus] *had plenty of allies, I mean the neighbouring chieftains, who possessed strongholds; among these places was Lysias, which is situated above the lake that lies near Apameia, as also Arethusa, belonging to Sampsiceramus and his son Iamblichus, chieftains of the tribe of the Emeseni; and at no great distance, also, were Heliupolis and Chalcis, which latter was subject to Ptolemaeus the son of Mennaeus, who possessed Massyas and the mountainous country of the Ituraeans. Among the allies of Bassus was also Alchaedamnus, King of the Rhambaeans, who were nomads this side the Euphrates River; and he was a*

friend of the Romans, but upon the belief that he was being treated unjustly by the Roman governors he retired to Mesopotamia and then went into the service of Bassus as a mercenary.[26]

Dio also details his military preparations:

When Sextus was dead, Bassus gained possession of all his army except a few; for the soldiers who had been wintering in Apamea withdrew into Cilicia before his arrival, and although he pursued them, he did not win them over. Returning then to Syria, he took the title of Praetor and fortified Apamea, so as to have it as a base for the war. And he proceeded to enlist the men of military age, not only freemen but slaves as well, to gather money, and to prepare arms.[27]

They recruited another legion, and both were drilled together.[28]

Thus Bassus was able to use Syria to forge together another Romano-native army, composed of both Roman legionaries and native allies to defend the region and expand the rebellion. In doing so he created another quasi-independent region, with himself ruling as its warlord, though he took the title of Praetor, much as we had seen in the First Civil War with Sertorius in Spain (and to a lesser degree M. Marius in Asia). Though in reality ruling as a warlord, Bassus would have used his letter from Metellus Scipio to legitimatise his rule, acting as Propraetor for the Pompeian Roman government. With Metellus dead there was no one to disprove this and the remaining Pompeians would have been happy to continue this fiction.

We are not told when Caesar was informed of the loss of Syria, most likely only after his victory at Thapsus. This must have come as a blow, not only losing a favoured cousin, but seeing his conquest of the Roman East unravel, in less than a year, and his plans for future campaigns undermined. Furthermore, we do not know which news reached him first – the rebellions in Spain or those of Syria – but we must assume it was those of Spain, given its proximity to North Africa. Thus Caesar faced a double blow of bad news after his major victory. Again with campaigns needed both in the East and the West, Caesar chose to return to Rome, to stabilise his political position and build on his victories in Africa before taking to the field again, dispatching Caesarian commanders in both regions to try and stabilise the situation. Naturally, whichever campaign Caesar chose to focus on, would risk the neglect and worsening of the other.

The Civil War Campaigns in Syria (46 BC)

Unlike the Spanish campaign however, the lack of Caesar's presence means that we have far fewer sources detailing the civil war campaigns fought there; there is no *de bello syriana*, therefore we have to piece together an overview from brief mentions elsewhere. Clearly having only just pacified the region the year before, Caesar had two clear aims. First (and most important) was the need to stop his control of the region deteriorating beyond the loss of Syria, and rebellion spreading throughout the Near and Middle East. The second aim would have been for his forces to crush the rebellion in Syria before it became too entrenched.

The geopolitical situation in the East presented both advantages and disadvantages to Caesar in respects of this rebellion. To the north lay Asia Minor, with three Roman provinces and the nearest Roman legionary forces. These were: the long-standing province of Asia itself (formerly the Kingdom of Pergamum); a more recent conquest, Roman Cilicia; and the newly-conquered Bithynia-Pontus, formerly home of the Pontic Empire. Yet Asia Minor had only just seen the Fourth Romano-Pontic War concluded the year before, with Caesar's victory over King Pharnaces II at the Battle of Zela.

The problem for Caesar was that after his reconquest of the region the previous year, he had made Syria the centrepiece of his control of the Eastern Republic, meaning he had limited forces and commanders elsewhere in the region. The nearest Roman province was that of Cilicia, on the southern coastline of Asia Minor, guarding the entrance into Asia Minor (see Map One). This was commanded by Q. Cornificius, to whom Caesar entrusted the temporary command of the war in Syria (replacing the murdered Sex. Iulius Caesar). Cicero himself comments on this appointment (in two letters to Cornificius himself) and highlights the key danger, himself having commanded in Asia in the aftermath of First Romano-Parthian War:

> *I think I gather from your letter that you are not likely to take any step rashly, nor to decide on any plan before you know in what direction that fellow* [Caecilius Bassus] *is likely to break out. That is what I had hoped, for I felt confidence in your wisdom, and now your very welcome letter makes me quite secure.*[29]

> *I learn from your letter that the war now raging in Syria and the province of Syria itself have been put in your hands by Caesar. I hope it may turn out to your honour and success. I feel confident that it will do so, for I have full reliance both on your activity and prudence. But what you say as to the suspicion of a Parthian invasion caused me great uneasiness. For I was able to conjecture the amount of your forces, and your letter confirms my calculation.*

> *Therefore I can only hope that that nation will not move until the legions reach you, which I hear are on their way. But if you have not the forces adequate for the struggle, do not forget to follow the policy of M. Bibulus, who kept himself shut up in a very strongly fortified and well-supplied town, as long as the Parthians were in the province. But you will settle these points better on the spot, and in view of the actual circumstances. For myself, I shall continue to feel anxious as to what you are doing, until I know what you have done.*[30]

Thus we have a first-hand account that Cornificius' major worry was not Bassus, but the Parthians, who just six years earlier had invaded Roman Syria in the aftermath of their victory at the Battle of Carrhae. It also confirms that Caesar had dispatched fresh legions to the region, but that Cornificius had to move with just the forces he had, aiming to dislodge Bassus before he became too entrenched or before the Parthians intervened.

It is the role of Parthia that made this rebellion in Syria so dangerous. Though Rome held the region to the north of Syria (Asia Minor) and the south (Roman Judea and Ptolemaic Egypt), to the East lay the expansionist Parthian Empire, who just seven years earlier had crushed seven Roman legions and killed one of Rome's three leading men (M. Licinius Crassus) and were intent on driving towards the Mediterranean. An alliance between the Pompeians and the Parthians would present the gravest challenge yet to the fledgling Caesarian Republic (see Chapter Seven).

Cornificius would have been supported by the other Roman Governors of Asia Minor; P. Servilius Isauricus (Cos. 48 and 41 BC) in Asia, and C. Vibius Pansa Caetronianus (Cos. 43 BC) in Bithynia and Pontus. Again without a surviving narrative source for this campaign we can only peace together fragments. The major clash between the Caesarian forces and the Pompeians seems to have occurred in 45 BC (see Chapter Seven) and Cornificius seems to have served the rest of the year without accomplishing anything of note and was replaced by C. Antistius Vetus.

Thus the status quo was maintained; Bassus held Syria for the Pompeians, but was blocked from the north by Cornificius and his colleagues and the south by the pro-Caesarian Judea and Egypt. It is likely that he was negotiating with the court of the Parthian King Orodes II, as subsequent events proved (again see Chapter Seven). Thus the year ended with stalemate in the Eastern Republic between the Caesarian and Pompeian forces.

Summary – Pompeius and Labienus - A Credible Pompeian Threat

The narrative that Caesar wished to weave at the time, and one which has unfortunately lasted to this day, is that the Pompeians were crushed at Pharsalus and after that represented no credible threat. As we have seen from the Thapsan campaign, this is a Caesarian fiction that would have been questioned at the time, as it must be now. The subsequent Pompeian campaigns were always going to be overshadowed by the loss of Pompeius, who was a clear rival for Caesar. Thus, without a rival at his level, the subsequent Pompeian leaders all seem to fall short as credible threats and not Caesar's equals.

Though this may be true in terms of modern historiography, this was not the case at the time. Metellus Scipio had a far greater political lineage than Caesar and with the backing of Numidia could put an army of 80,000 men in the field. Despite his own propaganda (and all that followed) Caesar was not invincible in battle; he was bold and that could be used against him, as it was at both Dyrrhachium (a clear defeat) and Ruspina (a near defeat). Furthermore, the Pompeians were not fighting against the whole Roman state, but a faction, led by one man, who had temporary control of the Republic, just as they had had.

Just as defeat at Pharsalus had seen the collapse of the Pompeian Alliance's control of the Republic, so one defeat of Caesar could easily see the same. As was clearly shown, despite Caesar's victory at Pharsalus in 48 BC, both Spain and the East collapsed into rebellion against his rule and the same happened again in 46 BC. The loss of both Spain and Syria showed that, despite his many military victories, Caesarian control of the Republic and its provinces was only wafer thin.

Again the Pompeians had been defeated heavily, this time in North Africa, and the aftermath had been far more costly than at Pharsalus. Yet again, however, the faction rose from the ashes and quickly established control of southern Spain and raised another army. Furthermore, they now had an additional base of operation in Syria – the richest eastern province bordered by the Parthian Empire.

The similarities in the revolts of Scapula and Aponius in Spain and that of Bassus in Syria are striking. The surviving sources draw our attention to their middle-ranking origins (Roman knights; the equestrian class) and that all three men organised a revolt seemingly independent of the main Pompeian faction itself, but done 'in the name of Pompeius'. This is a much-overlooked aspect when people view the modern cult of Caesar; namely, how wafer thin his control of the Roman world was and how easily provinces would revolt against him, despite his overwhelming success on the battlefield.

This also speaks to the success of Pompeius (Snr) in his conquest of the respective regions and his embedding of personal loyalty in each location amongst both the elites and the rank and file. Though each region swore loyalty to Caesar when he was physically present (with his army) they soon reverted to supporting the (dead) Pompeius when he left.

Whilst Metellus Scipio had by far a greater Republican pedigree than Caesar, Cn. Pompeius Magnus represented the opposite, a youth untainted by the Republican politics of the 50s BC, with its violence and descent into civil war. He represented the new generation of the ruling elite, one that could be looked upon to restore the 'Golden Age' of the Republic. If we want to understand how successful Pompeius could have been, we need look no further than Caesar Octavianus (later Augustus) who could draw upon the achievements and loyalty of his (adopted) father without any of the associations of the bloodshed and tyranny. Both men represented a blank slate, upon which all but the die-hard supporters of Caesar could paint their own hopes and aspirations.

The key to the rise of Pompeius and his taking control of the Republic would clearly be the death of Caesar in battle, after which the Caesarian control of the Republic would unravel. Clearly Pompeius himself had limited military experience, yet he would not face Caesar alone. Again the parallels to Caesar Octavianus are instructive. He rose to supreme control of the Republic defeating a far older and more experienced general (Antonius) despite not being a great general himself. Key to his military success over a far more experienced opponent was his reliance on an ally (in his case, Agrippa) who won his victories for him. Pompeius did indeed have his own Agrippa; none other than T. Labienus, one of Caesar's most successful lieutenants, a man trained in the Caesarian fighting style and who had come close to defeating him at the Battle of Ruspina.

Thus, just as the alliance of Octavianus (political) and Agrippa (military) defeated Antonius and took control of the Republic, so that of Pompeius and Labienus could have done the same. Thus once again, Caesar had to take to campaigning to save his control of the Republic, facing the Pompeians for the fourth time.

Chapter Four

The Renewed Civil War in Spain (46–45 BC)

Caesar's Future Plans

Following his victorious return from Africa and with the civil war reigniting in both Spain and Syria, Caesar had the Senate vote him an unprecedented Dictatorship for ten years in succession,[1] on top of his Consulship for 46 BC. Yet apparently this was not enough for Caesar who, in anticipation of his departure for Spain and the campaign against Pompeius, was again elected as Consul for 45 BC, but on this occasion as Sole-Consul, without even Lepidus as a colleague.

Breaking even further with Republican precedent, Caesar ensured that his election as Consul was the only Curule election held for 45 BC, with none of the other Curule offices (Praetors, Curule Aediles, Questors) being filled. This was an act that could not be justified by precedent as he himself had been elected as Consul. Thus all political power now (very visibly) sat with Caesar. In terms of governance, M. Aemilius Lepidus was again to rule Rome in his absence as his Master of the Horse, aided by an enhanced number of City Prefects (either eight or six, the number cannot be confirmed).[2] Despite this, there would also have been the Plebeian officers elected, a full complement of ten Tribunes and two Plebeian Aediles.

Nevertheless, we can here see an interesting blueprint for a Caesarian Republic, with Caesar as Sole Consul and perpetual Dictator and Rome ruled by direct Caesarian appointments rather than elected officials; a very efficient (and un-Republican) system. Needless to say, such efficiency would hardly endear Caesar to the more Republican-minded members of the ruling oligarchy, or even his own supporters, looking for political reward.

Furthermore, Caesar's thoughts seemed to turn to his heirs and two young men arrived in Rome. The first was a young baby accompanied by his mother, the Egyptian Pharaoh Cleopatra VII. Staying at Caesar's house in Rome, the boy was duly named Caesarion (Ptolemy XV in Egypt), confirming the rumours of Caesar having fathered a bastard whilst in Egypt. Thus Caesar added to his Consulship and Dictatorship by parading a royal mistress and royal offspring at the heart of the Republic. The second boy was late-teenage (sixteen/seventeen) and was named C. Octavius and he was now the closest living male relative of

Caesar, with his mother (Atia) being Caesar's niece. Nicolaus of Damascus, in a near contemporary biography of Augustus, wrote the following:

> *While Octavianus [Octavius] was convalescing, still weak physically though entirely out of danger, Caesar had to take the field on an expedition in which he had previously the intention of taking the boy. This however he could not now do on account of his attack of sickness. Accordingly, he left him behind in the care of a number of persons who were to take particular charge of his mode of life; and giving orders that if Octavianus should grow strong enough, he was to follow him, he went off to the war.*[3]

With these matters settled to his satisfaction, Caesar, again ever impatient, had no intention of wintering in Rome, set off for Spain in November of 46 BC.

The Situation in Spain

Although this was Caesar's second Spanish campaign against the Pompeian faction (the first coming in 49 BC), the two strategic situations were quite different. On the one hand, in 49 BC the Pompeians had complete control of both Spanish provinces, whereas in 46 BC they only held Farther Spain (Baetica), with the Caesarians holding Nearer Spain under Fabius Maximus and Pedius. This provided Caesar with a secure base of operations, rather than having to force his way into hostile territory. This also meant that whilst the first campaign was fought in Northern Spain, this one would be fought in the south.

Furthermore, in 49 BC, the Pompeians had been in charge of the province for five years (since Pompeius' Proconsulship of 54 BC), with no Caesarian presence whatsoever. Now the Pompeians were fighting in a region that they had just seized and did not yet have full control of. To counter this, the Pompeians now had thirteen legions (of varying quality) whereas Caesar only had six in 49 BC. We are not told how many legions Caesar took with him on this occasion, nor how many were already in Spain with Fabius and Pedius. We do not know the exact date Caesar left Rome, but we have two sources who tell us how long Caesar's march into Spain took; Orosius states it was seventeen days to Saguntum,[4] whilst Appian quotes twenty-seven days (perhaps to Corduba in Baetica), supported by Strabo.[5] This would put the date of Caesar's arrival in early- to mid-December 46 BC (by a modern calendar).

Up until that point the two factional armies had been avoiding each other. The Pompeians hadn't pushed into Northern Spain and the Caesarians hadn't pushed against the Pompeians. Pompeius (and Labienus) were clearly going to fight a defensive war, ideally learning the lessons of Caesar's first Spanish campaign, when the Pompeians nearly gained victory by wearing Caesar down.[6] Furthermore, Pompeius was engaged in a siege of the city of Ulia at the time of Caesar's arrival, being the only town in the province to remain 'loyal' to Caesar.

Caesar naturally made towards the Caesarian forces commanded by Fabius Maximus and Pedius, in order to link up, but seemingly took them by surprise:

> *Caesar was thereby encouraged and informed Q. Pedius and Q. Fabius Maximus, the two officers he had previously appointed to command his army, that he had arrived, adding instructions that the cavalry which had been raised in the province should support him. But he came up with them more expeditiously than they themselves anticipated, and so did not have the cavalry to support him as he himself had wished.*[7]

Once unified, the Caesarian army marched towards the Pompeian capital of Corduba (See Map 2).

The Battle of Carteia (Late 46/Early 45 BC)

However, the first clash of this campaign came, not on land, but on sea, as the Caesarian fleet of C. Didius contested control of the Spanish waters with the Pompeian fleet of Attius Varus. The two fleets met in battle off the naval port of Carteia, on the Bay of Gibraltar:

> *The sea, moreover, straightway became hostile to him* [Pompeius] *and Varus was defeated in a naval battle near Carteia by Didius; indeed, had he not escaped to the land and sunk a row of anchors upon which the foremost pursuers were wrecked as upon a reef, he would have lost his whole fleet.*[8]

> *Nowhere, therefore, were the encounters more bitter or the results so doubtful. First Varus and Didius, the lieutenant-generals, fought at the very mouth of the Ocean. But the ships had a harder struggle against the sea than against one another; for the Ocean, as though it were punishing the madness of civil war, destroyed both fleets by shipwreck.*
>
> *What a dread conflict was that in which waves, storms, men, ships, and arms all strove together at the same time! Mark too the terrible nature of the battlefield, the shores of Spain closing in on one side and those of Mauretania on the other, an outer and an inner sea, and the watchtowers of Hercules overhanging them, while all around was the rage of battle and of storm.*[9]

Thus it seems that Didius and the Caesarian fleet emerged victorious, but both fleets were wrecked by the storm, meaning neither side emerged with naval superiority over the other.

The Initial Clashes on Land

The *de bello hispaniensi* gives the initial deployment of the Pompeian brothers. Pompeius Magnus was besieging the town of Ulia (seemingly accompanied by Labienus), whilst his brother (Sextus) held the provincial capital Corduba (see Map 2).[10] Wishing to tie the elder Pompeius down whilst he moved on his brother, Caesar dispatched six cohorts (roughly 3,000 men) and the same in cavalry to relieve Ulia, under the command of L. Vibius Paciaecus. Again the location of Labienus is not explicitly noted during these early clashes, though he is later noted at the side of Pompeius Magnus at Ategua.[11] Caesar then moved to attack Corduba itself and drive Sextus Pompeius from the city or force his brother to come and give battle.

First Battle of Corduba (Late 46/Early 45 BC)

The first battle came when Caesar dispatched a force of cavalry and infantry (of unknown size) towards the city, where they were met by a force of Pompeian defenders:

> Now as they were approaching Corduba, a good large force came out of the town and cut the cavalry to pieces, and the heavy-armed infantry we have just mentioned now dismounted. They then fought a great battle, to such effect that out of the countless host but few men retired back into the town.[12]

Thus we can see that initially the Pompeians had the better of the clash, destroying the Caesarian cavalry, but were themselves nearly wiped out by the Caesarian infantry (again no casualty figures are given). The key outcome of the clash saw Sextus inevitably calling on his brother to break off his siege of Ulia and come to his aid, this fulfilling Caesar's aims.

Second Battle of Corduba (Late 46/Early 45 BC)

With the elder Pompeius' forces expected, Caesar did not try to take the city by storm and thus become sandwiched between the two Pompeian forces, but crossed the River Baetis, with his engineers having created a bridge, and camped by the city. Upon Pompeius' arrival, his army camped on the opposite bank of the river. As happened frequently in this civil war, both sides avoided a pitched battle but engaged in low level trench warfare:

The Renewed Civil War in Spain (46–45 BC)   67

> *In order to cut him [Pompeius] off from the town and the supplies it afforded, Caesar began to carry a line of fortifications to the bridge, and Pompeius adopted tactics on similar lines. Whereupon a race took place between the two commanders as to which of them should seize the bridge first; and this race gave rise to daily skirmishes on a small scale in which now our troops, now theirs, would come out on top. This situation had now developed into a more intensive struggle, and both sides being more passionately bent on holding their ground had embarked upon hand-to-hand fighting and formed a solid mass near the bridge; and as they approached the river's banks, they were flung headlong into it, packed tightly as they were. At this point the two sides vied with each other not merely in piling one death upon another but in matching mound of dead with mound. Several days were passed in this fashion.*[13]

Thus, although neither side committed to a full scale battle, they engaged in several days of low-level warfare, with an (unknown) number of casualties on both sides.

The Caesarian Withdrawal

Realising again that his forces were being caught up in low level warfare (as had happened in both Spain, Greece, and Africa), Caesar withdrew his forces from Corduba in an effort to regain the initiative and entice Pompeius into the open, where he could face him in full battle once again. Thus Caesar chose a new target, the Pompeian stronghold of Ategua, which lay to the southeast. Caesar thus began the immediate siege of the town, and behind him left various outlying forts manned by forces of cavalry and infantry.

Ateguan Skirmish (Late 46/Early 45 BC)

In his move to confront Caesar at Ategua, Pompeius' force came upon one such garrison and massacred it:

> *Yet, in these circumstances, it so chanced that when Pompeius did arrive there was a very thick mist in the early morning. And so in the resulting gloom the Pompeians surrounded Caesar's cavalry with a number of infantry cohorts and squadrons of horse and cut them up so severely that but few men barely managed to escape that massacre.*[14]

Again we are given no estimates for the numbers involved, nor the Caesarian losses.

The Battle of Camp Postumius (Early 45 BC)

Though there is no timescale given in the early passages of the *de bello hispaniensi*, it seems by now to have been early January 45 BC. Not wishing to engage with Caesar in open battle, Pompeius drew up with legions (all thirteen of them according to the *de bello hispaniensi*) on a nearby hill, but made no move to break the siege. In response to this Caesar established a forward position, creating a hillfort overlooking the Pompeian camp:

> *Pompeius had his camp established between the above-mentioned towns of Ategua and Ucubi, in sight of both of them; and some four miles distant from his camp there lies a hillock, a natural elevation which goes by the name of the Camp of Postumius; and there Caesar had established a fort for purposes of defence.*[15]

Believing that he had an opportunity to inflict a defeat upon Caesar, Pompeius determined to attack that hillfort and eliminate it.

> *Now Pompeius observed that this fort was screened by its natural position on the same ridge of hills and was some distance away from Caesar's camp; and he further observed that Caesar, cut off as he was from it by the River Salsum, was not likely to let himself be committed to sending support, considering the very difficult character of the ground. Accordingly, with the courage of his convictions, he set out at the third watch and proceeded to attack the fort.*
>
> *On their approach they suddenly raised a shout and began to launch heavy volleys of missile weapons, with the result that they wounded a large proportion of the defenders. Whereupon the latter began to fight back from the fort; and when the news was brought to Caesar in his main camp, he set out with three legions to succour our hard-pressed troops. When he reached them, the enemy retired in rout and panic, with many killed and several captured, including two centurions. Many in addition threw away their arms and fled, and eighty of their shields were brought back by our men.*[16]

Again, we have another heavy skirmish between the two forces. We know that Caesar responded with three legions, but we are not told how many of Pompeius' troops he used for the attack. What is clear is that this was a Caesarian victory (though again we need to be careful of the sources' bias as to the efficiency of the Pompeian troops). Again we do not know how many men Pompeius lost. What is clear is that the initiative still lay with Caesar. His forces were strengthened further by the subsequent arrival of additional cavalry from Italy.

The Pompeian Redeployment and Subsequent Cavalry Skirmishes (Early 45 BC)

Having failed to dislodge the Caesarians from that hillfort, Pompeius changed tactics, abandoning his own position, and repositioning himself nearer Corduba. It seems that the Caesarian possession of that strategic hill and the arrival of additional cavalry threatened Pompeius' lines of supply and communication and created the danger of being cut off from Corduba. Thus Pompeius' repositioning attempted to reduce this threat. In doing so, he also appears to have scored a minor victory on the way against some Caesarian allied cavalry.

That night Pompeius burned his camp and proceeded to march towards Corduba. A king named Indo, who had accompanied the cavalry, bringing with him troops of his own, pursued the enemy's column somewhat too eagerly, and in the process was cut off and killed by troops of the native legions.[17]

Caesar then deployed this newly-arrived cavalry to do just as Pompeius feared and cut him off from Corduba:

On the next day our [Caesarian] cavalry fared somewhat far afield in the direction of Corduba in pursuit of those who were carrying supplies from the town to Pompeius' camp. Fifty of the latter were captured and brought with their pack animals to our camp. That day Q. Marcius, who was one of Pompeius' Military Tribunes, deserted to us. At the third watch of the night there was very sharp fighting in the area of the town, and many fire-brands were discharged.[18]

Thus, as Caesar was besieging Ategua, low level warfare was continuing between the Pompeians and Caesarians from Corduba and Pompeius' new camp.

On the next day two soldiers from one of the native legions were captured by our cavalry: they asserted they were slaves. Immediately on their arrival they were recognised by troops who had formerly been with Fabius and Pedius and had deserted from Trebonius. No opportunity was afforded of reprieving them, and they were executed by our troops. At the same time some couriers were captured who had been sent from Corduba to Pompeius and had come to our camp in error: their hands were cut off and they were then let go.[19]

The Siege of Ategua (Early 45 BC)

From his new position, Pompeius attempted to pin the Caesarians between his two forces: his legions in their camp and the defenders of the town.

At the second watch the enemy observed his usual custom of hurling from the town a large quantity of firebrands and missiles, spending a good long time in the process and wounding a large number. When the night had now passed, they made a sally against the sixth legion when our men were busily occupied on a fieldwork and began a brisk engagement; but their sharp attack was contained by our troops despite the support which the townsmen derived from the higher ground. Having once embarked upon their sally, our opponents were none the less repulsed by the gallantry of our troops, although the latter were labouring under the disadvantage of a lower position; and after sustaining very heavy casualties they withdrew back into the town.[20]

On the next day Pompeius began to carry a line of fortifications from his camp to the river Salsum; and when a few of our horsemen on outpost duty were discovered by the enemy, who were in greater strength, they were driven from their post, and three of them were killed.[21]

Caesar, accordingly, being compelled, as I have said, to carry on warfare even in the winter, did not attack Corduba, which was strongly guarded, but turned his attention to Ategua, a city in which he had learned there was an abundance of grain. Although it was a strong place, he hoped by the size of his army and the sudden terror of his appearance to alarm the inhabitants and capture it. And in a short time he had cut it off by a palisade and surrounded it by a ditch.[22]

Déjà vu – Caesar's Slow Start to Civil War Campaigns

It is clear to see that once again, Caesar found himself in a stalemate, much as he had been at Dyrrhachium some three years before, and again in North Africa. Despite wanting to force Pompeius into open battle where his superior generalship and troop quality would tell, he found himself in a siege of a town (of little intrinsic value in itself) but fighting a low level war against Pompeius (and presumably Labienus), who was engaging in a counter siege. Again none of this was of benefit to his strategy of forcing a swift conclusion to the campaign.

If anything there are echoes of all three of Caesar's previous civil war campaigns here, Spain in 49 BC, Greece in 48 BC and Africa in 46 BC, where despite wanting a swift conclusion, he found himself dragged into low level warfare, grinding both sides down. Thus again he found himself playing to the tactics and strengths of his Pompeian/Labienan opponents, desperate to avoid a set piece battle.

The Pompeian Counter Siege

With the city resisting the Caesarian siege and the Pompeians beating off the Caesarian cavalry, Pompeius seems to have grown in confidence and extended his counter siege:

Earlier on that day Pompeius established a fort across the River Salsum without meeting any opposition from our troops; and this put him under a misapprehension and led him to boast inasmuch as he had occupied a position which was as good as in our territory. Likewise on the following day he again pursued his usual tactics and made a fairly extensive sweep, in the course of which at one point where our cavalry were picketed, several squadrons of ours with some light-armed troops were attacked and dislodged from their position; and then, because of their small numbers, both our horsemen and the light-armed troops were completely crushed amidst the squadrons of their opponents. This action took place in view of both camps, and now the Pompeians were boasting with yet greater triumph on the ground that they had begun to sweep further ahead while our men were retreating further back. But when on favourable ground our men took them on again with their customary outstanding gallantry, they cried out and refused to engage battle.[23]

In the Civil War, when the Spanish city of Ategua, belonging to Pompeius' faction, was under blockade, one night a Moor, pretending to be a Tribune's adjutant belonging to the Caesarian party, roused certain sentries, and got from them the password. He then roused others, and by continuing his deception, succeeded in conducting reinforcements for Pompeius through the midst of Caesar's troops.[24]

Thus the Pompeians were engaging in hit and run tactics, attacking the Caesarian forces when the situation favoured them and not engaging when it didn't (much to the apparent chagrin of the author of the *de bello hispaniensi*, who clearly seems to have been present). Again we can clearly see the guiding hand of Labienus here.

The Siege of Ategua – Another Skirmish

Again the *de bello hispaniensi* details another clash between the Caesarian and Pompeian cavalry at Ategua, naturally with inflated Pompeian casualties and deflated Caesarian ones:

When picked light-armed infantry took our cavalry by surprise by coming forward to engage them, and when this manoeuvre was observed in the course of the fighting, quite a number of our horsemen dismounted. As a result, in a short time our cavalry began to fight an infantry action, to such good purpose that they dealt death right up close to the rampart. In this battle on our opponents' side there fell 123 men; and of those who were driven back to their camp not a few had been stripped of their arms and many were wounded. On our side there fell three men; twelve infantrymen and five horsemen were wounded.[25]

The Siege of Ategua – The Pompeian Breakout

Wishing to capture the initiative, Pompeius ordered an attempted breakout by the Pompeian garrison of the town, with a bold night attack against the Caesarian camp.

Accordingly, after they had hurled firebrands and a quantity of missile weapons and spent a very large part of the night in so doing, they opened the gate which lay directly opposite Pompeius' camp and was in sight of it and made a sally with their entire forces. With them they brought out brushwood and hurdles to fill up the trenches, as well as hooks for demolishing and then burning the straw-thatched huts which had been built by our men to serve as winter quarters; they also brought silver and clothing besides, so that, while our men were busily engaged in looting it, they could wreak havoc upon them and then retire to Pompeius' lines. For in the belief that they could carry through their enterprise he spent the whole night on the move in battle formation on the far side of the River Salsum. However, although this operation had come as a surprise to our men, yet, relying on their valour, they repulsed the enemy, inflicted heavy casualties upon them, and drove them back to the town, taking possession of their booty and equipment and capturing some alive, who were put to death the next day.[26]

For Pompeius, encouraged by the nature of the place and thinking that Caesar because of the winter would not besiege it very long, paid no heed and did not try at first to repel the assailants, since he was unwilling to distress his own soldiers by the cold. Later, to be sure, when the town had been walled off and Caesar was encamped before it, he grew afraid and came with assistance. Falling in with pickets suddenly on a misty night, he killed a number of them; and since the inhabitants were without a general, he sent in to them Munatius Flaccus.

For this man contrived in the following way to get inside. He went alone by night to some of the guards, as if appointed by Caesar to visit the sentries,

Bust of Cn. Pompeius Magnus.

Bust of C. Iulius Caesar.

Bust of M. Tullius Cicero.

Bust of M. Antonius.

Bust of M. Porcius Cato.

Bust of Sextus Pompeius.

Coin of Metellus Scipio.

Coin issued by Caesar – Dictator for Life.

Coin issued by the Anti-Caesarian faction.

Coin of Octavius.

Bust of C. Octavius, as Augustus.

Theatre of Pompeius

and asked and learned the watchword; for he was not known, and inasmuch as he was alone, would never have been suspected of being anything but a friend when he acted in this manner. Then he left these men and went around to the other side of the circumvallation where he met some other guards and gave them the watchword; after this he pretended that he was there to betray the city, and so went inside through the midst of the soldiers with their consent and actually under their escort. He could not, however, save the place.[27]

Thus again another Pompeian attack had been beaten off by the Caesarians, and the stalemate continued.

The Surrender of Ategua

The failure of the Pompeian breakout was seemingly the last throw of the dice as far as Pompeius was concerned, and, apparently having no wish to become bogged down in protracted siege and counter-siege, gave orders for the garrison to abandon the town:

At a later period two brothers, Lusitanians, deserted and reported a speech which Pompeius had delivered, to the effect that, since he could not come to the assistance of the town, they must withdraw by night out of sight of their opponents in the direction of the sea.[28]

It seems that the Pompeian grip on Ategua was not as firm as Pompeius would have liked it. The *de bello hispaniensi* has a number of passages referring to pro-Caesarian sentiment in the town, and even reports a massacre (presumably of the pro-Caesarian townspeople).[29] This story is repeated in Valerius Maximus:

Munatius Flaccus, a more eager than reputable defender of Pompeius' party, when he was besieged by Caesar within the walls of Ategua in Spain, exercised his savage cruelty in a most truculent manner. For after he had killed all the citizens whom he thought well inclined towards Caesar, he threw them headlong from the walls. These things, intolerable to be heard, were performed by Lusitanians, at the command of a Roman; well-fortified by their assistance, Flaccus withstood the divine labours of Caesar, with a desperate obstinacy.[30]

In addition to other setbacks there was one occasion when the citizens hurled fire upon the engines and ramparts of the Romans, although without doing them any damage worth mentioning, while they themselves fared ill by reason of a violent wind which just then began to blow toward them from the opposite direction;

> *for their houses were set on fire and many persons perished from the stones and missiles, not being able to see any distance ahead of them for the smoke. After this disaster, as their land was being ravaged, and portions of their wall were collapsing as the result of mines, they began to riot. Flaccus first made overtures to Caesar on the basis of pardon for himself and his followers; but afterwards, when he failed of this owing to his refusal to surrender his arms, the natives sent envoys and submitted to the terms imposed upon them.*[31]

Such an attitude was understandable, as throughout this civil war the inhabitants of the various towns and cities that had unwittingly found themselves in the firing line were eager to avoid destruction and give their loyalty to the attacking force. Faced with a Caesarian siege that could easily end in the town's destruction, all but the hard-core Pompeian supporters would have been looking for a negotiated solution.

With the failure of the Pompeian breakout and the Pompeian garrison ordered to abandon the city (presumably to its fate), the inhabitants rose up and attacked the remaining garrison. Soon afterwards, both envoys from the city came to Caesar and seemingly members of the Pompeian garrison offered their surrender if their lives were spared. Thus the town surrendered to Caesar, most commonly dated to mid-February 45 BC. Caesar, therefore, had a modest victory, having broken the Pompeian counter siege, and forced Pompeius to withdraw. Yet this clash had taken up precious time and done nothing to bring Pompeius and Labienus to battle.

Continuing Deja Vu - The Pompeian Redeployment and Subsequent Cavalry Skirmishes (Feb 45 BC)

Having already planned to re-deploy from Ategua, Pompeius Magnus (and Labienus) moved their army eastwards towards the town of Ucubi, creating a number of fortifications to protect this position. Naturally Caesar followed and shadowed his position and the game of cat and mouse continued. Again the earlier pattern repeated itself, with cavalry skirmishes between the two armies.

> *At that time too about forty of their horse dashed out upon a watering party of ours, killing some of its members and leading others off alive: eight of their horsemen were taken prisoner.*[32]

With Pompeius wisely avoiding battle, both sides engaged in their familiar pattern of siege and counter-siege with fortifications built and attacked:

In the period which followed Caesar moved up his camp and proceeded to carry a line of fortifications to the River Salsum. At this point, while our men were busily engaged in the operation, a fair number of the enemy swooped down upon them from higher ground and, as our men carried on with their work, there were not a few casualties among them from the heavy volleys of enemy missiles.[33]

The Battle of Soricaria (5 March 45 BC)

It seems that the Caesarian fortifications succeeded in forcing the Pompeians to take to the field, albeit with a small force and a clash took place between forces from the two sides, with a Pompeian attack on Caesarian siege lines:

On the next day the forces of both sides converged upon Soricaria. Our men proceeded to build fortified lines. When Pompeius observed that he was in process of being cut off from the fortress of Aspavia, which is five miles distant from Ucubi, this circumstance peremptorily demanded that he should enter the fray; yet, for all that, he gave his opponents no opportunity of engaging him on favourable ground, but from a hillock.

They set about capturing a lofty knoll, and made such good progress that Caesar had no option but to approach unfavourable ground. When accordingly the forces of both sides had launched an attack upon this lofty knoll, our men forestalled the enemy and hurled them back on to the level ground. This led to a successful action by our troops: on all sides their opponents gave ground, and our men were engaged in a massacre of no mean proportions. It was the high ground, not the enemy's valour, which proved the latter's salvation; and even relying upon its aid they would, but for the approach of evening, have been deprived of all support by our less numerous forces. As it was, their casualties comprised 323 light-armed and 138 legionaries, apart from those who were stripped of their arms and equipment.[34]

Thus again, if we are to believe the unknown author of the *de bello hispaniensi*,[35] the Caesarians emerged victorious. Yet again, however, the deadlock was not broken, and the two sides fell into the familiar pattern, again to the apparent frustration of the author of the *de bello hispaniensi*:

On the following day Pompeius' forces followed a similar routine and returned to the same spot, where they employed those old established tactics of theirs; for with the exception of his cavalry at no point did his troops venture to commit themselves to favourable ground. While our men were engaged on their task of fortification, the enemy cavalry forces began to launch attack.[36]

> *Later on, when our men were busily engaged on a fieldwork, a number of our cavalry were killed while collecting wood in an olive grove.*[37]

The Pompeian Withdrawal from Ucubi

The *de bello hispaniensi* presents a garbled account of a Pompeian withdrawal from Ucubi, but the reason is not clear:

> *Some slaves deserted to us, who reported that since March 5th, the day when the battle took place at Soricaria, there had been grave alarm, and Attius Varus had been in command of the fortified zone. On that day Pompeius moved his camp and established it in an olive grove over against Spalis.*[38]

What this 'grave alarm' was we will never know, and it is doubtful that the runaway slaves knew themselves. Nevertheless, Pompeius' position at Ucubi had been seen to be more precarious than he had perhaps wished, as seen by the necessity of the clashes at Soricaria, and therefore withdrawal to a new position made perfect strategic sense.

Pompeius appears to have marched his forces to the south-west towards the town of Carruca (see Map 2). Caesar naturally followed, but attacked another Pompeian-held town on the way (Ventipo). Interestingly the town of Carruca barred their gates to Pompeius and was burnt down for its resistance, with the Pompeian army moving on to the town of Ursao, in the plain of Munda.

The End of the Stalemate – The Tension in the Pompeian Tactics

Now some four months into the Spanish campaign, Caesar was apparently no nearer his goal of bringing Pompeius Magnus to battle and ending the campaign with (what he planned to be) a swift victory. As had happened in the previous Spanish campaign, along with those in Greece and Numidia, the Pompeians, no doubt at the urging of Labienus, adopted a guerrilla campaign of hit and run, spearheaded by another of Labienus' strengths, the use of cavalry (Labienan tactics). The frustrations in the Caesarian camp can be seen in the writings of the unknown author of *de bello hispaniensi*.

Yet despite the apparent success in stringing Caesar along, ultimately as in 49, 48 and 46 BC, we have to ask ourselves what the Pompeian strategy for victory was? It was all well and good to not rush headlong into battle against Caesar, his undoubted strength, but we must legitimately ask what Pompeius and Labienus' ultimate goal was? In 49 BC, the Pompeians in Spain weren't aiming for victory, just to tie Caesar down to allow Pompeius to amass his 'grand army' in Greece. In 48 BC Pompeius was clear that he needed a victory over Caesar in front of his Senatorial and Eastern allies to cement his new position. In 46 BC, we see perhaps two conflicting plans, with Labienus planning on wearing Caesar down in the desert with guerrilla warfare, whilst Metellus Scipio was seemingly intent on avenging Pharsalus and defeating Caesar in open battle. This conflict ultimately saw a long running guerrilla campaign abandoned suddenly when Metellus Scipio spied the time to strike and may well have led to the split between the two men.

As we have seen, both in 48 and 46 BC the Pompeians choosing to abandon the policy of grinding Caesar down for a 'more glorious' (and perhaps more Roman) desire to win in battle led to their downfall. Caesar's clear tactical strength lay in fighting set piece battles, outside of which his impatience always seemed to get the better of him. Time and again, both in Gaul during the Romano-Gallic War, and in the three civil war campaigns to date, Caesar had struggled when his opponents refused to give battle and adopted guerrilla tactics. No one knew this better than T. Labienus, who had fought by Caesar's side throughout the Romano-Gallic War and faced him in two civil war campaigns.

Yet, just as in 46 BC, the Pompeian tactics in Spain appeared to suddenly change and on the plains of Munda, the Pompeian army suddenly turned and offered battle; an act which surprised even Caesar:

On the following day Caesar was minded to take the road with his forces when scouts came back with the news that Pompeius had been in battle formation since the third watch.[39]

Naturally, we will never know for sure what brought about this change of tactic, perhaps another falling out between the wilier Labienus and his policy of guerrilla warfare and the more traditional Pompeius who needed a victory to both emulate and avenge the honour of his father. Dio, however, cites pressure from his native allies:

Upon the capture of this city [Ategua] *the other tribes also no longer held back, but many of their own accord sent envoys and espoused Caesar's cause, and many received him or his lieutenants on their approach. Pompeius, in consequence, being at a loss what to do, at first moved about and wandered from place to place through the country; later on he became afraid that as a result of this very course the rest of his adherents would also leave him in the lurch, and he chose to risk a decisive battle, although Heaven had beforehand indicated his defeat very clearly.*

> *To be sure, the drops of sweat that fell from the sacred statues, and the rumbling noises of legions, and the many creatures that were born outside their own species, and the torches darting from the east to the west, all of which signs occurred in Spain at that one time, did not make it clear to which of the two leaders they were revealing the future. But the eagles of Pompeius' legions shook their wings and let fall the thunderbolts which they held in their talons, in some cases of gold; thus they seemed to be hurling the threatened disaster directly at Pompeius and to be flying off of their own accord to Caesar. But he made light of it, for Destiny was leading him on; thus he established himself in the city of Munda in order to give battle.*[40]

Moving aside from prodigies and other divine portents, Pompeius seemed to suffer from the same issue that had plagued his predecessors as leader of the Pompeian faction (both his father and Metellus Scipio); namely, that despite the success of grinding Caesar down, his supporters expected him to defeat Caesar in battle, thus, once again, expediency was sacrificed for the grander (and more honourable) set piece victory in battle.

Summary – The Weight of Expectation and the Curse of the Pompeians

Thus, for a third time in a row, and against the evidence of all recent military history (not to mention common sense), a Pompeian leader felt obliged to abandon the successful Labienan tactics of wearing Caesar down and exploiting his frustrations, and give battle against a general with a proven superior battlefield ability and success rate. In Pompeius' case in 48 BC, there must have been doubts in his mind about the wisdom of such a move at that time, but he had been boxed in by Caesar refusing to follow the timetable Pompeius set and so became trapped by the logic of his own masterplan; namely, to publicly defeat Caesar in battle. Thus it was a calculated gamble and one that failed, costing him his life.

The fact that both Metellus Scipio and Pompeius Magnus (jnr) followed the same path, despite the clear evidence of Pharsalus, and abandoned sound tactics, speaks more for the impact of the Roman (and allied) psyche than it does to common sense. In reality neither man had the need to see Caesar defeated in battle, just ensure his failure or death and let the Caesarian faction and its rebellion wither away. Instead, both gave in to the weight of expectation and the ghost of their predecessors rather than take the harder route and continue with the Labienan tactics of grinding Caesar down.

In terms of Labienus, he was doomed (now in all senses of the word) to see his advice ignored yet again and the mistakes of the past repeated, knowing more than any man alive Caesar's strengths and weaknesses, and that his skill on the battlefield was his strength. Ultimately it was the fourth (and final) Pompeian leader, Sextus, who broke this vicious circle of expectation and refused to follow his predecessors, greatly explaining his longevity (leading the faction for the next decade): that and the absence of Caesar himself. However, at the field of Munda, his brother took the fateful decision to trust in the gods and hope, rather than in common sense, and against all the evidence, offered to give battle against Caesar.

Chapter Five

The Battle of Munda – Caesar's Final Battle (45 BC)

Thus, having again abandoned the guerrilla tactics that had served them so well, the Pompeians chose to give battle, on what we now equate to 17 March 45 BC, at a now-lost location near the city of Munda (see Map 2). We are fortunate to have a seemingly first-hand account of the battle, written by the unknown author of the *de bello hispaniensi*, along with descriptions in a number of other surviving sources. Caesar himself is said to have stated that it was his most hard-fought battle and the one in which he came closest to defeat (again displaying his usual arrogance and ignoring his defeat at Dyrrhachium).

The Battlefield

Though the exact location of the battlefield is now lost, the author of the *de bello hispaniensi* provides us with a detailed analysis of the site itself:

> Between the two camps ran a plain, extending for some five miles, so that there were two factors which made for the protection of Pompeius' troops, the town, and the lofty nature of the ground. Extending from the town the plain ground nearest to it levelled out and ran down to where a stream ran in front of it, which made the ground there extremely awkward for Caesar's troops to approach the Pompeians; for the soil to the right of the river's course was marshy and full of bog-holes.[1]

Thus, the Pompeians (most likely T. Labienus – see below) chose the battlefield for this encounter and one which ensured their tactical advantage. The site was close to the ancient Romano-Spanish city of Munda and allowed the Pompeians to utilise the city in their defensive line, much as they had done in the early North African campaign the year previously.

The Pompeian Army

Again, the unknown author of the *de bello hispaniensi* provides several descriptions of the Pompeian army (more so than his own):

> *He [Pompeius] had the eagles and standards of thirteen legions; but among those which he thought afforded him any solid support two were native legions, having deserted from Trebonius; a third had been raised from the local Roman settlers; a fourth was one which was once commanded by Afranius and which Pompeius had brought with him from Africa, while the rest were made up of runaways or auxiliaries. As for light-armed units and cavalry, our troops were in fact far superior both in quality and quantity.*[2]

> *Their battle line was composed of thirteen legions, and was screened on the flanks by cavalry as well as 6,000 light-armed troops, while in addition there were nearly as many again auxiliary troops besides.*[3]

Thus on the face of, if we utilise the standard numbers for legions at the time (and assuming that they were fully manned), Pompeius had approximately 75,000 men under his command and an unknown number of cavalry. Clearly Pompeius had the larger army, yet the key issue lay not with the numbers, but the quality. As the author of the *de bello hispaniensi* is at pains to point out, a huge proportion of Pompeius' army were not veteran legionaries, but native troops, with only four of the thirteen legions Roman, or Romano-Spanish veterans. Interestingly, Dio chooses to draw our attention to the native elements of each army, which not only included Spanish natives, but African ones as well:

> *Both leaders had in addition to their citizen and mercenary troops many of the natives and many Moors. For Bocchus had sent his sons to Pompeius, and Bogud in person made the campaign with Caesar. Still, the contest turned out to be like one between the Romans themselves, not between them and other nations.*[4]

This is an interesting nugget of information, as Bocchus (II) and Bogud were the joint kings of the Mauri, long standing enemies of Numidia, who, as early as 47 BC, had supported Caesar (the enemy of their enemy – Numidia) and even previously sent their forces to Spain to quell the pro-Pompeian uprising. Their attack on Numidia in 46 BC did much to weaken the Numidian campaign against Caesar and in return they received a good portion of the defeated Numidia as a reward. Yet, less than a year later, we find the two kings on opposite sides and one (Bocchus II) even siding with the Pompeians. Clearly a falling out between the two had occurred.

The other aspect which Dio chooses to highlight is the motivation of the Pompeian veterans at Munda, most of whom had previously fought Caesar in 49 BC in his first Spanish campaign, having both surrendered and been pardoned:

> *Pompeius' men were inferior in these respects, but, becoming strong through their despair of safety, should they fail to conquer, they were full of eagerness. For inasmuch as the majority of them had been captured with Afranius and Varro, had been spared, and afterwards delivered to Longinus, and had revolted from him, they had no hope of safety if they were beaten, and hence were reduced to desperation, feeling that they must now win or else perish utterly.*[5]

Thus, having been pardoned once and facing Caesar again, they clearly believed that no prisoners would be taken, and this tallies with the various acts of brutality meted against prisoners which can be seen in the narrative of the preceding campaign, as depicted in the *de bello hispaniensi*. This brutality clearly is at odds with the other Caesarian civil war campaigns, during which Caesar is noted for not mistreating the common Pompeian soldiery. Yet, Spain clearly tested his patience, having revolted almost immediately following his conquest in 49 BC and now sustaining a Pompeian revival. Such a diehard attitude on behalf of the Pompeian soldiery would go a long way to making up for the inexperience of the rest of the legions and perhaps explain the high casualty rates in the subsequent battle.

The exact disposition of the Pompeian legions is not given, and it would be interesting to note the locations of the veteran Roman legions versus the newly-raised ones. Ideally the Pompeian leadership would have wanted to ensure that there was an equal distribution of veteran legions in each part of the army, to bolster the morale of the freshly raised ones who had never faced battle before.

The Pompeian Leadership

Whilst the narrative of the *de bello hispaniensi* refers frequently to Pompeius and his brother, the roles of the other two men in the Pompeian ruling Triumvirate – T. Labienus and P. Attius Varus – have been obscured. Labienus is only mentioned on two occasions, the second being his subsequent fate in the battle. The only mention in the three-month-plus campaigns prior to the battle comes in relation to the news of the massacre of pro-Caesarians at Ategua.[6] Yet the *de bello hispaniensi* does him a disservice (perhaps deliberately so, given his ex-Caesarian status).

The tactics used by the Pompeians in the previous months were classic Labienan ones; hit and run, dragging Caesar into trench warfare, or pointless sieges, and constantly changing position to deny him an advantage, all seen previously in the desert campaigns that preceded Thapsus. For Labienus it must have been a distressing case of déjà vu, when a less experienced superior officer abandoned these tactics and gave battle, as had happened, with disastrous consequences, at Thapsus. Nonetheless, as set out below, the Pompeian battle dispositions seem to bear all his hallmarks, and though not the overall Pompeian commander, the battle that followed was one which clearly followed his plan.

The role of P. Attius Varus is equally obscured. Again he only rated two mentions in the *de bello hispaniensi*, the second being his fate in the battle. The first related to him being in command of a 'fortified position' at the earlier Battle of Soricaria. Though more recently a naval commander, he had fought the Caesarians both in Italy and North Africa, and was the overall commander of the Pompeian victory at Bagradas River in 49 BC, which saw the invading Caesarian army destroyed (though this was mostly thanks to the Numidian army). What role he played in these subsequent Spanish campaigns is not clear.

Finally, we have the figure of Cn. Pompeius Magnus himself, seemingly the man responsible for the fateful decision to risk the entire campaign on a set piece battle at Munda. Having limited practical military experience himself, and having made the final decision, it is likely that it was Labienus who chose the ground and the tactics the Pompeian army would deploy on the day (see below), with him being the figurehead, with his father's legacy weighing heavily on him.

The Caesarian Army

Repeating the pattern that we have seen throughout these civil war campaigns to date, it seems that the Caesarian army was the smaller of the two, with the unknown author of the *de bello hispaniensi* reporting the following for the size of the Caesarian army:

our forces comprised eighty cohorts and 8,000 cavalry.[7]

If we utilise the traditional number for a Roman cohort that gives us a figure of just over 38,000 Caesarian soldiers, along with 8,000 cavalry: nearly 45,000 men, compared to the 65,000 plus of the Pompeian army. Interestingly, the *de bello hispaniensi* intimates that the Caesarians held the advantage in cavalry numbers, unlike Pharsalus and Thapsus, and hence the Pompeian caution and use of the topography of the battlefield (see below).

Again, it is Dio who points out that Caesar's forces were bolstered by a Maurian contingent led by one of their Kings (Bogud),[8] though his brother, and co-ruler (Bocchus II), had sent a contingent to fight with the Pompeians. The only description we have for the disposition of the Caesarian army is as follows:

On our side the men of the Tenth legion held their proper post, the right wing; while the men of the Third and Fifth legions together with all the rest of our forces; the auxiliary troops and the cavalry; held the left wing.[9]

The Pompeian Tactics

Although Pompeius had seemingly ruled that the Pompeians would give battle and abandon their hit-and-run tactics, most likely overriding the advice of Labienus, the latter's influence can clearly be seen in the tactics the Pompeians employed on that day. Much to the annoyance of the author of the *de bello hispaniensi*, the Pompeians did not engage the Caesarians on equal terms but used the natural advantages afforded to them both by the topography of the battlefield (occupying the heights and protected by the stream) and by the closeness of the city of Munda. The latter tactic can be seen to be a copy of those used in the North African campaign (at the city of Uzitta), where the Pompeian army used the city to anchor their defensive line:

Consequently, when Caesar saw their battle line deployed, he had no doubt that his opponents would advance to the level ground to do battle in the middle of the plain. This area was in full view of all. Moreover, with a level plain like that and a calm, sunny day, it was a tempting situation for cavalry, a wonderful, longed-for and well-nigh heaven-sent opportunity for engaging battle. Our men were delighted, though some also had misgivings, at the thought that the welfare and fortunes of everyone were being brought to the point that no one could tell for certain what would prove to be the luck vouchsafed them an hour later.

And so our men advanced to do battle; and we supposed that the enemy would do likewise: but our opponents would not venture to advance far from the defences of the town: on the contrary, they were establishing themselves in the town close to the wall. And so our men advanced. From time to time the favourable nature of the ground would sorely tempt the enemy to press on to victory under such conditions; but nonetheless, they would not depart from their accustomed tactics so as to forsake either the high ground or the town. And when our men, advancing at a moderate pace, came up closer to the stream, their opponents remained consistently on the defensive on the steep ground.[10]

Given the lack of battle experience possessed by Pompeius Magnus, we can clearly see the influence of Labienus in these Pompeian tactics, who, even though he had likely been overruled on giving battle, refused to meet Caesar on equal terms and maintained every advantage that could be found. Thus Caesar, if he wanted his victory, was going to have to fight on unequal terms; uphill and disrupted by the terrain of the battlefield.

The Caesarian Advance and Subsequent Stalemate

That being the case, it fell upon the Caesarian army to attack and try to dislodge the Pompeian forces from their fixed position. Thus the Caesarian army attacked uphill, accompanied by the usual fusillade of javelins:

> *The shout was raised, and the battle joined. Hereupon, although our men were superior in point of valour, their opponents offered a very spirited resistance from their higher position; and so furious proved the shouting on both sides, so furious the charging with its attendant volley of missiles, that our men well-nigh lost their confidence in victory. In fact, as regards attacking and shouting, the two chief methods of demoralising an enemy, both sides stood on equal terms of comparison. But though they accordingly brought to the contest an equal fighting capacity in both these departments of battle, yet the enemy masses were pinned down by our volleys of heavy javelins and fell in heaps.*[11]

Given its understandable partisanship, reading the *de bello hispaniensi* presents us with an ultimately one sided affair that was seemingly over quickly. Yet it is only when you read the other surviving accounts of the battle (most notably those of Appian and Dio) that you begin to see the true picture:

> *When battle was joined fear seized upon Caesar's army and hesitation was joined to fear. Caesar, lifting his hands toward heaven, implored all the gods that his many glorious deeds be not stained by this single disaster. He ran up and encouraged his soldiers. He took his helmet off his head and shamed them to their faces and exhorted them. As they abated nothing of their fear, he seized a shield from a soldier and said to the officers around him, "This shall be the end of my life and of your military service." Then he sprang forward in advance of his line of battle toward the enemy so far that he was only ten feet distant from them. Some 200 missiles were aimed at him, some of which he evaded while others were caught on his shield. Then each of the Tribunes ran toward him and took position by his side, and the whole army rushed forward and fought the entire day, advancing and retreating by turns until, toward evening, Caesar with difficulty won the victory. It was reported that he said that he had often fought for victory, but that this time he had fought even for existence.*[12]

Thereupon the allies on both sides were quickly routed and fled; but the legions themselves struggled in close combat to the utmost in their resistance of each other. Not a man of them would yield; they remained in their places slaying and perishing, as if each individual were to be responsible to all the rest as well for the issue of victory or defeat. Consequently, they were not concerned to see how their allies were battling but fought as eagerly as if they alone were struggling. Neither sound of paean nor groan was to be heard from any one of them, but both sides merely shouted "Strike! Kill!", while their deeds easily outran their words.

Caesar and Pompeius, who witnessed these struggles from horseback from certain elevated positions, had no ground for either hope or despair, but with their minds torn by doubts, were equally distressed by confidence and by fear. The battle was so evenly balanced that they suffered tortures at the sight as they strained to spy out some advantage and shrank from discovering some setback. In mind, too, they suffered tortures, as they prayed for success and against misfortune, alternating between strength and fear. Therefore, they were unable to endure it long but leaped from their horses and joined in the conflict. Thus they preferred to share in it by personal exertion and danger rather than by tension of spirit, and each hoped by his participation in the fight to turn the scale somehow in favour of his own troops; or, failing that, they wished to die with them.

The leaders, then, took part in the battle themselves; yet no advantage came of this to either army. On the contrary, when the men saw their chiefs sharing their danger, a far greater disregard for their own death and eagerness for the destruction of their opponents seized both alike. Accordingly, neither side for the moment turned to flight, but matched in determination, they proved also to be matched in physical strength.[13]

The Turning Point – The *de bello hispaniensi* and the Military Analysis

Thus the two evenly matched sides fought throughout the day, with both sets of commanders fighting in the thick of it. Interestingly, we are presented with two different (but not mutually incompatible) accounts of what finally turned the battle. Firstly, we have the eyewitness account of the *de bello hispaniensi*. As seen below, this account has the battle turning on account of the Pompeian wings being eventually worn down, firstly by the veterans of the Tenth Legion on the Caesarian right, overpowering their counterparts, and then the Pompeians weakening their right to reinforce the legions facing the Tenth, thereby weakening the wing facing the Caesarian cavalry. Thus with both wings weakened, the Pompeian army eventually was slowly enveloped and crushed, with a considerable number of the Pompeians fighting to the death:

Our right wing, as we have explained, was held by the men of the Tenth Legion; and despite their small numbers, their gallantry none the less enabled them by their exertions to inspire no little panic among their opponents. They proceeded, in fact, to exert strong pressure on the enemy, driving him back from his positions, with the result that he began to transfer a legion from his right, to give support and to prevent our men from outflanking him.

As soon as this legion had been set in motion Caesar's cavalry began to exert pressure on the enemy left wing, so that, no matter how gallantly the enemy might fight, he was afforded no opportunity of reinforcing his line. And so, as the motley din, shouts, groans, the clash of swords, assailed their ears, it shackled the minds of the inexperienced with fear. Hereupon, as Ennius puts it, "foot forces against foot and weapons grind against weapons"; and in the teeth of very strong opposition our men began to drive the enemy back. The town, however, stood them in good stead.[14]

The Turning Point – Dio and the Human Element

Thus we have an account written by a military man, who puts the defeat in military terms, with the eventual pressure on the Caesarian right prevailing on the Pompeians to disrupt their formation and weaken one wing to support the other, which seems to have bought them time, but ultimately weakened their other wing, ensuring their eventual over-powerment. Dio, however, presents a more political analysis and rather than the inevitability of military tactics and experience, prefers to ascribe a more human factor for the defeat:

All would have perished or at nightfall they would have parted with honours even, had not Bogud, who was somewhere outside the conflict, set out for Pompeius' camp, whereupon Labienus, observing this, left his station and proceeded against him. Pompeius' men, then, supposing him to be in flight, lost heart; and though later, of course, they learned the truth, they could no longer recover themselves.[15]

Thus, for Dio's source, it was Bogud and his Maurian contingent who set off the final collapse of the Pompeian forces caused, not by superior Caesarian fighting ability and the slow grind of an all-day battle, but by his (un-Roman?) move to attack Pompeius' camp, forcing Labienus to leave his position in battle, a move interpreted by his men as signalling a collapse which brought about a real collapse. Thus in this narrative, it was a 'perfidious' move by Bogud and a mistake by Labienus which brought about a tragic misunderstanding and that is why the Pompeians lost: due to a comedy of errors.

Pro and Anti-Caesarian Narratives

Naturally, we can see that the Dio version represents the Anti-Caesarian narrative: that it was down to bad luck, not superior tactics or fighting ability that the Caesar won the day. The role of Labienus is interesting, as it assumes that, spotting Bogud's move on their camp, he would break off from a life-and-death struggle with Caesar to block him. Given his subsequent fate, this is a clear scapegoating of the Pompeians' best general, showing that this is not only an Anti-Caesarian narrative, but a pro-Pompeian one, with Pompeius Magnus exonerated by the reckless actions of a (lower class) subordinate.

Yet, as we can see, there are deficiencies in both narratives. The *de bello hispaniensi* has a short battle won by the superior tactics and fighting strength of the Caesarian army. Yet he omits any reference to Caesar having to rally his men or even the presence of his African allies. Dio by contrast, has the North Africans routed early in the battle and the rest of the day taken up by an evenly-balanced slogging match between the two sets of legionaries, but with the ultimate victory coming from a Maurian flanking manoeuvre which set off a Pompeian mistake and subsequent collapse.

There is common ground between the two accounts, namely that the victory came on the wings due to a deliberate Pompeian weakening of their forces stationed there. In the *de bello hispaniensi* this is due to the Pompeian right wing having to be weakened to reinforce their left wing, and in Dio it is due to Labienus detaching men from a wing[16] (which one is not stated) to chase after the Maurian flanking manoeuvre. Thus a Pompeian flank was weakened, leading to the army's envelopment and collapse. If Labienus were the commander of the Pompeian wing that sent reinforcements to the opposite flanks, then we have the same action in both narratives, with them only disagreeing on his motive.

The Turning Point – The Other Surviving Sources and Caesar's Intervention

Yet, aside from these two main narratives, we have a number of other surviving accounts of the battle, and they present an interesting third narrative; that of the Caesarian army on the brink of being routed and only being saved by Caesar's personal intervention.

> *The last battle was fought at the Munda River. There huge forces contended, and the slaughter of the combatants was so great that even Caesar, since his own veterans were not ashamed to yield ground, seeing that his battle line was being cut to pieces and forced back, was beginning to entertain the idea of*

suicide, anticipating the disgrace of coming defeat, when suddenly the army of the Pompeiians broke and turned to flight.[17]

Orosius, primarily based on the lost books of Livy has the clearest evidence yet that at one point the Pompeians were in the ascendancy and the Caesarian forces were being pushed back, until Caesar rallied them. He speaks of a sudden collapse, which supports the Dio version more than that of the *de bello hispaniensi*. The same story, with more detail (the number of Pompeians detached from the army) can be found in an unusually detailed account in Florus:

On this occasion Caesar's usual good fortune was lacking, and the struggle was for a long time doubtful and anxious; so much so that Fortune seemed clearly to be deliberating some strange issue.

Caesar himself too before the battle was unusually depressed, either from a consideration of human weakness, or because he felt doubtful whether his good luck, having lasted so long, would continue, or else because, having started on the same career as Pompeius, he feared that the same fate might befall him. In the battle itself too an incident occurred which was unparalleled in men's memory.

When the two armies, being evenly matched, had long been simply cutting one another down, suddenly, at the height of the battle, silence fell upon both hosts, as though by mutual agreement.

And as if everyone was asking himself "What was to be the end of it all?" Finally, an unaccustomed disgrace presented itself to Caesar's eyes: his tried band of veterans, after fourteen years of service, gave ground, and though they had not gone so far as to flee, yet it was obvious that shame rather than valour made them resist.

Sending away his horse, Caesar rushed forward like a madman to the forefront of the battle, where he seized hold of those who were fleeing, heartened the standard-bearers, uttered prayers, exhortations, and rebukes, and, in a word, dashed this way and that through the ranks with glances, gestures and shouts.

In the turmoil he is even said to have meditated making an end of himself and to have shown clearly by his expression that he wished to take his own life; only, at that moment, five cohorts of the enemy, which had been sent by Labienus to protect the camp, which was in danger, crossed the battlefield and suggested an appearance of flight.

Caesar either actually believed that the enemy was fleeing or else craftily made use of the incident and gave them heart against an enemy, who they thought was fleeing and already conquered, while he discouraged the foe. His men, thinking that they were winning the day, followed more boldly, while the Pompeians, thinking that their own side was in flight, began to flee.[18]

Again we have a narrative in which, not only were the two sides evenly matched, but the Pompeians had the advantage, and Caesar's veteran legions began to falter. This Caesarian collapse was only prevented by Caesar himself personally intervening to raise his men's morale.

The Labienus story is actually a more reasonable version of events than the one presented in Dio, as Labienus did not leave his post, but merely dispatched five cohorts (nearly 2,500 men – if at full strength) to protect the Pompeian camp, presumably from a fresh Caesarian flanking manoeuvre (Bogud). Florus' account of this incident also has the additional detail that it gave the Caesarians heart, as well as demoralising the Pompeians.

The other surviving accounts add little details but focus on the near collapse of the Caesarian army during the battle:

The great battle was joined near the city of Munda, and here Caesar, seeing his own men hard pressed and making a feeble resistance, asked in a loud voice as he ran through the armed ranks whether they felt no shame to take him and put him in the hands of boys. With difficulty and after much strenuous effort he repulsed the enemy and slew over 30,000 of them, but he lost 1,000 of his own men, and those the very best. As he was going away after the battle, he said to his friends that he had often striven for victory, but now first for his life.[19]

Caesar's usual fortune followed him to Spain; but no battle in which he ever engaged was more bitterly fought or more dangerous to his cause. Once, indeed, when the fight was now more than doubtful, he leapt from his horse, placed himself before his lines, now beginning to give way, and, after upbraiding fortune for saving him for such an end, announced to his soldiers that he would not retreat a step. He asked them to consider who their commander was and in what a pass they were about to desert him. It was shame rather than valour that restored their wavering line, and the commander showed more courage than his men.[20]

Personally he always fought with the utmost success, and the issue was never even in doubt save twice: once at Dyrrhachium, where he was put to flight, and said of Pompeius, who failed to follow up his success, that he did not know how to use a victory; again in Spain, in the final struggle, when, believing the battle lost, he actually thought of suicide.[21]

Many engagements took place, the last near the city of Munda, in which Caesar was so nearly defeated, that, upon his forces giving way, he felt inclined to kill himself, lest, after such great glory in war, he should fall, at the age of fifty-six, into the hands of young men. At length, having rallied his troops, he gained the victory.[22]

The deified Iulius, when his troops gave way at Munda, ordered his horse to be removed from sight, and strode forward as a foot-soldier to the front line. His men, ashamed to desert their commander, thereupon renewed the fight.[23]

In an engagement with the younger Pompeius, Caesar, seeing his men give way, jumped from his horse, and called aloud: "Are you not ashamed, my fellow-soldiers, to run away and leave me in the hands of the enemy?" The troops felt the reproof, rallied, and renewed the fight.[24]

The Narrative of Caesar's Hardest Battle

Thus, we get a totally different picture from the other surviving (and later) sources than we do from the contemporary *de bello hispaniensi*. In that work, the battle was one sided and the Caesarians won with relative ease and in a short time. In the other sources, however, the battle ebbed and flowed, lasted all day, and at one point the Caesarian forces were on the point of collapse and had to be revived by Caesar himself, who apparently contemplated both defeat and suicide, rather than defeat and execution.

It is this narrative that Munda was the closest Caesar came to defeat, and contemplated suicide that we find (in varying degrees) in the accounts of Orosius (based on Livy), Appian, Plutarch, Florus, Velleius, Suetonius and even Frontinus (see above). In all these accounts, Caesar comes across suitably heroically, with the dramatic dismissal of his horse and his exhortations to his veterans, yet all agree that the veteran Caesarian army was rocking and being pushed back before they rallied and eventually won the day, either by wearing down his opponents or Labienus' dispatch of reinforcements being mistaken for a retreat.

Clearly the author of the *de bello hispaniensi*, who seems to have been present, had no wish to present this image to the Roman world, even though these elements presented Caesar in a heroic light, personally turning round the fortunes of the Caesarian army in a heroic display of leadership. This silence in fact speaks volumes that the battle was indeed far closer than the Caesarians would subsequently have liked to admit and at one point a defeat looked more likely.

The Suicide of Caesar

The story that Caesar contemplated suicide, rather than face defeat, is perhaps the most intriguing aspect from these additional sources. Ultimately, we will never know whether they are later embellishments or whether they represent an unknown source that recorded Caesar's own reminiscences of the battle, perhaps in some now lost narrative source or letters. Plutarch has the interesting comment:

> *As he was going away after the battle, he said to his friends that he had often striven for victory, but now first for his life.*[25]

Thus it is possible that this narrative comes from a friend of Caesar, who either published it in a history or in letters, presumably after Caesar's death. This story can be found in a range of later surviving sources: Suetonius, Florus, Eutropius and Orosius. The most frustrating aspect is the inclusion in the works of Orosius, who though writing some 400 plus years later maintains an enviable preservation of historical details lost from other surviving sources and greatly used the (now-) lost books of Livy on this period, leading to the question: did Livy have this story in his history, as early as the late-first century BC?

All we have for this period is the *Periochae* ('Summary') of Livy, which has the following intriguing statement: '*Caesar won at great risk his greatest victory near the town of Munda.*'[26] The inclusion of the 'great risk' element intriguingly leads us to the supposition that Livy too had this story that, contemplating defeat, Caesar's thoughts turned to suicide, another one of history's greatest 'what ifs'.

So, What Did Happen?

Clearly, we have to look beyond the bland whitewash that is the *de bello hispaniensi* and recover the view that this was one of (if not the most) hard fought battles that Caesar ever fought and one in which he was nearly defeated and lost his life. As noted earlier, for once Caesar was not allowed to choose the battlefield (as he had at both Pharsalus and Thapsus) and the terrain favoured his opponents.

It is clear that the two sides were evenly matched for much of the day and that at one point, as shown most clearly by Florus' account, the Caesarian veteran legions began to buckle and turn to flight. Had Caesar not personally rallied them, then the battle would have indeed been lost. Though this Caesarian intervention was clearly *a* turning point in the battle, we cannot say with any certainty whether it was *the* turning point in the battle.

All through these accounts we have both armies evenly matched right up until the evening, when the Pompeian army finally collapsed, with an element of the army being routed and another standing its ground and dying where it fought. So what caused this final collapse? Here we have two logical possibilities, as presented in our two main sources; a twist of the old 'revolution or evolution' argument – in this case inevitable pressure finally bearing fruition – or a sudden (unforeseen) event.

From the (unreliable) eye witness account we have a Pompeian wing (their left) buckling under renewed fighting from the Caesarians and needing to be reinforced, which weakened their other wing, with both eventually succumbing. This narrative can be supported by the other sources in so much as the renewed pressure on the Pompeian wing was the result of Caesar's ability to prevent his own forces from routing and exhorting them into one last renewed push, forcing the Pompeians to buckle. Was it really the sight of 2,000 men moving to the rear in formation that demoralised the Pompeians, or the sight or the Caesarian army buckling and then actually stopping their retreat and turning to fight anew that finally forced them to buckle?

To my mind, this makes more sense than stories of thinking their army in retreat. After a long day in the field, the Pompeian forces saw the Caesarian armies begin to buckle and took heart and probably advanced down the hill at them, hoping to finish them off. Thanks to Caesar's personal intervention, the Caesarian army then stopped its retreat, turned, and pushed unexpectedly at the advancing Pompeians, catching them off guard and perhaps slightly out of formation. This surprise Caesarian counter attack both demoralised the Pompeians, who were sensing victory, and caught them unawares and perhaps out of their strict formation, causing their wing to buckle.

This then forced Labienus to send reinforcements to that beleaguered wing, allowing Caesar to press home the cavalry attack on the now-weakened opposite wing. With both Caesarian wings winning their respective battles, the Pompeian army was slowly enveloped, with many (including Labienus himself) choosing to stand and fight (and die) rather than retreat. Given the casualties, it seems a large proportion of the Pompeian army stood its ground as the two wings folded in on them and died where they stood.

This is outlined in the battle diagrams.

94 The Battle of Munda (45 BC)

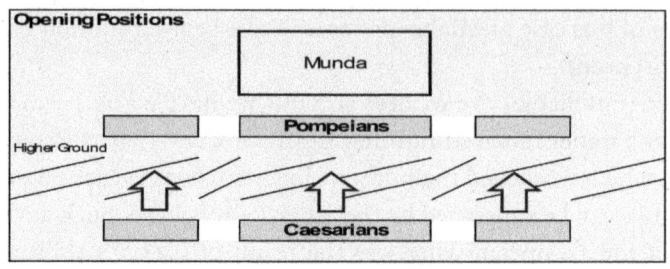
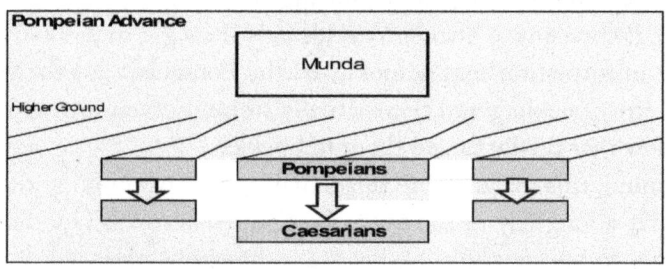
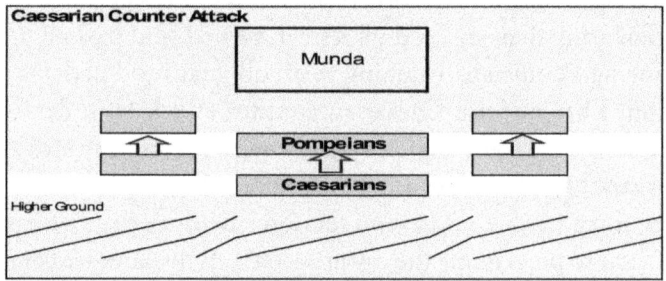
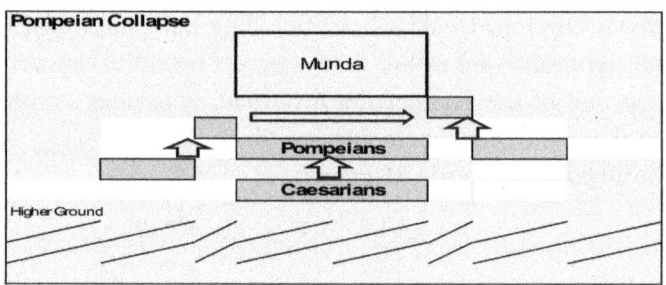
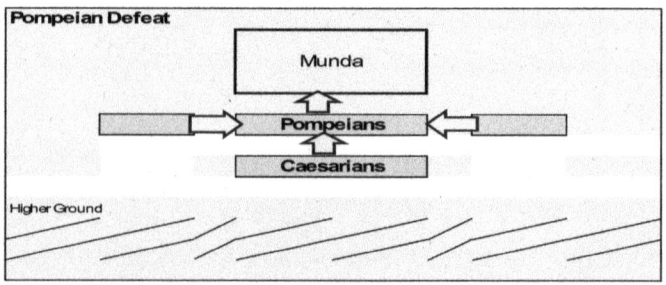

The Casualties

The *de bello hispaniensi* reports the following losses (repeated by Plutarch):

In this battle there fell some 30,000 men, if anything, more, as well as Labienus and Attius Varus, both of whom were buried where they fell, and about 3,000 Roman knights besides, some from Rome, some from the province. Our losses amounted to about 1,000 men, partly cavalry, partly infantry, while our wounded totalled about 500. Thirteen legionary eagles belonging to the enemy were captured; and in addition he had the following standards and rods of office.[27]

Thus just under half of the Pompeian army was killed in battle, along with two of its three commanders, the greatest casualties they had suffered in battle so far, testament to their desire to stand and fight on this occasion.

As detailed, two of the three ruling Pompeian Triumvirate stood their ground and died in battle; T. Labienus and P. Attius Varus. It is likely that had they wished, both men could have retreated from the battle (as happened at both Pharsalus and Thapsus, and as the Pompeian brothers were able to), yet both seemingly chose to stand their ground and die in battle. Both men would have been aware that pardons were highly unlikely, but both veteran commanders clearly ruled out the idea of living to fight again, perhaps aware that this was their closest and ultimately final chance to defeat Caesar in battle; two more martyrs for the Republican cause. Appian describes the grisly aftermath:

The heads of Varus, Labienus, and other distinguished men were brought to Caesar.[28]

The Pompeian brothers however, for whom this had been their first battle (and defeat), clearly did not share the pessimism of the older generation, and with the name of their father to uphold, both successfully fled the battle, to try to fight another day. Sensibly, the two brothers split up, with Sex. Pompeius travelling to the nearby Pompeian capital of Corduba, presumably to rally the remaining Pompeian forces and prevent the collapse of Pompeian Spain. Cn. Pompeius Magnus, however, along with a small force of cavalry, chose to retreat to the Pompeian port of Carteia, home of the Pompeian fleet, presumably to take to the seas.

Naturally the author of the *de bello hispaniensi* chose to play down the Caesarian casualties, with only 1,000 dead, which really doesn't tally with the other descriptions of the battle, nor does it resemble an army that was on the edge of being routed. The Caesarians, however, clearly did not wish the official account of the battle to allow its listeners and readers to realise how close a run thing the outcome was. Plutarch repeats the *de bello hispaniensi*:

> *[Caesar] slew over 30,000 of them, but he lost 1,000 of his own men, and those the very best.*[29]

Dio, however, presents the following, which does not contain figures, but gives the scale of the losses on both sides:

> *So great was the total loss of Romans on both sides that the victors, at a loss how to wall in the city* [Munda] *to prevent any from running away in the night, actually heaped up the bodies of the dead around it.*[30]

The Immediate Aftermath – The Siege of Munda

All sources agree that the Pompeian casualties would have been higher had they not been able to fall back to the city of Munda itself, around which the Pompeian army had fought. As the *de bello hispaniensi* notes:

> *The town, however, stood them in good stead. And so they were routed and put to flight on the very day of the Liberalia* [17 March] *nor would they have survived, had they not fled back to their original starting point.*[31]

Thus the bulk of the renaming Pompeian forces withdrew into the city of Munda and held it against an immediate Caesarian attack. Again it is interesting to note that the remaining Pompeian forces, with none of their senior commanders present, chose to fight on rather than surrender, perhaps again the result of a number of them having been previously pardoned by Caesar in 49 BC.

Nonetheless, whatever their motivation, the Pompeian remnants in Munda represented a clear challenge to Caesar, who launched an immediate attack on the city, necessary to cement his victory and prevent them from buying the other Pompeian forces in Spain time to recover. There are a number of accounts of the subsequent siege:

> *Those who, after surviving this rout, had made the town of Munda their refuge, and our men were of necessity compelled to blockade them. Shields and javelins taken from among the enemy's weapons were placed to serve as a palisade, dead bodies as a rampart; on top, impaled on sword points, severed human heads were ranged in a row all facing the town, the object being not merely to enclose the*

enemy by a palisade, but to afford him an awe-inspiring spectacle by displaying before him this evidence of valour. Having thus encircled the tomb with the javelins and spears taken from the corpses of the enemy, the Gallic troops now proceeded to assault it.[32]

Some fled to the city, some to the rampart. The latter body vigorously fought off their assailants and fell only when attacked from all sides, while the former long held the wall safe, so that it was not captured till all had perished in sallies.[33]

Appian presents a garbled account, wrongly naming the city of Corduba:

After a great slaughter the Pompeians fled to Corduba, and Caesar, in order to prevent the fugitives from preparing for another battle, ordered a siege of that place. The soldiers, wearied with toil, piled the bodies and arms of the slain together, fastened them to the earth with spears, and encamped behind this ghastly wall. On the following day the city was taken.[34]

Despite Appian's account however, it seems that the Siege of Munda was not resolved quickly and will be covered later. The important issue to note here is that the bulk of the surviving Pompeian forces were holed up in the town of Munda and still fighting. Not only did this take the shine off the earlier victory, but it allowed time for the two surviving Pompeian commanders, the brothers Cnaeus and Sextus, firstly to escape and then to regroup. Caesar had another battlefield victory, but again he faced the inevitable question of whether he could turn it into a battlefield victory in the wider civil war.

Summary – So Nearly the Pompeian Victory and the Death of Caesar

Hopefully, we have been able to demonstrate that, rather than as Caesarian (and most modern) historiography would have us believe, the Spanish campaign was not merely Caesar 'mopping up' the last remnants of the Pompeian faction, but was in fact the closest Caesar had come to defeat to date (aside from Dyrrhachium). Various accounts reveal that the Caesarian legions were pushed back and were beginning to break, with Caesar himself apparently contemplating ending it all, by his own hand, as his notable nemesis (Cato) had. Yet Caesar had the tactical acumen both to see the danger and the charisma to be able to make his army not only stand and fight but to renew their assault on the Pompeians, seemingly the key turning point in the battle which converted potential defeat into unexpected victory. Upon such actions, the whole history of the western world turned. This battle came within a whisker of being a Pompeian victory, accompanied by the death of Caesar and the establishment (for however long) of the Pompeian Principate of Cn. Pompeius Magnus.

It is interesting to note that the battle took place on 17 March, and just under a year on from his final victory, Caesar would be dead (15 March).

Section III

Rising from Defeat – The Pompeian Revival (45–44 BC)

Chapter Six

The Rise of Sextus Pompeius and the Pompeian Victories in Spain and Africa (45–44 BC)

Thus Caesar had his third (and final) victory in a major civil battle; and his thoughts now turned to converting that victory into a wider ending to the civil war (at least in the Western Republic). As we have seen, it was only during the aftermath of the battles of Pharsalus and Thapsus that Caesar was able to do the most damage to the Pompeian order, though both times they regrouped. Again Caesar faced the same issue. Although the battle had claimed the notable head of perhaps the most dangerous Pompeian general; T. Labienus, the sons of Pompeius, the figureheads of the Republican resistance to Caesar, escaped from the battlefield. Furthermore, a significant proportion of the Pompeian army remained in control of the city of Munda, resisting the Caesarian siege.

The Siege of Corduba

Leaving a force behind to progress the siege of Munda, Caesar naturally made quickly for the Pompeian capital of Corduba, where he hoped to find the Pompeian brothers. According to the *de bello hispaniensi*, however, a Pompeian officer escaped from Munda and rode to Corduba to warn the brothers.[1] Thus warned, the brothers abandoned the city:

> *On learning of these events, the latter* [Sex. Pompeius] *divided what money he had with him among his present cavalry force, told the townsfolk that he was setting out for peace talks with Caesar, and left town at the second watch. Cn. Pompeius, attended by a few horsemen and some infantry, pressed forward on the other hand to the naval fortified base of Carteia, a town which lies 170 miles away from Corduba.*[2]

However, despite the escape of the two Pompeian leaders, a number of survivors from the Battle of Munda had fled to Corduba and they prepared to resist Caesar. Notable amongst the survivors was a certain T. Quintius Scapula. He first appears in the civil war narrative during the Spanish revolt of 47 BC, mentioned in the

Pseudo-Caesarian account *de bello alexandrino*, as a 'provincial of the highest standing and influence'.[3] He appears as a leader of the revolt against the Caesarian governor, Q. Cassius Longinus. He next appears alongside Pompeius Magnus and Labienus on their journey to Spain from Africa the year previously.[4] It is Dio who provides his full name and places him as one of the key Pompeian officers in the revolt of the Spanish legions that forced the Caesarian Governor (C. Trebonius) from Spain.[5] Again Dio paints him as a charismatic figure and one of the key Pompeian leaders:

> *The followers of Scapula, on learning of this, went there and chose him general with full powers, after which they were most devoted to him and showed the greatest zeal, regarding his successes as the successes of each one of them and his disasters as their own.*[6]

Having taken part in and survived the Battle of Munda, he chose to follow the Catonian example and chose an ostentatious suicide rather than surrender to Caesar, which the author of the *de bello hispaniensi* describes in some detail:

> *Now the ringleader of all this unrest, as well as the head of a gang of slaves and freedmen, was Scapula; and when he came to Corduba as a survivor from the battle he summoned his slaves and freedmen, had himself built a lofty pyre, and ordered a banquet to be served on the most lavish possible scale and the finest tapestries likewise to be spread out; and then and there he presented his slaves with money and silver. After himself, in due course he fell to upon the banquet, and ever and anon anointed himself with resin and nard. Accordingly, at the latest possible moment, he bade a slave and a freedman, the latter was his concubine, the one to cut his throat, the other to light the pyre.*[7]

Thus another Pompeian leader chose death rather than surrender, though Scapula's lower social status meant that he was never elevated into the Pantheon of Republican martyrs. Despite the loss of three key leaders however, the Pompeian forces chose to oppose Caesar, initially contesting the bridge across the river, despite which Caesar was able to cross and placed his camp by the city. Again the eye-witness account of the *de bello hispaniensi* states that the city was defended by two scratch Pompeian legions (the Ninth and Thirteenth), so some 8,000-plus men (though we have to doubt that they were full strength given their scratch nature).[8]

The author of the *de bello hispaniensi* paints the two legions as being divided, with the Thirteenth willing to defend the town and the Ninth preferring to surrender, which most likely reflects the origins of the legionaries, freedmen vs survivors of Munda.⁹ As he details, the two legions fell into fighting each other, making the city an easy target for Caesar:

> *The Thirteenth legion proceeded to defend the town, whereas the men of the Ninth, as soon as they became involved in the fray, seized some of the towers and battlements. Once again, they sent envoys to Caesar, requesting that he should send in his legions to support them; and when the refugees got to know of it they proceeded to set fire to the town. However, they were overpowered by our men and put to death, to the number of 22,000 men, not counting those who lost their lives outside the battlements. Thus did Caesar gain possession of the town.*¹⁰

Thus Corduba (the Pompeian capital) fell easily to Caesar, unlike Munda, which still resisted.

Continued Pompeian Resistance – The Siege of Hispalis

With Corduba captured and Munda under siege, Caesar moved to subdue the rest of Baetica. His next major target seems to have been the prominent city of Hispalis, which lay to the west of Corduba, also on the Guadalquivir River. Again, unlike in 49 BC when he had previously defeated the Pompeians in Spain, and unlike in Greece in 48 BC or North Africa in 46 BC, victory in battle did not seem to persuade the locals to abandon either their support for the sons of Pompeius nor their armed resistance to Caesar, showing the depth of Pompeian support in the region.

Nevertheless, the same tensions that had surfaced in Corduba, between those who wanted to continue to fight and those who wanted to come to terms, were present in most Spanish cities. An excellent example of this can be seen in the case of Hispalis, a long standing Romano-Spanish city. Initially the city sent envoys to Caesar and welcomed a garrison into the city, but the pro-Pompeian party (led by a man known only as Philo) struck back. Again the *de bello hispaniensi* provides a narrative of the subsequent events:

> *Now inside the town there was a good large group of supporters of Pompeius, who thought it scandalous that a garrison should have been admitted unbeknown to a certain Philo, the man who had been the most ardent champion of the Pompeian faction and was a very well-known figure throughout Lusitania. This man now set out for Lusitania without the knowledge of our garrison troops, and at Lennium met Caecilius Niger, a foreigner, who had a good large force of Lusitanians. Returning to Hispalis, he penetrated the fortifications by*

night and thus gained re-admission to the town; whereupon they massacred the garrison and sentries, barred the gates, and renewed hostilities.[11]

Thus Caesar encountered a degree of Pompeian resistance that he had hitherto not seen in his campaigns, despite scoring his fourth major victory over a Pompeian army. Clearly, with sieges being waged at both Munda and Hispalis, Caesar was again in danger of losing momentum and allowing the Pompeians to stir up the whole of southern Spain. In the case of Hispalis, he undertook to bring the matter to a swift conclusion through a ruse; namely allowing the Lusitanians to spring a 'surprise' attack on his lines which he had encouraged and prepared for:

At Hispalis the Lusitanians kept up the fight without a moment's pause; and when Caesar observed their stubbornness, he was afraid that, if he made strenuous efforts to capture the town, these desperadoes might fire the town and destroy the walls. So after holding consultations he allowed the Lusitanians to make an attack by night, a course which the latter never supposed was deliberate policy. Accordingly, they made the attack, and in the process fired some ships which were alongside the River Baetis. While our men were occupied with the fire, the Lusitanians took to flight and were cut down by our cavalry. This led to the recovery of the town; whereupon Caesar proceeded to march to Asta, from which township envoys came to him to surrender it.[12]

So he [Caesar] made a campaign against them, and by appearing to conduct the siege in a rather careless fashion he gave them some hope of being able to escape. After this he would allow them to come outside the wall, where he would ambush and destroy them. In this way, he captured the town, which had been gradually stripped of its men.[13]

Thus Hispalis fell to Caesar, allowing him to continue receiving the submission of the other cities. Yet, as we have seen, these submissions were tokenistic at best and the threat of a Pompeian revival must have been ever present.

The End? - The Death of Cn. Pompeius Magnus

Key to the success of the Pompeiian cause was the figure of Cn. Pompeius 'Magnus', the 'new hope' of the Republic, son of Rome's most successful general and untainted by any of his father's political manoeuvrings. As long as he survived and continued to fight then both the Pompeian and the Anti-Caesarian factions would have a figurehead to rally round. Initially Pompeius seems to have succeeded in evading Caesar, first riding to Corduba to consult with his brother and then to the port of Carteia, home to the Pompeian fleet, though with the Caesarian fleet of C. Didius offshore (see Chapter Four).

We do not know for certain what the plan was, but it seems that the brothers decided to divide their efforts, with Sextus remaining in Spain to tie Caesar and his legions down in a guerrilla war (as had happened successfully during the First Civil War), whilst Cnaeus took to the seas. With Africa lost, the obvious destination for him was the Eastern Republic and in particular the Roman province of Syria, currently held by the 'Pompeian' forces commanded by Caecilius Bassus. Not only was it the only Roman province still in Pompeian hands, but it was the lynchpin of Roman control of the Near East, a region that had only been conquered for Rome some twenty years earlier by Pompeius' father. Syria was also the cornerstone of Rome's defence against their eastern rival, the Parthian Empire.

Thus Syria made an ideal base for a Pompeian recovery and that must have been his destination. Unfortunately, however, the déjà vu aspect of this scenario cannot have been lost on anyone, as it was the exact same journey that his father took after his defeat at Pharsalus. On this occasion however, the son had two advantages his father did not. Firstly, Syria was held by legions loyal to Pompeius (unlike in 48 BC), and secondly Caesar was not hot on his trail (again as in 48 BC). Yet, there was another more recent historical precedent that Pompeius followed, namely the fate of the previous Pompeian commander, Q. Caecilius Metellus Scipio. Scipio too had survived defeat at the Battle of Thapsus and successfully taken to the seas to evade Caesar and retreat to Pompeian held territory (Spain in his case).

Unfortunately for Metellus, he had not evaded the Caesarian fleet and his ship had been boarded, an action which ended with Metellus choosing to join the Pantheon of Republican martyrs and take his own life. Thus there were clear warnings for Pompeius Magnus as he contemplated his retreat and he must have been hoping it would be third time lucky for a retreating Pompeian leader.

In the first instance, Pompeius faced a city where a familiar story played itself out between Pompeian loyalists and those wishing to curry favour with Caesar, as the author of the *de bello hispaniensi* illustrates:

There was the party which had sent envoys to Caesar: there was another party which espoused the cause of Pompeius. Civil discord being thus stirred up, they seized the gates: much blood was shed: Pompeius, who was wounded, seized twenty warships, and took to flight.[14]

Thus Pompeius had succeeded in his first aim and had put to sea with a sizeable fleet. He now needed to succeed in the second stage – evading the inevitable Caesarian pursuit by both land and sea – and it was at this point that Pompeius' luck ran out:

> As soon as the news of his escape reached Didius, who was at Gades in command of a squadron, he forthwith began to give chase; and from Carteia too, the hunt was likewise taken up immediately by infantry and cavalry marching in swift pursuit. On the fourth day of their voyage Pompeius' party put in to land since they had been ill provided and without water when they sailed from Carteia. While they were getting water Didius hastened up with his fleet, captured some of their ships, and burned the rest.[15]

Thus C. Didius and the Caesarian fleet caught up with the Pompeian fleet and destroyed it, stranding Pompeius in Spain. Thus the decision to land for water proved to be a costly one, for Pompeius and the Pompeian cause and ultimately the Republic. As in 48 BC, a minor naval action proved to be the turning point, achieving what Caesar could not in battle. In 48 BC the key turning point came when Cassius' fleet not only failed to stop Caesar crossing the Bosphorus but defected to him, allowing him to catch up with Pompeius by sea. Now it was Didius' attack on the Pompeian fleet that hastened the end of the Pompeian retreat. For the third time in a row, the Pompeian leader had failed to successfully escape after being defeated in battle, and on none of those occasions did Caesar have a direct hand in it himself.

Stranded on land and with a Caesarian force pursing him from Cateria, Pompeius only had one option – move inland, and try to link up with his brother in the Spanish interior. Unfortunately for him, he had sustained additional injuries, making such an escape far more difficult:

> Pompeius took to flight with a few companions and occupied a certain spot which possessed natural defences. When the cavalry and infantry cohorts which had been despatched in his pursuit learned of this from scouts they had sent on ahead, they pushed on day and night. Now Pompeius was seriously wounded in the shoulder and left leg; added to which he had also sprained his ankle, which hampered him very much. So a litter was employed to carry him off to this redoubt and, once arrived there, he continued to be carried about in it. One of the Lusitanians who had been despatched from his escort on reconnaissance in accordance with normal military routine was now spotted by the Caesarian force, and Pompeius was promptly surrounded by the cavalry and cohorts.[16]

Cn. Pompeius' Final Battle

Despite this, Pompeius actually managed to fight off the Caesarian forces for a time:

> *It was a difficult place to approach, which in fact was the very reason why Pompeius had chosen himself a naturally fortified position, so that, no matter how great a force was brought up to it, a handful of men might be able to defend it from higher ground. On their arrival our men came up close to it only to be driven back with javelins. As they gave ground the enemy pressed upon them the more eagerly and called an immediate halt to their advance. When this manoeuvre had been repeated several times, it became obvious that it was a very risky business for our men. The enemy then began to fortify their position with a rampart, our men, however, acting with speed and despatch, carried a similar rampart along the high ground, to enable them to encounter their opponents on an equal footing. When the latter observed this move, they took refuge in flight.*[17]

Given the disparity between the size of the two forces and Pompeius' wounds, the end was inevitable:

> *Pompeius, as we have pointed out above, was wounded and had sprained his ankle, and this handicapped him in flight; moreover, the difficult nature of the ground made it impossible for him to have recourse to riding horseback or driving to assist his escape to safety. On all sides our troops were carrying on the work of slaughter. Cut off from his entrenchment and having lost his supporters, Pompeius now resorted to a ravine, to a spot where the ground was eaten away; and there in a cave he proceeded to hide himself, so that, short of his being given away by a prisoner, it was no easy matter for our men to find him. By such means in fact he was discovered there and put to death. When Caesar was at Gades, the head of Pompeius was brought to Hispalis on April 12th, and there publicly exhibited.*[18]

> *Being pursued thither he fled by a rough and thorny road that aggravated his wound, until tired out he took a seat under a tree. Here his pursuers came upon him, and he was cut down while defending himself bravely.*[19]

> *Cnaeus Pompeius, a fugitive from the battlefield and wounded in the leg, was overtaken, as he was seeking some solitary and inaccessible place of refuge, by Caesonius [Caesennius Lento*[20]*] near the town of Lauro, and was killed, still showing enough spirit to resist.*[21]

> *He met Caesennius Lento and was defeated; and taking refuge in a wood, perished there.*[22]

Thus, the third Pompeius commander met with death during a retreat after a defeat in battle, with Pompeius Magnus ironically following his father in an ignominious death; beheaded in a cave, as opposed to beheaded on a beach. The 'New Hope' of the Pompeian faction and the wider Anti-Caesarian movement lost yet another figurehead and the Pantheon of Republican martyrs gained another member.

In practical terms this cemented Caesar's victory in Spain; the young pretender, upon whose shoulders Caesar's enemies could place so much, was now dead. The question was whether the two factions (Pompeian and Anti-Caesarian) could rally around a new leader. Ultimately (by the 30s BC) the answer was yes, but in the short term, the chance of both factions recognising a single leader fell with the death of Pompeius Magnus. The Anti-Caesarian party in Rome would find new (ex-Pompeian leaders) in the forms of Brutus and Cassius, whilst the Pompeian faction turned to the surviving son of the original Pompeius Magnus, Sextus Pompeius, now gone to ground in the Spanish interior but bearing the bloodline (and Republican credentials) that could one day make him a challenge to Caesar.

Unnamed Battle – The Defeat of Didius

Though Caesennius Lento was the man who killed Pompeius, he fell under the command of C. Didius, and it was Didius who sent Pompeius' head to Caesar (a fate that had befallen Pompeius' father). Didius was the Roman commander who had fought one of the first actions in the Spanish Campaign when he defeated the Pompeian navy at Carteia (either in late-46 or early-45 BC). It was Didius whose timely attack on Pompeius' fleet brought Pompeius' retreat to an end. Yet Didius did not live long enough to be rewarded by Caesar, as he almost immediately fell in battle with the pro-Pompeian Lusitanians. The only account we have of this battle (its location is not mentioned) is by the *de bello hispaniensi*, though Dio makes reference to it:[23]

> *Filled with delight at the death of young Pompeius, Didius, whom we mentioned above, withdrew to a nearby stronghold, beached some of his ships for a refit, and …*
>
> *Those Lusitanians who survived the battle rallied to their standard and, when a good large force had been mustered, duly proceeded against Didius. Although he displayed no lack of care in guarding his ships, yet their constant*

The Rise of Sextus Pompeius in Spain and Africa (45–44 BC)

sallies enticed him on occasions to leave his stronghold, with the result that in the course of almost daily battles they laid a trap for him, dividing up their forces into three groups. There were some who were detailed to burn the ships; some to repel an enemy relief force, when the ships had once been fired: these parties were posted in such a way as to be entirely hidden from view, whereas the remainder marched into battle in full view of all.

Accordingly, when Didius advanced with his forces from his stronghold to drive them back, the signal was displayed by the Lusitanians, the ships were set on fire, and simultaneously those who had advanced to battle from the stronghold, they were now pursuing the same retreating bandits, who had turned tail on that same signal, were surprised by the ambushing party, which raised a shout and surrounded them from the rear.

Didius met a gallant death with many of his men; some in the course of the fighting seized some pinnaces which were close inshore, while quite a number, on the other hand, swam off to the ships moored in deep water, weighed anchor, and then began to row them out to sea, thereby saving their lives. The Lusitanians gained possession of the booty. Caesar left Gades and hastened back to Hispalis.[24]

Clearly, the Lusitanians had enough forces to pin Didius and his men down in a stronghold and ambush and destroy his force (of an unnamed size). Thus the Pompeians had allies who could still ambush and wipe out Caesarian forces in the region and avenge Pompeius' death.[25,] showing how thin Caesar's grip on Spain was, despite his victory.

The Last Stand of the Pompeian Army – The Siege of Munda

The siege of Munda, however, home to the remnants of the defeated Pompeian army, proved to be a harder proposition. There are a number of references to the siege of Munda throughout the *de bello hispaniensi*, which is a testament to the length of the siege (several weeks) and intensity of the fighting. There are fewer references in the other sources, keen to move onto other matters, though the famously gruesome depiction of the initial Caesarian rampart of corpses can be found in other sources:

Those who, after surviving this rout, had made the town of Munda their refuge, and our men were of necessity compelled to blockade them. Shields and javelins taken from among the enemy's weapons were placed to serve as a palisade, dead bodies as a rampart; on top, impaled on sword points, severed human heads were ranged in a row all facing the town, the object being not merely to enclose the enemy by a palisade, but to afford him an awe-inspiring spectacle by displaying before him this evidence of valour. Having thus encircled the tomb with the javelins and spears taken from the corpses of the enemy, the Gallic troops now proceeded to assault it.[26]

The fugitives had retreated to Munda, and Caesar immediately ordered that his conquered foes should be besieged, a rampart was constructed of corpses piled up and held together by the javelins and missiles which were thrust through them, an expedient which would have been horrible even if it had been used against barbarians.[27]

When the divine Iulius's army, the unconquered right hand of an unconquered general, besieged Munda, and they lacked timber to raise up a rampart, they made up the height, which they needed, with the bodies of their dead enemies. And because they lacked stakes, they drove in their spears and javelins to strengthen them, as necessity taught them a new method of fortification.[28]

Caesar, hurrying after the Pompeian brothers, left Q. Fabus Maximus in charge of the siege, which saw a number of separate actions. We have no timeframe for how long the siege took, but it clearly lasted a number of weeks:

While he was occupied here, the survivors of the battle who had been shut up [in Munda], as we described above, made a sally, only to be driven back into the town with very heavy losses.[29]

As for the survivors of the battle who had taken refuge in the town of Munda, a somewhat protracted siege led a good large number to surrender; and on being drafted to form a legion they swore a mutual oath that during the night at a given signal their comrades in the town should make an attack, while they carried out a massacre in the camp. But this plot was discovered; and when at the third watch on the following night the password was given, they were all cut down outside the rampart.[30]

Fabius Maximus, who had been left behind by Caesar to attack the enemy garrison at Munda, besieged that town in a continuous series of operations by day and night. Now that they were cut off the enemy fell to fighting amongst themselves; and after a welter of bloodshed they made a sally. Our troops did not fail to take this opportunity of recovering the town and captured the remaining men alive, to the number of 14,000.[31]

The Rise of Sextus Pompeius in Spain and Africa (45–44 BC)   111

Thus it seems that the Pompeian army made several attempts to break the siege, with upward of 20,000 men still in the city (seen from the number of prisoners, those who surrendered, and those who died). We are not told the size of the Caesarian besieging force, but it would have needed to be comparable or else face being overwhelmed.

As we can see from the excerpts above, the Pompeians launched three attacks on the Caesarian besiegers, each one being defeated. It was on the third and final attack that Fabius was able to defeat enough of the Pompeians to take the city, even then taking 14,000 Pompeian soldiers prisoner. Thus Fabius Maximus ended the last act of the Battle of Munda and defeated the remnants of the Pompeian army, for which Caesar rewarded him with a (disputed) Triumph and a Consulship. Not that Fabius lived long to enjoy the fruits of his labour, dying mysteriously on the last day of his Consulship (at the end of 45 BC). Orosius (and his earlier source) sums up the siege of Munda:

> *The city of Munda, after its inhabitants had suffered severe casualties from Caesar's assault, was finally captured with great difficulty.*[32]

The Siege of Ursao

Yet the capture of Munda and the final defeat of the Pompeian army did not end the civil war campaigns in Spain. The *de bello hispaniensi* moves on to detailing another siege, this time of the nearby town of Ursao:

> *Our men now set out for Ursao, a town which was buttressed by massive fortifications, to such an extent that in itself the place seemed adapted to assail an enemy by virtue of its natural site as well as its artificial fortification. Added to this, apart from a single fountain in the town itself, there was no water to be found anywhere in the neighbourhood under eight miles from the town; and this was a great advantage to the townsfolk. Then again there was the additional circumstance that materials for a rampart, ... and timber, which they habitually used for the construction of towers and mantlets, was not to be found under six miles' distance from the town; and in order the more to safeguard himself against an attack upon it, Pompeius had had all the timber in the neighbourhood felled and dumped inside it. Thus our troops were under the necessity of detaching men to carry timber thither from Munda, the town they had just recently captured.*[33]

What happened during this siege in unknown, as the manuscript of the *de bello hispaniensi* breaks off after one more chapter, mid-flow in the middle of a Caesarian speech. That the town fell eventually is a given,[34] but again it shows that despite Caesar's victory much of southern Spain still held out for the Pompeian cause, by now represented by the younger and surviving Pompeian brother, Sextus, who seems to have had a hand in organising the defence of the town.

Sex. Pompeius and the Withdrawal of Caesar

As noted above, the unexpected ending of the manuscript of the *de bello hispaniensi*, halfway during a Caesarian harangue of the locals of Hispalis for their disloyalty towards Rome (for that read Caesar), robs us of our narrative for the remainder of the Spanish campaign. The siege of Ursao was still continuing, the Lusitanians had raised an army that had defeated Didius, and the surviving Pompeian brother (Sextus) was still leading the resistance. Yet the loss of the *de bello hispaniensi*, whilst regrettable, is no deterrent to reconstructing the subsequent campaigns and in many ways allows us to do so without an outright partisan Caesarian view clouding the issue. Whilst the unknown author of that tract, and no doubt Caesar himself, would have been congratulating themselves on ending the civil wars in Spain (and in general), they did in fact accomplish no such thing and the civil war campaigns continued in Spain right up to Caesar's assassination, and beyond.

Nevertheless, Sextus' initial strategy was one of caution: rather than raising the banner of the Pompeian cause immediately, he took the sensible route and laid low, indulging in piracy with the remnants of the Pompeian fleet and awaiting the inevitable event that would change the Pompeian fortunes – namely the withdrawal of Caesar from Spain, along with the bulk of his armies. As we have seen throughout these civil war campaigns, the Caesarian faction needed the presence of Caesar himself, whether leading in battle or to cow the locals into temporary submission. However, as we have also seen, once that immediate presence disappeared then so did the leadership and the loyalty. Pompeius and his remaining supporters rightly banked that Spain had already revolted from Caesarian control twice since 49 BC and without Caesar there could easily do so once again. Thus once again, we see the weakness of the Caesarian position.

For Caesar however, there was little choice, the Pompeian army had been destroyed and the rising star of Cn. Pompeius Magnus had been cut down, removing a potentially dangerous rival. At the time, the surviving younger brother had taken to piracy and seemed no threat, which is reflected in the sources:

> *Hirtius has written to tell me that Sextus Pompeius has quitted Cordoba and fled into Northern Spain, and that Cnaeus has fled I don't know whither, nor do I care. 1 I know nothing more.*[35]

Sextus for the present kept hid and lived by piracy, but Caesar having ended the civil wars hastened to Rome, honoured, and feared as no one had ever been before.[36]

With Pompeius the situation was as follows. Being the younger son of Pompeius the Great, he was at first disregarded by Caius Caesar in Spain as not likely to accomplish anything of importance on account of his youth and inexperience. He roamed about the ocean with a few followers, committing piracy and concealing the fact that he was Pompeius.[37]

This was the business in which these men were now engaged. I shall now relate how Sextus had fared. When he had fled from Corduba on the former occasion, he first came to Lacetania and concealed himself there. He was pursued, to be sure, but eluded discovery because the natives were kindly disposed to him out of regard for his father's memory.[38]

Given the deteriorating situation in the Eastern Republic (see Chapter Seven), Caesar clearly had no option but to leave Spain in the control of his subordinates and return to Rome, to secure his position and plan his next campaign (see Chapter Eight). Equally, he probably had no desire to stay in Spain when faced with the lure of the East. So, with the last of the outright hostile cities conquered, Caesar laid down some new pro-Caesarian colonies and then set off for Rome, with the bulk of his legions, arriving back in October.[39] One additional point to note is that late in his campaign, he was joined by none other than his great nephew C. Octavius, now one of his only surviving relatives.

The Renewed War of Sex. Pompeius Magnus (45–44 BC)

Once again, however, it is important to stress that the absence of Caesar did not mean an end to the civil war campaign, much as Caesarian propaganda would have willed it (then or now). With Caesar (and his army) out of the way, Pompeius now swung into action and returned to Spain to revive the Pompeian fortunes, much as his brother and Labienus had done the year previously. Again we are denied a clear chronology of the subsequent campaigns, but we do have Dio's and Appian's accounts of them, which saw cities once again declare for the Pompeian cause and the massing of at least seven fresh Pompeian legions (from a province awash with veterans):[40]

When larger numbers joined him [Pompeius] for the purpose of pillage, and his force became powerful, he revealed his name. Presently those who had served with his father and his brother, and who were leading a vagabond life, drifted to him as their natural leader, and Arabio, who had been deprived of his ancestral kingdom, as I have related previously, came to him from Africa. His forces being thus augmented, his doings were now more important than robbery, and as he flew from place to place the name of Pompeius spread through the whole of Spain, which was the most extensive of the provinces; but he avoided coming to an engagement with the governors of it appointed by Caius Caesar. When Caesar learned of his actions, he sent [C.] Carrinas with a stronger army to fight him. Pompeius, however, being the quicker of the two, would show himself and then disappear, and so he wore out his enemy and got possession of a number of towns, large and small.

Then Caesar sent [C.] Asinius Pollio as successor to Carrinas to prosecute the war against Pompeius. While they were carrying on warfare on equal terms, Caesar was assassinated, and the Senate recalled Pompeius.[41]

Later, when Caesar had set out for Italy and only a small army was left behind in Baetica, Sextus was joined both by the natives and by those who had escaped from the battle; and with them he came again into Baetica, because he thought it a more suitable region in which to carry on war. There he gained possession of soldiers and cities, particularly after Caesar's death, some voluntarily and some forcibly; for the commander in charge of them, Caius Asinius Pollio, had no strong force. He next set out against Spanish Carthage, but since in his absence Pollio made an attack and did some damage, he returned with a large force, met his opponent, and routed him, after which the following accident enabled him to terrify and conquer the rest also, who were contending fiercely. Pollio had cast off his general's cloak, in order to suffer less chance of detection in his flight, and another man of the same name, a distinguished knight, had fallen. The soldiers, hearing the name of the latter, who was lying there, and seeing the garment, which had been captured, were deceived, thinking that their general had perished, and so surrendered. In this way Sextus conquered and gained possession of nearly the whole region. When he had thus become powerful, Lepidus arrived to govern the adjoining portion of Spain, and persuaded him to enter into an agreement on the condition of recovering his father's estate. And Antonius, influenced by his friendship for Lepidus and by his hostility toward Caesar, caused such a decree to be passed. So Sextus, in this way and on these conditions, departed from Spain.[42]

You say that Pompeius has been received at Carteia, so we shall presently see an army sent against him. Which camp am I to join then? For Antonius makes neutrality impossible. The one is weak, the other criminal. Let us make haste therefore.[43]

They also report that Sextus has been at New Carthage with only one legion, and that on the very day on which he captured the town of Barea he received the news about Caesar. That after the capture of the town there was great rejoicing and recovery of spirits, and people flocked to him from every side; but that he returned to the six legions which he had left in lower Spain. He also wrote to Libo saying that be cared for nothing unless he were allowed to return to his own house. The upshot of his demands was that all armies wherever stationed should be disbanded. That is nearly all about Sextus.[44]

Thus we can see that, in Caesar' absence, the Pompeian faction under Sex. Pompeius flourished and undid all of Caesar's hard work. Despite celebrating an unwise Triumph for his victory in Spain (see Chapter Eight), Caesar faced the humiliation of having to appoint a commander to fight a campaign against the surviving Pompeius. This was formalised in 44 BC when C. Asinius Pollio, a long-standing Caesarian lieutenant, was appointed as Proconsul for Farther Spain to fight Pompeius.

The Civil War Campaigns (45 BC) – Pompeius vs. Carrinas

The first Caesarian general sent against Pompeius was C. Carrinas, son of a Marian general in the First Civil War who was executed in the aftermath of the Battle of Colline Gate. Clearly a lifelong opponent of the Sullan faction and Pompeius, this Spanish campaign is his first appearance in the ancient sources. Presumed to be a Praetor in 46 BC, this seems to have been his first campaign. Only given a few months at the end of 45 BC, we have no further detail other than Appian's limited account below:

When Caesar learned of his actions, he sent [C.] Carrinas with a stronger army to fight him. Pompeius, however, being the quicker of the two, would show himself and then disappear, and so he wore out his enemy and got possession of a number of towns, large and small.[45]

We have no details for the size of the army Caesar supplied him with, but it cannot have been more than the remnants of the Caesarian garrisons in Spain. His short-lived campaign seems to have been highly ineffective with Pompeius refusing to give battle (finally) and using his speed and local support to run rings around him, with a number of towns and cities declaring once more for the Pompeian cause. Thus Carrinas' first campaign came to a swift conclusion when he was replaced by the close Caesarian ally C. Asinius Pollio, who fared even worse than he did. Nevertheless, he went on to become a staunch

Caesarian general, finally winning a Triumph under Octavianus in 29 BC for a Gallic campaign.

The Civil War Campaigns (44 BC) – Pompeius vs. Pollio

The formal appointment of a Proconsulship for Farther Spain to fight Pompeius and the selection of a close Caesarian adherent in the form of C. Asinius Pollio shows how seriously Caesar took this renewed Pompeian threat. Clearly, he could not return to Spain and re-fight the same campaign he had just celebrated a Triumph for, nor could he allow himself to be distracted from his proposed Eastern campaigns. Pollio had been with Caesar at the Rubicon in 49 BC, was one of the only survivors of the disastrous Caesarian invasion of Africa that year, and had accompanied Caesar in his Greek and African campaigns. He may well have fought in Spain in 45 BC also. We are not told how many additional forces he took with him to Spain in 44 BC, as Appian only states that he '*had no strong force*'.[46]

Unlike his predecessor he managed to bring Pompeius to battle, but that seems more due to Pompeius' growing strength and confidence rather than any skill on his part.

Unnamed Battle (44 BC)

We only have Dio's account for the battle that followed between the two men:

> *He next set out against Spanish Carthage, but since in his absence Pollio made an attack and did some damage, he returned with a large force, met his opponent, and routed him, after which the following accident enabled him to terrify and conquer the rest also, who were contending fiercely. Pollio had cast off his general's cloak, in order to suffer less chance of detection in his flight, and another man of the same name, a distinguished knight, had fallen. The soldiers, hearing the name of the latter, who was lying there, and seeing the garment, which had been captured, were deceived, thinking that their general had perished, and so surrendered. In this way Sextus conquered and gained possession of nearly the whole region.*[47]

Often overlooked in favour of the more famous Battle of Munda, this battle saw a clear Caesarian defeat (a second for Pollio) and the collapse of Caesarian control of Farther Spain, totally undoing the victory at Munda. Initially, it seems that Pollio's strategy was a wise one, diverting Pompeius' move on New Carthage by attacking Pompeian-held territory. However, Pompeius returned and felt confident enough to face a Caesarian commander in battle (as long as it wasn't Caesar). The result was a total Pompeian victory, with Pollio disgracefully fleeing the battle incognito and the Caesarian army surrendering.

Thus, less than a year after Munda the Pompeians had control of Father Spain once more, a bastion of opposition to the Caesarian Republic. With Caesar determined to move eastward and reconquer Pompeian-held Syria and renew the Romano-Parthian War, Sextus Pompeius had a free hand to build on his Spanish conquests and even raise a threat to Caesarian-held Italy once more. It was only Caesar's timely demise that brought this campaign to a negotiated conclusion, with the remaining Caesarian commanders in no hurry to face Pompeius, and the Anti-Caesarian factions in the Senate anxious to bring back a commander to act as a counter balance to the Caesarians.

Thus in 44 BC, little more than a year from the Battle of Munda, Sextus Pompeius was invited back to Rome, pardoned by the Senate, and compensated for the loss of his father's property (some fifty million drachmas) in a deal brokered by Caesar's two most powerful lieutenants (Lepidus and Antonius), where he received a hero's welcome, a remarkable turnaround in Pompeian fortunes.

The Pompeian Invasion of North Africa (44 BC)

However, Spain was not the only theatre of conflict that saw a revival in Pompeian fortunes and events of the previous years overturned. As previously documented,[48] North Africa had been a Pompeian stronghold, a situation which had been overturned in 46 BC by Caesar's victory at the Battle of Thapsus. One of the consequences of this victory was the dismemberment of the Kingdom of Numidia, the strongest native kingdom in the region. Numidian independence was extinguished, and the territory split three ways. The eastern portion of the country became a new Roman province, Africa Nova; the western portion was given to Bocchus II of the Mauri; and a central portion was given to the Roman warlord, P. Sittius, who had done so much (whilst in the pay of the Maurian Kings) to aid Caesar by invading Western Numidia and defeating the Royal Numidian army, not to mention murdering F. Cornelius Sulla and L. Afranius in the aftermath of Thapsus (see Chapter Two).

Little is known about this private kingdom of Sittius, for good reason; formed in 46 BC, it was extinguished in 44 BC by the Numidian prince Arabio. He first appears in our surviving sources in Spain fighting alongside Sex. Pompeius (see above) in 45 BC after the Battle of Munda, though he may well have been present before this. Arabio was a Numidian prince of the ruling royal family, son of a Masinissa, a Numidian prince. With the death of King Juba (and presumably

Masinissa himself), Arabio found himself as the heir to the vacant Numidian throne and thus a natural Pompeian ally.

By early 44 BC, with Sextus Pompeius having the upper hand in Spain, he clearly felt the time was right to open up a second front and thus sponsored Arabio's invasion of his lost homeland. In particular, they targeted the small and vulnerable kingdom of Sittius, allowing them to avenge his role in the Pompeian/Numidian defeat two years before. Only Appian refers to this event, and even then, only in retrospect:

> *When Caius [Iulius] Caesar pursued the Pompeians to Africa Sittius joined him and destroyed Juba's famous general, Saburra, and received from Caesar, as a reward for these services, the territory of Masinissa, not all, but the best part of it. Masinissa was the father of this Arabio and the ally of Juba. Caesar gave his territory to this Sittius, and to Bocchus, the king of Mauritania, and Sittius divided his own portion among his soldiers. Arabio at that time fled to the sons of Pompeius in Spain but returned to Africa after Caesar's death and kept sending to the younger Pompeius detachments of his men, whom he received back in a state of good training, and so expelled Bocchus from his territory and killed Sittius by stratagem.*[49]

Thus Arabio was able to successfully invade Caesarian North Africa and recovered two-thirds of the Numidian kingdom, defeating and killing Sittius in central Numidia and driving Bocchus II from Western Numidia (leaving only Eastern Numidia, which was now a Roman colony). Thus the Caesarian destruction of Numidia in 46 BC was also overturned and a new Numidia re-emerged, another Pompeian ally re-established.

Summary – What Caesarian Victory?

Thus, not only was Munda the closest Caesar came to defeat, but never had a Caesarian victory been overturned so quickly. Even before Caesar had left Spain, one of his armies (that of Didius) had been defeated by the locals. At the time however, Caesar had achieved his campaign aims; a Pompeian revival had been crushed and a political rival murdered. Spain had always been a Pompeian stronghold and even with two Pompeii dead, the province would never afford him more than token loyalty. Yet for Caesar this would have been enough. He needed to return to Rome and begin preparations for an Eastern campaign, first to deal with the Pompeian-held province of Syria and then the Parthian Empire. He would have given little thought to the last Pompeian, Sextus, who had taken to the seas. It was an understandable oversight but one that came back to undermine his hard-fought victory.

As we have seen, before the year was out another Pompeian rebellion had broken out in Spain, forcing him to appoint a fresh commander to deal with it. When the magistracies for 44 BC were confirmed, this Caesarian failure was enshrined for all to see, with the appointment of a Proconsul for Farther Spain to fight Sextus and the Pompeian rebellion. Yet the situation deteriorated further and neither Caesarian commander was able to defeat Pompeius, who unlike his brother took the guidance of T. Labienus to heart. Pompeius soon re-established Pompeian control of Baetica, raised an army of at least seven legions, and took control of a number of the major cities including New Carthage.

Thus in just over six months (October to March) Sextus Pompeius overturned the Caesarian victory at Munda and by the time of Caesar's assassination was in control of a large portion of southern Spain, setting up a rival Pompeian Republic, with himself as a rival to Caesar. Thus we can see that in those five months Sextus stepped out of his brother's shadow and went from overlooked second son to the new leader of the Pompeian forces in the Republic. We will never know what Caesar's plans were for Sextus, but a third Spanish campaign was unlikely, with Caesar clearly facing the prospect of leaving a Pompeian controlled province on his (and Italy's) western flank whilst he campaigned in the East. It was as if the Battle of Munda had never occurred.

Chapter Seven

The Civil War in Syria and the Parthian Intervention (45–44 BC)

The Eastern Republic and the Civil Wars

With all the ancient sources' attention being focused on Caesar in the Western Republic, we must not overlook events in the Eastern Republic and their impact on the ongoing civil war. The provinces and allied kingdoms which comprised Rome's Eastern Republic had long been a powerbase for Pompeius and the Pompeians. At this point, the region had only been under Roman control for the last twenty years, having been conquered by Pompeius during Rome's Great Eastern War (74–62 BC).[1] In 49/48 BC, the region supplied the bulk of Pompeius' Grand Army which faced (and was defeated by) Caesar at the Battle of Pharsalus. Inevitably, it was to his power base in the East that Pompeius retreated in the aftermath of that battle, but equally inevitably, he found a cold welcome from his clients, returning as a defeated general without an army and being chased by Caesar with his.

With the Caesarian army marching through the region to reach Caesar in Egypt, having become entangled in the latest Ptolemaic Civil War, naturally the cities and kingdoms of the region swore a token allegiance to Caesar instead. Aside from the Roman and Egyptian Civil Wars affecting the power balance in the region, there was also the fallout from the First Romano-Parthian War which had seen a seven legion strong Roman army destroyed at Carrhae (53 BC)[2] and Parthian armies sweeping into Roman Syria for the first time, just seven years earlier (52 BC). To make matters worse, as we have seen, Pontic armies under King Pharnaces II swept into Asia Minor from the Bosporan Kingdom of the Crimea, sparking off the Fourth (and final) Romano-Pontic War.[3] Thus we can see the total disruption that the cities and kingdoms of the region faced in this period.

Caesar's victory at the Battle of Zela in 47 BC over the Pontic army of Pharnaces II not only ended the Fourth Romano-Pontic War, but sent a clear statement to the Parthian Empire and Pompeius' supporters in the region that the Eastern Republic would not only be defended, but was central to Caesar and his future campaigns, who clearly had one eye on the post-civil war Roman world. To

The Civil War in Syria and the Parthian Intervention (45–44 BC)

cement this control, Caesar left his cousin (and possible successor) Sex. Iulius Caesar in control of the Roman province of Syria, the lynchpin to Rome's control of the whole region, with a legion to defend the Eastern Republic from both its internal and external enemies. Unfortunately for Caesar, reality never bent to his desires and his control of the region was proved (as always) to be wafer thin.

Just the following year, with Caesar far away in the deserts of North Africa playing cat and mouse with the Pompeian forces of Metellus Scipio and Labienus, Sex. Iulius Caesar was murdered and Syria rose in revolt, declaring their loyalty to the Pompeian Republic under the command of Q. Caecilius Bassus, a hitherto unknown Roman officer who was now the Pompeian governor of Syria, though in reality another in the long line of Romans who carved out their own territories during a civil war.

Bassus' position was an interesting one, with a mixture of strategic strengths and weaknesses. On the strength's side, he had control of the only Roman legions in the Middle East and the lynchpin province of Syria, the former heartland of the Seleucid Empire, controlling the trade routes from the East. He could also tap into the lingering loyalty of the Pompeian cause, then resurgent in North Africa. In terms of weaknesses, to the North lay the Caesarian legions of Asia Minor (Asia, Pontus, Cilicia), whilst to the south lay the Caesarian ally of Ptolemaic Egypt (with a Judean buffer state in between). Having clearly identified with the Pompeian cause, he was now tied to its fortunes in North Africa. Furthermore, as had already been amply demonstrated, loyalty to their Roman overlords was not well embedded amongst the natives and tended to be to whoever had their army in the region at the time.

There was also one very large unknown factor, namely the Parthian Empire. With the First Romano-Parthian War in abeyance, following a failed Parthian invasion of Syria in 51 BC, would the Parthians see this as a chance to annex Syria, wait to see whether the Caesarians regained control, or even create a Parthian client state and support Caecilius Bassus? At this point, all three possibilities were in play.

As we have seen, Syria declared for the Pompeian cause just before it took a massive hit with the defeat at the Battle of Thapsus in North Africa in April 46 BC. Yet this did not seem to shake Bassus' control of the Roman legions of the region, given that the news could be suppressed for a while, and the result downplayed. The swift Pompeian revival in Spain actually benefited Bassus twofold; firstly, it showed that the Pompeians had not been crushed (arguably) and were still fighting (and thus worth supporting), and secondly it diverted Caesar away from moving on Syria. So, just as events in the Eastern Republic benefited the Pompeians in the West during 47 BC by allowing them time to rebuild, so now events in the Western Republic benefited the Pompeians in the

East. It also clearly highlighted the problems that Caesar faced during this civil war, namely he could only be in one place at one time and whatever region he was not personally present in could not be relied upon.

The Campaigns of 44 BC – Caesarians vs Pompeians

Thus, it fell to Caesar's generals to recover Syria for Caesar, and again, as we have seen, in terms of quality and effectiveness they were a mixed bag. The two most prominent Caesarian lieutenants were Aemilius Lepidus and Antonius, both in Rome during this period, with the former ruling Rome in Caesar's name and the latter in disgrace. Naturally, given the inattentiveness of our surviving sources to this theatre of campaign, there is little clarity in terms of chronology, but it seems that this Caesarian counter attack did not take place until 45 BC, with Caesar perhaps organising it from Rome before he left for Spain and the Mundan campaign.

We do know the identity of the three Caesarian Governors in Asia Minor in 45 BC, the most senior of which was C. Antistius Vetus, who was named as Caesar's Quaestor in Roman Syria. Antistius came from a long standing middle ranking Plebeian family and his father seems to have been the Praetor of 70 BC, under whom a young Caesar served in Spain in 69 BC. He was possibly a Tribune in 56 BC, but next appears with this appointment which seems to have been his first military command. Supporting him were the Governors of Asia, Bithynia/Pontus and Cilicia, who were P. Servilius Isauricus, Q. Marcius Crispus and L. Vocatius Tullus respectively.

The most senior of these men was clearly P. Servilius Isauricus, who had been Consul in 48 BC alongside Caesar himself, and had commanded the Caesarian forces who suppressed the Pompeian insurrection of Caelius and Milo in Italy that year. Despite this, he could hardly be classed as a leading Caesarian general, but nevertheless brought *gravitas* to the proceedings as a close adherent of Caesar and an ex-Consul. Of the other two men, both were unknown entities, though Volcatius Tullus was the son of a Consul (66 BC). Thus there seems to have been little military experience amongst the Caesarian commanders assigned to recover Syria for the faction. It is difficult to separate the campaigns of 45 and 44 BC, as all the surviving sources which provide detail roll the two together. Nevertheless, from the sources below we can determine an outline of the campaign:

> When Sextus was dead, Bassus gained possession of all his army except a few; for the soldiers who had been wintering in Apamea withdrew into Cilicia before his arrival, and although he pursued them, he did not win them over. Returning

then to Syria, he took the title of Praetor and fortified Apamea, so as to have it as a base for the war. And he proceeded to enlist the men of military age, not only freemen but slaves as well, to gather money, and to prepare arms. While he was thus engaged, one Caius Antistius besieged him. Later they had a fairly equal struggle, and when neither party was able to gain any great advantage, they parted, without any definite truce, to await the bringing up of allies. Antistius was joined by such persons of the vicinity as favoured Caesar and by soldiers who had been sent from Rome by Caesar, while Bassus was joined by Alchaudonius the Arabian. It was he who had formerly made terms with Lucullus, as I have stated, and later joined with the Parthians against Crassus. On this occasion he was summoned by both sides but entered the space between the city and the camps and before making any answer called for bids for his services as an ally; and as Bassus outbid Antistius, he assisted him, and in the battle proved greatly superior in his archery. Even the Parthians, too, came at the invitation of Bassus, but on account of the winter failed to remain with him for any considerable time, and hence did not accomplish anything of importance.[4]

He has had a letter from Vetus, dated on the last day of the year, announcing that 'when he was investing Caecilius Bassus, and was on the point of compelling him to surrender, the Parthian Pacorus arrived with an immense force: that accordingly Bassus was snatched from his hands, for which he blames Volcatius'. Accordingly, I think that a war there is imminent.[5]

Meanwhile at Apamea the Romans had trouble on their hands leading to civil war. Caecilius Bassus, out of devotion to Pompeius, assassinated Sextus Caesar and took command of his army; whereupon Caesar's other generals, to avenge the murder, attacked Bassus with all their forces. Antipater, for the sake of his two friends, the deceased, and the surviving Caesar, sent them reinforcements under his sons. The war dragged on and Murcus arrived from Italy to succeed Antistius.[6]

About the same time disturbances broke out in Syria for the following reason. Bassus Caecilius, one of Pompeius' sympathisers, formed a plot against Sextus Caesar, and after killing him, took over his army and made himself master of the country; thereupon a great war began near Apamea, for Caesar's generals marched against him with a force of cavalry and infantry. Antipater also sent them reinforcements together with his sons, being mindful of the benefits they had received from Caesar and on that account thinking it just to avenge Sextus and exact satisfaction from his murderer.[7]

Thus we can create an outline for the Syrian campaign of 45 BC. As expected, Antistius Vetus led the Caesarian army, of unknown size but possibly the same three legions we find there the following year, against Bassus, who had at least two legions (as stated by Appian[8]). In this he was joined by the Caesarian Governor of nearby Cilicia, L. Volcatius Tullus. The Caesarian Governors of Asia and Bithynia-Pontus seemingly remained in position, presumably to defend the (only recently re-conquered) region from threats from either the north (Bosporus) or the east (Armenia-Parthia). In the face of the Caesarian advance, Bassus avoided open conflict and retreated to his headquarters in the strategically-key city of Apamea in western Syria, which he had been preparing for some time.

As we have seen above, this campaign drew in at least three different sets of locals. From neighbouring Judea came Jewish forces under the command of the sons of Antipater, the Caesarian-appointed Roman Procurator (Governor), one of which may well have been Herod (later to become the infamous King Herod). From Arabia came Arabian mercenaries led by their chief Alchaudonius, who sold his services to the highest bidder, in this case Bassus, and according to Dio played a key role in beating off Antistius' forces.[9]

The third force of natives was by far the most important, namely a Parthian force led by non-other than Pacorus, heir to Orodes II, the Parthian Emperor. His intervention raised the stakes considerably, as this was the first time that the Parthians had intervened in the Roman Civil War, something that the Romans had always feared would happen. This intervention, on the side of the Pompeians, was a telling one, and done for sound strategic reasons. Caesar had made no secret of his desire to attack Parthia once the civil war was done with an eye to conquest, so for the Parthians, it made sense to deny him the use of Syria as a launch pad for an invasion and keep the civil war going for as long as possible.

Dio, a later source, stated that the intervention accomplished little, but Cicero, writing at the time, stated that the Parthian invention saved Bassus, who was on the point of surrendering to Antistius when the Parthians arrived.[10] He stated that this came from a letter from Antistius himself and that the Parthian force was massive. He also laid the blame for this successful intervention at the feet of Volcatius Tullus, his subordinate, though no further details are given. It is possible that Volcatius was commanding another Caesarian force in the East of the country and (understandably) failed to prevent the Parthians reaching Apamea, or perhaps failed to warn Antistius. In any event, the Parthian intervention saved Bassus and the Pompeians and meant that the Caesarian (Antistian) campaign ended in failure. Unsurprisingly, Antistius' failure brought about his replacement and recall.

Thus the year ended with a Parthian army at Apamea, presumably forcing a Caesarian withdrawal and retrenchment, awaiting the new commander and new campaigning season. Whether the Caesarians withdrew into Cilicia is not known, but the year 45 BC ended with the Pompeians and their Parthian allies in control of Syria. It does seem that Pacorus and the bulk of the Parthians withdrew for winter, but we can imagine that they left behind a notable Parthian contingent to support Caecilius Bassus, including their famed horse archers. Furthermore, the threat of further intervention against the Caesarians was now ever present, escalating the situation in Syria even further and making it, rather than Spain, the key campaign for Caesar.

The Campaigns of 44 BC – Anti-Caesarians vs Pompeians

Nevertheless, it would take time to gather forces for a renewed Romano-Parthian War and Caesar needed to stabilise the situation in Rome and the Western Republic (Spain and North Africa) before setting off eastwards himself (see Chapter Eight). Therefore, Caesar appointed a new commander for the Syrian campaign, L. Staius Murcus, as Proconsul. Murcus was a long time Caesarian legate, having served with him in Greece in 48 BC (at Oricum[11]) and again in Africa in 46 BC.[12] He was presumably elevated to the Praetorship in 45 BC and was now considered a safe pair of hands by Caesar, who could stabilise the deteriorating situation in Syria until Caesar himself arrived. Ultimately, Caesar's judgement of his character was at fault, as Murcus joined the new Anti-Caesarian faction in the conspiracy against Caesar (see Chapter Eight), and if we rely on Appian was actually present in the Senate House when Caesar was murdered.[13]

Hastily withdrawing from Rome, Murcus arrived in the east and took up the command of the Caesarian legions, though we are not told whether he brought any fresh forces. Of the other Caesarian Governors of the region, we know that P. Servilius Isauricus was replaced by C. Trebonius in command of Asia and that Q. Marcius Crispus was replaced by L. Tillius Cimber in Bithynia-Pontus, both men prominent Anti-Caesarians and members of the assassination plot. Volcatius Tullus' fate is unknown, but given letters circulating in Rome about his incompetence it is likely he too was replaced.

The campaign which Murcus inherited clearly now looked completely different. When he was appointed, it was to stabilise the situation in Syria and keep Bassus and the Parthians pinned down until Caesar arrived with the main Roman army. With Caesar dead, there would be no reinforcements coming from Rome. As Murcus was part of the newly-reformed Anti-Caesarian faction of Brutus and Cassius, it is surprising that this civil war campaign continued, especially with the post-Caesarian Senate coming to terms with Sex. Pompeius himself in Spain (see Chapter Six).

No such accommodation was reached in Syria however, and if anything this campaign took on a surreal edge with the Caesarian legions being led by one of Caesar's murderers, making it a civil war between the Anti-Caesarians and the Pompeians. Understandably, given events in Rome, there are even fewer sources for the campaigns of this year, but again we can piece together a framework:

> *Bassus prevailed for a time, to be sure, but was later again held in check by Marcius Crispus and Lucius Staius Murcus.*[14]

> *However that may have been, Caesar sent Staius Murcius against him with three legions. Bassus defeated him badly. Finally, Murcus appealed to Marcius Crispus, the governor of Bithynia, and the latter came to his aid with three legions.*[15]

> *Caesar sent Staius Murcus against them with three legions, but they resisted bravely, Marcius Crispus was then sent from Bithynia to the aid of Murcus with three additional legions, and thus Bassus was besieged by six legions altogether.*[16]

> *When Caius Cassius, taking over their strong legions from Statius Murcus and Marcius Crispus, both Praetorians who had been saluted as imperator by their troops.*[17]

Thus the campaign of 44 BC seems to have been a carbon copy of the previous one, with Caecilius Bassus retreating in the face of a Caesarian invasion of Syria, presumably back to Apamea. At some point however there was a battle between the two men as Appian states that Bassus defeated Murcus badly (see above). Murcus then called on the departing Governor of Bithynia-Pontus, Q. Marcius Crispus, who bought three legions (presumably all that was left of the Caesarian forces in Asia Minor), now bringing the Anti-Caesarian force to six legions. The statement from Velleius that both commanders had been hailed as Imperator by their forces does indicate that these two men won a subsequent victory over Bassus. Thus the campaign of 44 BC ended in stalemate once more, with both sides holding a victory over the other and Bassus still holed up in Apamea.

There was no subsequent Parthian intervention to support Bassus, which is likely to have been a combination of Bassus being in a stronger position than in 45 BC and the Parthians being reticent about the political situation in Rome in the aftermath of Caesar's assassination. Certainly there would be no renewed Roman invasion of Parthia, now that the last of Rome's Triumvirate of leading generals (Crassus, Pompeius and Caesar) was dead and the Roman Civil War looked like it would spread beyond Spain and Syria.

The Civil War in Syria continued into 43 BC, beyond the scope of this present work, and became absorbed by the larger conflict between the Caesarian and Anti-Caesarian factions. Ultimately the clash between Bassus and Murcus was ended by negotiation, led by none other than the former commander of Syria in the First Romano-Parthian War, C. Cassius Longinus. He assumed command of Syria, at the request of the Senate, and absorbed and united the armies of both Bassus and Murcus and defeated the new Caesarian Governor of Syria, P. Cornelius Dolabella.

Thus the Pompeian control of Syria was ended by negotiation and the province came into the possession of the Anti-Caesarian faction, who took over the role of lead protagonists against the Caesarian faction until their defeat in 42 BC at the Battles of Philippi, after which Syria briefly came under the control of the new Caesarian Triumvirate and in particular M. Antonius, until it was overrun by the Parthian invasion of 40 BC led by Pacorus and briefly became part of the Parthian Empire. Antonine control of Syria was restored following the Parthian defeat at the hands of P. Ventidius Bassus.[18] Full Roman control was not restored until 31–30 BC when the Antonine Empire was defeated by Caesar's adopted son Octavianus Caesar.

Summary

As we can see, Syria remained under Pompeian control from 46 to 43 BC, a control which two Caesarian campaigns could not dislodge. Ultimately Caesar's murder prevented him from recovering this province, as he planned to do in 44 BC, but we have shown that the civil war continued in the East, despite the Caesarian narrative that Munda brought an end to the civil war. At Caesar's death, the Pompeians continued to fight in both Spain and Syria, both of which campaigns were only ended by negotiation with the Senate. These negotiations brought a temporary end to the Pompeian/Caesarian fighting in the Third Civil War, which was then overtaken by a Caesarian Civil War, a Civil War between the Caesarian and Anti-Caesarians factions and another Caesarian Civil War (in 43, 42 and 41–40 BC respectively). It was left to Sex. Pompeius to take up the Pompeian cause against the Caesarian faction in the aftermath of the Battle of Perusia, a campaign that culminated in the Battle of Naulochus in 36 BC and the fifth and final major Pompeian defeat, some thirteen years after the start of the Third Civil War.[19]

Section IV

Caesar The Great (Failure)?

Chapter Eight

Caesar: The Five Month King

In the surviving sources it is Velleius who draws our attention to the short length of Caesar's reign after his return to Rome from Spain:

But it was the lot of this great man, who behaved with such clemency in all his victories, that his peaceful enjoyment of supreme power should last but five months. For, returning to the city in October, he was slain on the ides of March.[1]

As we have seen, throughout these early years of the Third Roman Civil War, Caesar had always shown a marked distaste for remaining in Rome and fulfilling the duties of Princeps that his military victories had brought him. The period after his victory at Munda looked like it would be no different; a short gap between campaigns where he cemented his political position and planned the next campaign. Ultimately however, this period was to be very different, as Caesar never left Rome, meeting the same fate as his two former Triumviral colleagues and rivals, Crassus and Pompeius, by being murdered. The key difference on this occasion was that it was in Rome at the hands of his own faction, rather than in the East at the hands of his enemies.

The Ides of March represents the ultimate failure of Caesar in the civil war campaigns, whose skill on the battlefield was not mirrored off it. The victories at Pharsalus, Thapsus and Munda ultimately counted for nothing and were undone by the events that followed, events that need to be analysed to understand how Caesar won the war but lost the peace.

A New Rival – Marius and the Succession Question

Even before Caesar had returned from Spain, a new political tumult took place, and whilst there was no bloodshed on this occasion, unlike those of 49, 48, and 47 BC, this was just as dangerous to Caesar politically. This disorder centred on an individual whose claim threatened one of the key foundations of Caesar's political support: his claim to be the inheritor of his uncle's (C. Marius') political legacy. Caesar's early political successes in the 60s BC owed everything to him claiming the mantle of inheritor of his uncle C. Marius, the general who had saved Rome from the northern tribes in the Great Northern War (113–101 BC) and who was the dominant figure in Rome and briefly Princeps of the Republic. Marius claimed the dubious distinction of dying of natural causes in 86 BC, after having captured and sacked Rome during the First Civil War.

Naturally, Marius' power and patronage was claimed by his (probably) only son C. Marius, who rose to the Consulship in 82 BC, whilst still in his late-20s. In many ways, the rise and fall of C. Marius (jnr) mirrored that of Cn. Pompeius (jnr), becoming the figurehead of a civil war faction in decline. After being defeated in battle (Sacriportus) he found himself besieged in Praeneste and committed suicide rather than be captured by the Sullan forces. With no sons of his own, the main line of the Marian family was extinguished. The rest of the Marian family fared little better in the First Civil War, with Sulla capturing Rome and purging his enemies.

One of the main victims of the Sullan proscriptions was the elder Marius' nephew (son of his brother) M. Marius Gratidianus, who was executed in 82 BC when Sulla captured Rome.[2] The only other Marius of note was the mysterious M. Marius who was the figurehead of a Marian faction in the East in the 70s BC during the First Civil War and who was 'allied' to Mithridates, to legitimise Mithridates' invasion of the Roman East (much as the Parthians were soon to do with Q. Labienus). His removal meant that there were no male Marians left to claim the political patronage of the elder Marius. Thus it fell to Caesar, Marius' nephew by marriage (Marius having married Iulia, Caesar's aunt) to claim this political inheritance, champion the memory of the dead Marius (whilst overlooking his more unsavoury moments, such as the sack of Rome) and use this campaign as a launch pad against the ruling Sullan faction in the 60s BC.

Yet in 45 BC, whilst Caesar was in Spain, a figure emerged claiming to be the son of Marius (jnr) and thus the grandson and heir of the late elder Marius.[3] Most later sources claim that the man was an imposter of low birth and there are numerous 'real' names ascribed to him. Initially however Cicero, in one of his surviving contemporaneous letters takes his claim seriously:

Yesterday, soon after your departure, I think, some people, who looked like city men, brought me a message and a letter from Caius Marius, son, and grandson of Caius. He begged me in the name of our relationship, in the name of Marius on whom I had written and by the eloquence of his grandfather, L. Crassus, to defend him: and he stated his case in full. I wrote back that he had no need of an advocate since his relative Caesar was omnipotent.[4]

Though by 44 BC, he had changed his tune:

A few days afterwards the Senate was delivered from the danger of bloodshed, and a hook was fixed into that runaway slave who had usurped the name of Caius Marius.[5]

Valerius Maximus has the best passage on the impact this re-emerged Marius had on Rome:

Herophilus, a horse doctor, by claiming that Marius the seven times Consul was his grandfather, so advanced himself, that many colonies of veteran soldiers, and eminent free towns, and almost all the guilds adopted him as their patron. Moreover, when C. Caesar, after overcoming the younger Cn. Pompeius in Spain, had admitted the People into his garden, Herophilus was saluted in the next space between the pillars by an almost equally enthusiastic crowd. And if the divine might of Caesar had not prudently prevented the trouble, the commonwealth would have suffered as much from him as from Equitius. But though he was banished out of Italy by him, after Caesar was taken up into heaven, Herophilus returned to the city, and dared to attempt a plot to kill the Senate.[6]

Interestingly, there is no agreement in the surviving sources as to the identity of this man. Valerius Maximus names him as Herophilus, Appian as Amatius[7] and Livy as Chamiates.[8] Later sources are unanimously convinced that he was an imposter, though there is always the possibility that he was a genuine son of Marius that had been kept in hiding for his safety. The most interesting question however, is: imposter or not, why did he choose this point in time to emerge and make his claim?

The surviving sources condense this incident down in terms of timescales, but he clearly chose to debut on the political stage when Caesar was absent (as he frequently was) in Spain, perhaps never to return. As has already been covered, unlike his rival Pompeius, Caesar had no heirs and the more power he amassed, the more this vexed question of succession rose in importance. As already noted, the year 46 BC had seen the death of the two members of the Iulii Caesarones family: Sextus, who was clearly being groomed by Caesar for a leadership role and Lucius.[9] This left distant relatives on the female side; notably Q. Pedius and C. Octavius. Ironically, Caesar did have a natural born son, Caesarion/Ptolemy XV, but he was a foreign born bastard in Roman law and in public and political opinion. He may have had a Roman bastard, given the rumours about both D. and M. Iunius Brutus, but again this was no substitute.[10]

Again, even within the Caesarian faction itself, there was no outstanding candidate to take his place. As we have noted, throughout this civil war, in Caesar's absence the Caesarian faction tended to be ineffective. Caesar's current deputy was M. Aemilius Lepidus, son of a former Consul who had died during the First Civil War after marching on Sullan-controlled Rome. He had been Consul with Caesar in 46 BC and his Master of the Horse from 46–44 BC.

There was also M. Antonius, Caesar's Master of the Horse in 48–47 BC and the man who again had ruled Rome in Caesar's absence. Antonius had been demoted due to his mishandling of the bloodshed in Rome in 48 BC, a convenient Caesarian scapegoat, and had spent the intervening years in political obscurity, though this was to change shortly (see below).[11]

Thus Marius emerged onto the political scene and soon won over support from Caesar's veterans, the People, the Italian cities, and we can imagine those Anti-Caesarian elements amongst the Senate. Marius' appeal was similar to that of Cn. Pompeius (Younger) and later C. Octavius. Here was a man of impeccable political lineage but none of the taint of bloodshed of the elder generation, especially that of Caesar. Furthermore, the close family ties between the Caesarian and the Marian families, so assiduously fostered by Caesar himself, could now be turned against him. Thus Marius could claim to be the closest relative of Caesar and thus his heir.

Unfortunately for Marius, Caesar did not die at Munda, but returned home to find a new relative and rival. Details are scant, but Valerius Maximus (above) details a meeting between the two men, following which Marius was exiled from Italy. Presumably Caesar also refused to recognise him as the grandson of Marius and accused him of being an imposter, which would explain Cicero changing his tune. Nevertheless, Caesar had left a dangerous political rival alive and was planning to leave Rome for the East, clearly allowing him the opportunity to return and play havoc in Rome (as he was to do in 44 BC).

The Murder of M. Claudius Marcellus (45 BC) – A Covert Assassination Programme?

On 26 May 45 BC, a formerly exiled Roman oligarch, and Pompeian supporter, M. Claudius Marcellus (Cos. 51 BC) was murdered in Athens on his return from exile by a member of his retinue. Cicero writes a contemporaneous account, having dined with Marcellus in Athens just three days beforehand:

> *On the third day after that* [meeting], *just as I was intending to start from Athens, at the tenth hour of the night my friend Publius Postumius called on me with the information that my colleague M.* [Claudius] *Marcellus just after dinner had been stabbed with a dagger by his friend P. Magius Cilo, and had received two wounds, one in the stomach, a second in the head behind the ear; but that hopes were entertained that he might survive; and that Magius had killed*

himself afterwards. He added that he had been sent by Marcellus to tell me this, and to ask me to send some physicians. Accordingly, I summoned some physicians, and immediately started just as day was breaking. When I was not far from Piraeus, a slave of Acidinus met me bearing a note containing the information that Marcellus had expired a little before daybreak. So there is a man of most illustrious character cut off in a most distressing manner by the vilest of men.[12]

Marcellus was a long-time opponent of Caesar who had supported Pompeius in the political shenanigans that marked the opening of 49 BC and led to the outbreak of the civil war. Having joined Pompeius in Greece and mostly likely having been present at the Battle of Pharsalus, he fled to the island of Mytilene in the aftermath and took no further part in the war, avoiding Caesarian retaliation. Petitioned by the Senate, Caesar granted his pardon and allowed him to return from Rome, but, as we have seen, he never made it back, meeting his end whilst en route. Yet whilst Cicero clearly places the murder on a 'madness' affecting the assassin (Magius, one of Marcellus' retinue), he does later admit that rumours in Rome were circulating that it had been on Caesar's orders, reminiscent of the murder of L. Iulius Caesar the year previously.

Today I am expecting Spinther; for Brutus has sent him to me. He writes to clear Caesar in regard to the death of Marcellus, on whom no suspicion would have fallen, even if his assassination had been the consequence of a plot. As it is, there is no doubt whatever about Magius. Does not his madness account for the whole thing? I don't clearly understand what he means.[13]

Thus, despite the public shows of clemency (in Rome at least), many in Rome suspected Caesar of running a covert assassination programme, settling old scores out of sight of the Senate and People.

Countdown to the Ides of March – The Motive

Clearly, Caesar's priorities were not Roman politics. Having temporarily defeated the Pompeians in Spain, his next military priority was the East, both in terms of finishing the ongoing civil war campaigns in Syria and then re-igniting the Romano-Parthian War. As we have already seen, these two campaigns had become intertwined when the Parthians had led an army into Roman Syria to support the Pompeian leader Q. Caecilius Bassus. This gave Caesar the excuse he needed to rekindle the Parthian War, avenge the Roman loss at Carrhae, and emulate his great hero Alexander the Great and conquer the East.

To those ends he set about planning his expedition to the East with his usual focus, but unwisely (and ultimately fatally) chose his usual utilitarian and military approach to Roman politics, resulting in a series of clear political missteps that created the atmosphere for the emergence (or re-emergence) of a new civil war faction and the planning of the most famous assassination in history.

The Unwise Triumphs

The first misstep was the holding of a Triumph for his 'victory' in Spain. Ever eager to show off his martial prowess, Caesar chose to celebrate a number of Triumphs for his Spanish campaign, regardless of the political message it sent. The year previously Caesar had celebrated four Triumphs, none ostensibly over his civil war opponents (Gaul, Egypt, Pontus, and Numidia). It was considered in bad taste to celebrate a Triumph over a Roman enemy and Caesar had come under criticism for including images of Metellus Scipio and Cato in his Numidian Triumph. Yet just a year later, Caesar not only celebrated a Triumph for his victory in Spain but allowed his two legates (Q. Fabius Maximus and Q. Pedius) to do so as well, totally against Roman custom and practice, as they were not Imperium holders in their own right, but legates of Caesar (and thus under his imperium).

Thus on the one hand, Caesar again showed off to the People his martial prowess and gave them three public celebrations, but on the other he created resentment amongst the Senatorial oligarchy by celebrating a Triumph won clearly over his civil war enemies, and by breaking tradition by allowing his deputies to do so as well.[14] With the clear benefit of hindsight, the surviving sources point out his mistakes:

This was the last war that Caesar waged; and the Triumph that was celebrated for it vexed the Romans as nothing else had done. For it commemorated no victory over foreign commanders or barbarian kings, but the utter annihilation of the sons and the family of the mightiest of the Romans, who had fallen upon misfortune; and it was not meet for Caesar to celebrate a Triumph for the calamities of his country, priding himself upon actions which had no defence before gods or men except that they had been done under necessity.[15]

For, although he had conquered no foreign nation, but had destroyed a vast number of citizens, he not only celebrated the triumph himself, incidentally feasting the entire populace once more, as if in honour of some common blessing, but also allowed Quintus Fabius [Maximus] and Quintus Pedius to hold a celebration, although they had merely been his lieutenants and had achieved no individual success. Naturally this occasioned ridicule, as did also the fact that they used wooden instead of ivory representations of certain achievements together with other similar Triumphal apparatus. Nevertheless, most brilliant triple Triumphs and triple processions of the Romans were held in honour of those very events, and furthermore a thanksgiving of fifty days was observed.[16]

Again, in itself, at worst Caesar could only be accused of bad taste and a willingness to flout tradition, but it was the first political misstep in a five-month-long campaign of missteps.

The Unwise Lifetime Dictatorship

Naturally, with the Mundan military matters dealt with, Caesar's thoughts turned to the future constitutional settlement. In the short term he finally appointed the magistrates for the year, with Q. Fabius Maximus adding a Consulship to his Triumph, clearly harking back to a more traditional Republic, given his family's history. He was joined by another Caesarian 'loyalist' C. Trebonius. In the medium term Caesar again appointed himself Consul (for the fifth time) for the following year, alongside M. Antonius, whose years in the political doghouse were now seemingly over. Yet Caesar's mistrust of Antonius' abilities were clearly to be seen when he made it known that, when he left on campaign, he would surrender his Consulship (again another blow against tradition) and in his place would be appointed none other than P. Cornelius Dolabella, the former Tribune who had clashed bloodily with the Antonine administration in 47 BC. To say this was a combustible mix would be a political understatement, and Antonius made his feelings on the matter well known:

> *But since Antonius vehemently opposed the plan, heaped much abuse upon Dolabella, and received as much in return, for the time being Caesar desisted, being ashamed of their unseemly conduct. And afterwards, when Caesar came before the people to proclaim Dolabella, Antonius shouted that the omens were opposed.*[17]

As we have seen, whenever Caesar left Rome the Caesarian administration had a tough time preserving law and order and preventing political bloodshed, with outbreaks of political violence and revolt in 49, 48 and 47 BC. As we have previously discussed, Antonius' abilities to rule Rome had already been proven to be deficient, and to leave him in charge along with the man he had come to blows with in 47 BC was a political disaster in the making.

A far greater misstep came when Caesar considered his long term political position. It was clear to all that his victory at Munda had not ended the civil war, which was still raging in Syria and was beginning to re-emerge in Spain. In some ways this suited Caesar, as it meant there was still a crisis so Rome still needed the emergency office of the Dictator. To the military mind, this was logical, but to a Roman oligarch's political mind, this should have set alarm bells ringing. With this in mind, Caesar accepted the office of *Dictator Perpetuus* in late-January/early-February 44 BC:

> *However, the Romans gave way before the good fortune of the man and accepted the bit, and regarding the monarchy as a respite from the evils of the civil wars, they appointed him dictator for life. This was confessedly a tyranny, since the monarchy, besides the element of irresponsibility, now took on that of permanence.*[18]

Caesar also planned a new variation on the office of Master of the Horse, the Dictator's official deputy, which had previously been occupied by both M. Aemilius Lepidus and in years past by M. Antonius. Caesar, it now seemed, envisioned the role as an additional annual magistrate (and one not subject to the usual rules of the *cursus honorum*) having designated his great-nephew and heir C. Octavius for 44 BC and Cn. Domitius Calvinus for the following year.

Thus, Caesar was now Dictator for Life (however long it was to last). Though he was only following the path trod by others, notably Sulla, none of his predecessors had the lack of political sense to advertise this fact. To Caesar, this was practical and utilitarian, to his enemies and even his friends, this was political suicide. The Republic, founded on the mythos of the overthrow of the monarchy, now had a new permanent ruler. Caesar was seemingly blind to this danger, but someone close to him should have seen it and advised him against it, with Lepidus being the most level headed of his chief supporters.

The Unwise Honours

This perpetual Dictatorship was accompanied by a host of extravagant honours granted by the Senate and People, including having a month named after him, the title of *Parens Patriae*, father of the country, the role of guardian of public morals (a notable piece of hypocrisy, given his private life), Tribunician sacrosanctity, and that magistrates should swear to uphold his acts, along with a host of others. It is Plutarch who best sums up the trap that Caesar was walking into:

It was Cicero who proposed the first honours for him in the senate, and their magnitude was, after all, not too great for a man; but others added excessive honours and vied with one another in proposing them, thus rendering Caesar odious and obnoxious even to the mildest citizens because of the pretension and extravagance of what was decreed for him. It is thought, too, that the enemies of Caesar no less than his flatterers helped to force these measures through, in order that they might have as many pretexts as possible against him and might be thought to have the best reasons for attempting his life.[19]

Again, a wiser political mind would have rejected these honours, and done so publicly, as Pompeius did with the Dictatorship in 52 BC. Yet Caesar accepted them all, probably with his usual levels of enthusiasm – that of a general preparing for a long campaign, determined not to be distracted by the noise of politics. For once, Cicero could see what Caesar could not: Rome's oligarchy, which had always suffered from the temporary eclipses of great men, would not suffer a permanent one.

Caesar the King and the Unwise Clash with the Tribunes

It is possible that Caesar eventually realised the danger, and one incident shows that he had some political sense, but even then, it only seems to have made matters worse. The surviving sources cover the matter in detail:

When he kept refusing the title [of king] and rebuking in a way those who thus accosted him yet did nothing by which it would be thought that he was really displeased at it, they secretly adorned his statue, which stood on the rostra, with a diadem. And when the Tribunes, Caius Epidius Marullus and Lucius Caesetius Flavius, took it down, he became violently angry, although they uttered no word of abuse and moreover actually praised him before the populace as not wanting anything of the sort. For the time being, though vexed, he held his peace.

Subsequently, however, when he was riding in from the Alban Mount and some men again called him king, he said that his name was not king but Caesar; but when the same Tribunes brought suit against the first man who had termed him king, he no longer restrained his wrath but showed great irritation, as if these very officials were really stirring up sedition against him. And though for the moment he did them no harm, yet later, when they issued a proclamation declaring that they were unable to speak their mind freely and safely on behalf of the public good, he became exceedingly angry and brought them into the Senate House where he accused them and put their conduct to the vote. He did not put them to death, though some declared them worthy even of that penalty, but he first removed them from the Tribunate, on the motion of Helvius Cinna, their colleague, and then erased their names from the Senate. Some were pleased at this, or pretended to be, thinking they would have no need to incur danger by speaking out freely, and since they were not themselves involved in the business, they could view events as from a watch tower. Caesar, however, received an ill name from this fact also, that, where he should have hated those who applied to him the name of king, he let them go and found fault with the tribunes instead.[20]

But the most open and deadly hatred towards him was produced by his passion for the royal power. For the multitude this was a first cause of hatred, and for those who had long smothered their hate, a most specious pretext for it. And yet those who were advocating this honour for Caesar actually spread abroad among the people a report that from the Sibylline books it appeared that Parthia could be taken if the Romans went up against it with a king, but otherwise could not be assailed; and as Caesar was coming down from Alba into the city they ventured to hail him as king. But at this the people were confounded, and Caesar, disturbed in mind, said that his name was not King, but Caesar, and seeing that his words produced a universal silence, he passed on with no very cheerful or contented looks.[21]

To an insult which so plainly showed his contempt for the Senate he added an act of even greater insolence; for at the Latin Festival, as he was returning to the city, amid the extravagant and unprecedented demonstrations of the populace, someone in the press placed on his statue a laurel wreath with a white fillet tied to it; and when Epidius Marullus and Caesetius Flavius, Tribunes of the Plebs, gave orders that the ribbon be removed from the wreath and the man taken off to prison, Caesar sharply rebuked and deposed them, either offended that the hint at regal power had been received with so little favour, or, as he asserted, that he had been robbed of the glory of refusing it. But from that time on he could not rid himself of the odium of having aspired to the title of monarch, although he replied to the commons, when they hailed him as king, 'I am Caesar and no king,' and at the Lupercalia, when the Consul Antonius several times attempted to place a crown upon his head as he spoke from the rostra, he put it aside and at last sent it to the Capitol, to be offered to Jupiter Optimus Maximus. Nay, more, the report had spread in various quarters that he intended to move to Ilium or Alexandria, taking with him the resources of the state, draining Italy by levies, and leaving the charge of the city to his friends; also that at the next meeting of the Senate Lucius Cotta would announce as the decision of Fifteen, that inasmuch as it was written in the books of fate that the Parthians could be conquered only by a king, Caesar should be given that title.[22]

Caesar: The Five Month King   141

Thus, even though Caesar publicly refused the title of King, that connection was now openly being made in public, with many assuming that Caesar's refusals were not genuine, but part of a strategy to encourage the Senate and People to appoint him. It is doubtful that Caesar cared what title he had in Rome, eager as he was to get away from the city and the politics and back into the field. However, these perceived regal aspirations (his son was a Pharaoh, as was his mistress by the way) and the deposition of two Tribunes who opposed this regal movement set the question in many peoples' minds, especially those of the Senatorial oligarchy.

Caesar had an odd relationship with the Tribunes of the Plebs, far preferring the idealised Republican view of the office rather than the practical reality. In the opening of his work on the civil wars, Caesar defended his actions to his troops as defending the ancient privileges of the Tribunate:

He [Caesar] complains that a new precedent had been introduced into the state whereby the right of Tribunicial intervention, which in earlier years had been restored by arms, was now being branded with ignominy and crushed by arms. Sulla, he said, though stripping the Tribunicial power of everything, had nevertheless left its right of intervention free, while Pompeius, who had the credit of having restored the privileges that were lost, had taken away even those that they had before.

There had been no instance of the decree that the magistrates should take measures to prevent the state from suffering harm (the declaration and decision of the senate by which the Roman People are called to arms) except in the case of pernicious laws, Tribunicial violence, a popular secession, or the seizure of temples and elevated positions: and he explains that these precedents of a former age had been expiated by the downfall of Saturninus and of the Gracchi. No event of this kind had occurred at the time in question or had even been thought of. He exhorts them to defend from his enemies the reputation and dignity of the commander under whose guidance they have administered the state with unfailing good fortune for nine years, fought many successful battles, and pacified the whole of Gaul and Germany.

Thereupon the men of the Thirteenth Legion, which was present (he had called this out at the beginning of the disorder; the rest had not yet come together), exclaim that they are ready to repel the wrongs of their commander and of the Tribunes.[23]

After the Senate decreed many of the highest honours (such as the right to be called 'father of the fatherland' together with an eternal inviolability and dictatorship), several grudges rose against him: because he did not rise from his throne in front of the temple of Venus Genetrix when the Senators arrived to present him with these honours; because, when his fellow Consul M. Antonius, dancing with the Luperci, placed a diadem on his head, he placed it on his throne; and because he expelled the Tribunes of the Plebs Epidius Marullus and Caesetius Flavus from office after they had caused hostility towards him, arguing that he was aiming at one man rule.[24]

Yet no sooner had he occupied Rome in early 49 BC, than he threatened to murder a Tribune (L. Caecilius Metellus) who opposed his ransacking of the State Treasury. Now, five years later, the supposed defender of the Tribunate had ordered/supported the deposition of two Tribunes who upheld Republican values and opposed the moves to offer him a kingship. Caesar might not have been king in name, but it was obvious to all that he was in practice.[25] The only question was, what were his opponents going to do about it; let him leave Rome and hopefully die on the sands of Parthia, as Crassus had done, or take action before Caesar the King left to conquer the East and retrace the footsteps of Alexander the Great?

Countdown to the Ides of March – The Method

As well as providing the motive for what took place on the Ides of March, Caesar's actions during this period also provided both the method and the opportunity, creating the circumstances of the revival of a civil war faction he had crushed in Africa just eighteen months before. As previously stated, by the time of the Battle of Thapsus in 46 BC, the opposition Caesar faced consisted of three different but intertwined factions; the Pompeians, the Anti-Caesarians and the Romano-Numidians. The aftermath of Thapsus saw the destruction of the latter two, with the suicide of Cato and the surrender of the Three Hundred (bankers and merchants) signalling the end of the active Anti-Caesarian Senatorial faction.

Yet opposition to Caesar did not fade within the Senate, with the survivors, whether those who never evacuated to Greece in 49 BC or those who were pardoned after the defeats at Pharsalus and Thapsus, keeping their heads down and gracing Caesar with silent acquiescence. Having grown up under the proscriptions of Sulla himself, Caesar chose to deliberately, and publicly, not follow his predecessor and eliminate his enemies through (open) extra judicial murder, to show clemency in the hope that these silent opponents would approve. In that, as in so much of Roman political life, he was to be proved wrong, fatally so.

The Unwise Pardons and Promotions

Having already pardoned so many of his former opponents from the Anti-Senatorial faction, including both Brutus and Cassius, in 44 BC Caesar again decided to publicly demonstrate his clemency with another round of pardons, in the mistaken belief that the civil wars were over, contrary to the reality in both Spain and Syria:

> *For in all other ways, at least after the civil wars were over, he showed himself blameless; and certainly it is thought not inappropriate that the temple of Clemency was decreed as a thank-offering in view of his mildness. For he pardoned many of those who had fought against him, and to some he even gave honours and offices besides, as to Brutus and Cassius, both of whom were now Praetors.*[26]

> *Caesar, however, removed the ban from the survivors of those who had warred against him, granting them immunity on fair and uniform terms.*[27]

> *Caesar also recalled the exiles, except those who were banished for some very grave offence. He pardoned his enemies and forthwith added many of those who had fought against him to the yearly magistracies, or to the command of provinces and armies.*[28]

Thus, Caesar brought more of his political enemies back into Rome, just as he was planning on vacating it. Furthermore, as Appian notes, the magistrates of 44 BC, which Caesar selected, contained a number of his former enemies, most notably M. Iunius Brutus as Urban Praetor and C. Cassius Longinus as Praetor Peregrinus. As previously noted, both men had fought with Pompeius in Greece, with Brutus fighting at the Battle of Pharsalus, and Cassius spurning the opportunity to crush Caesar when crossing the Bosphorus.

Nevertheless, despite elevating his former enemies, and publicly doing so, he ensured that neither man received military commands, with both receiving Rome-based Praetorships. However, this would mean that both men would be in Rome whilst Caesar was travelling to the East, and as already noted, he had ensured that there would be a combustible combination of Consuls with the former enemies, M. Antonius, and P. Cornelius Dolabella holding office in his absence.

Therefore, Caesar had ensured (or at least thought he had) that the military forces of the Western Republic would be in loyalist hands, with Gallia Narbonensis and Nearer Spain in the hands of L. Aemilius Lepidus, and

D. Iunius Brutus Albinus holding Cisalpine Gaul. Both men would be critical to not only containing Sex. Pompeius in Spain, but ensuring stability in Italy and that of the Caesarian government with the threat of military intervention.[29]

The Re-emergence of the Cult of Pompeius

Again, Caesar sought to further move himself away from the shadow of Sulla by not only spurning his example when it came to the memory of his opponents, but publicly doing the opposite. During Sulla's rule the monuments to his arch rival (and former mentor) C. Marius (Caesar's uncle) were destroyed and any public mention of his memory banned. Caesar, the nephew of Marius, who had previously used this public ban to aid his own career (by acting against it), clearly wanted to ensure that this example was not followed. To those ends, he actively fostered the cult of Pompeius (an act of supreme hypocrisy).

> *The statues of Pompeius, which had been thrown down, he would not suffer to remain so, but set them up again, at which Cicero said that in setting up Pompeius' statues Caesar firmly fixed his own.*[30]

> *Caesar ordered that the statues of Pompeius and Sulla, which had been demolished by their enemies, should be replaced.*[31]

Again, whilst he was clearly trying to reconcile his former enemies to his rule and distance himself from the legacy of Sulla, the fact that his commanders were still fighting Pompeius' son in Spain would have been lost on no one. All this would have done is stir up feelings for the Republic's lost martyr amongst the Senatorial elite, many of whom had served with him. The most famous statue restored was in the Theatre of Pompeius himself, site of the Senatorial meetings of 15 March.

This resurrection of the Cult of Pompeius built on that of the other Republican Martyr, that of Cato, with Caesar unwisely reacting to Cicero's agitating[32] by releasing a work attacking a man who could not defend himself and weakening his own position by doing so:

> *Cicero had written an encomium on Cato which he entitled 'Cato'; and the discourse was eagerly read by many, as was natural, since it was composed by the ablest of orators on the noblest of themes. This annoyed Caesar, who thought that Cicero's praise of the dead Cato was a denunciation of Caesar himself. Accordingly, he wrote a treatise in which he got together countless charges against Cato; and*

*the work is entitled 'Anti-Cato'. Both treatises have many eager readers, as well on account of Caesar as of Cato.*³³

In many ways, it is clear that this was a situation in which Caesar would have been 'damned if he did and damned if he didn't', yet he did not need to respond in either case but could have ignored the issues. Active *damnatio memoriae* as seen under Sulla could have been avoided without resurrecting feeling for both Pompeius and Cato by his actions.

Countdown to the Ides of March – The Opportunity

Yet, though Caesar's actions were politically unwise and undermined his political position, he still had military control of the Republic, supported by the People of Rome and a tight faction of supporters. Though the Pompeians were still fighting in both the Eastern and Western Republics, both were contained, and the fighting was taking place on the peripheries of the Roman world. Thus, as it was, Caesar should have been secure. The fact that he was not was down to key individuals who reacted to the circumstances and atmosphere which Caesar had created to take action and change history.

The First Hint of Conspiracy – the Trebonian Plot

With military action clearly out of the question and no possible route through either the courts or the Assemblies, there was only one course of action open to Caesar's opponents: assassination. For almost a century, the Republic had seen a litany of political murders, from the public – such as Ti. Sempronius Gracchus in 133 BC – to the secret – such as that of P. Scipio Aemilianus in 129 BC. Yet it had also seen very public failures, as with the Sullan conspiracy in Rome during the Second Civil War in 63 BC.

Yet the first hints of a conspiracy can be traced back to late-45 BC and came from within the Caesarian faction itself and not its enemies. This plot, if we are to believe it, centred upon a key Caesarian commander, C. Trebonius. Trebonius had been a prominent Caesarian supporter for years, serving under Caesar in Gaul from 54 BC. He had seen notable service throughout the civil war to date, but always on the periphery, whether it be as the commander of the Caesarian siege of Masillia in 49 BC, the Praetor who clashed with Caelius in Rome in 48 BC, or the Proconsul of Spain in 47–46 BC. For this loyal, yet undistinguished, service he had been rewarded by Caesar with a Consulship in late 45 BC.

Nevertheless, as later demonstrated, he came to the conclusion that Caesar needed to be removed. Ultimately, we will never know why, as unlike his former colleague Labienus, who also served under Caesar in Gaul but chose to oppose him in 49 BC, Trebonius had remained loyal throughout the civil war period, yet by 45 BC (the time of his Consulship), his thoughts apparently turned to assassination. As always there is no hard evidence, merely hints in Cicero's vitriolic attack on Antonius, the *Philippics*, which was then built on as fact in later sources, such as Plutarch:

> *Moreover at this very time an assassin sent by him* [Antonius] *was said to have been caught at Caesar's house dagger in hand; of which Caesar complained and openly attacked you in the Senate.*[34]

> *The rest were for making him* [Antonius] *one of them, but Trebonius opposed it. For, he said, while people were going out to meet Caesar on his return from Spain, Antonius had travelled with him and shared his tent, and he had sounded him quietly and cautiously; Antonius had understood him, he said, but had not responded to his advances; Antonius had not, however, reported the conversation to Caesar, but had faithfully kept silence about it.*[35]

Thus there is no hard evidence for a Trebonian plot, even less of one that included M. Antonius. Nevertheless, given the fact that Trebonius was one of the most prominent Caesarians to take part in the assassination plot of 44 BC, there may well have been some truth to these accounts, at least of Trebonius' own involvement. Antonius' involvement is even more open to question, but a silent acquiescence and the chance to inherit the mantle of leader of the Caesarian faction if some 'tragic accident' were to befall Caesar is not beyond the realm of possibility given what we know about his character and actions to date. He had just been rehabilitated by Caesar after years of being scapegoated for the failures of 48 BC. If true, it shows that even his own faction was beginning to have doubts about Caesar's new role in the Republic and that their own futures might be brighter without him.

The Resurrection of a New Civil War Faction – The Leaders

If the Caesarians could not bring themselves to successfully murder their own leader, then the ex-Pompeians had no such qualms and it fell to two failed ex-Pompeians to create a new faction and succeed where so many of their former colleagues had failed, and perhaps in doing so exonerate their own previous failings.

The two men in question were both middle-rank Senators, from differing backgrounds and experience but between them they were able to forge the new, and second, Anti-Caesarian faction. They were, of course, C. Cassius Longinus and M. Iunius Brutus. Of the two it was Cassius who had had the most political and military experience to date, but notably receives less modern historiographical coverage.[36] The Cassii Longinii were a long-established Plebeian family, part of the new wave of such families to emerge from the bloodshed of the Second Punic War, which did so much to thin out the Senatorial nobility and allow new political families to emerge. They had been regular holders of the Consulship (with five between 171 and 96 BC)[37] but again, like many of the mid-rank families, had failed to achieve the highest office in the disruptions caused by the civil wars.

Caius came to prominence during the First Romano-Parthian War, as a supporter of, and Quaestor to, M. Licinius Crassus. As the most senior surviving officer following the defeat at Carrhae in 53 BC, it was Cassius who assumed command of the surviving Roman forces in Syria in 52–51 BC, defeating a Parthian incursion into the province and stabilising the Roman position. Upon his return to Rome, he began his move through the *cursus honorum*, becoming a Tribune in 49 BC, and thus was present for the fateful political events that forced Caesar's hand into declaring war on his own state. Despite his military experience, his junior rank saw him as a (successful) commander of a Pompeian fleet during the 49–48 BC period. The aftermath of Pharsalus saw his most notable contribution when his fleet intercepted Caesar as he was crossing the Bosphorus in pursuit of Pompeius. It was the defection of his fleet that not only allowed Caesar to avoid being defeated/killed and prevented from pursuing Pompeius, but actually allowed Caesar to gain a fleet and thus dramatically shorten the pursuit, forcing Pompeius to make the fateful change of plan and land in Egypt (upon which he was subsequently murdered).

Thus Cassius, more than any man (other than Pompeius himself), bore the failures to prevent Caesar's rise to power. Following Pompeius' murder he apparently gave up the fight and sought Caesar's pardon, though if we are to believe Cicero (in his vitriolic *Philippics*), Cassius actually made an attempt to atone for his failures by attempting to assassinate Caesar whilst he was still in the East:

[Cassius], *a man who even without the assistance of these other most illustrious men, would have accomplished this same deed in Cilicia, at the mouth of the River Cydnus, if Caesar had brought his ships to that bank of the river which he had intended, and not to the opposite one.*[38]

We are given no other details, and many have rightly questioned how serious a plot it was, or whether Cassius revealed this 'earlier effort' only after his final success.[39] Certainly Caesar kept him around in the East, given his experience as

Rome's most successful eastern commander, and he served as a Legate to Caesar during the Fourth Romano-Pontic War. Returning to Rome with Caesar, he took no part in the African campaign of 46 BC, remaining in Rome. Obviously keeping his nose clean, on Caesar's return to Rome he was appointed to the 'safe' position of Praetor Peregrinus for 44 BC, occupying the role of trophy-pardoned Pompeian, but being kept well away from military forces.

By contrast, his partner had what purported to be a far grander lineage, but little practical experience. M. Iunius Brutus came from a family that bore the same name as the near-mythical founder of the Republic, L. Iunius Brutus, though it is doubtful that was what the first Brutus intended (overthrowing his uncle, the last Roman King, L. Tarquinius Superbus, in a palace coup). The claim by the Iunii Bruti of the late Republic to be descended from the 'Founder of the Republic' was widely recognised at the time (at least in public), but questioned ever since given their Plebeian status and their disappearance from the historic record of Roman magistrates until after the Second Punic War.[40] Ironically, their first Consulship for over 100 years was the year before the Cassii Longinii achieved their first (178 BC). Again, they had only recorded three Consulships since their 're-emergence' in the aftermath of the Second Punic War and only one during the First Civil War (77 BC).

It was Brutus' father's role in the First Civil War that did much to shape his subsequent career. A Plebeian Tribune in 83 BC under the Cinnan regime, he survived the Sullan proscriptions of the late-80s, but was a legate of the civil war general M. Aemilius Lepidus (father of Caesar's lieutenant) and took part in the Lepidian attack on Rome in 77 BC which ended in defeat. Captured by Pompeius, he was subsequently put to death by the latter, earning his son the role of son of a traitor, at least under the Sullan regime.

Roughly the same age as Cassius, the two men were both elected as Quaestors for 53 BC, though he served a quiet period in office in Cilicia under his father-in-law, Ap. Claudius Pulcher (Cos. 54 BC), whilst Cassius was fighting in Mesopotamia and Syria. Following his return from the east in late-51 BC, and still a junior Senator, he seemingly held no further office until the outbreak of civil war in 49 BC when he swallowed his family's hatred for Pompeius and joined the bulk of the Anti-Senatorial faction in Greece in their (distasteful) support of Pompeius over Caesar, as the lesser of two evils.

Unlike Cassius, we have no surviving record of his activities in the 49–48 BC period other than Caesar's apparent eagerness to ensure his safety after the Battle of Pharsalus, which he probably participated in. Much will have been made in later sources of the relationship between Caesar and Brutus and much 'evidence' will have been introduced into the later sources to make it more personal and thus more dramatic when it came to the events of the Ides, including the rumour that a youthful Caesar was in fact Brutus' father.

Nevertheless, he surrendered to Caesar immediately after Pharsalus rather than fight on, and certainly prospered under the Caesarian regime, becoming the Governor of Cisalpine Gaul in 46–45 BC and the prominent Urban Praetor for 44 BC. However, it was on his return to Rome that he took the very public act of divorcing his wife Claudia and marrying his cousin, Porcia, daughter of the recently-deceased 'Republican martyr' M. Porcius Cato, causing a minor scandal at the time. This was a very public statement of his Republican sympathies which would not have gone down well with Caesar and may explain why he was 'honoured' with a Praetorship that kept him in Rome, under sight, with no military commitments.

Not only were Brutus and Cassius both elected to city-based Praetorships in 44 BC, but the two men were distantly related (as were most Roman oligarchs in some degree) through Cassius' wife, Iunia, being the half-sister of Brutus. Thus, these two men, who had known each other for many years, came together to act as the nucleus of the leadership of a new faction, the resurrected Anti-Caesarian faction, that Cato, Brutus' father in law, had spearheaded.

Though subsequent histories have made this a Duumvirate of the two men, there were at least two other key faction leaders: D. Iunius Brutus Albinus (Pr. 45 BC) and C. Trebonius (Cos. 45 BC). Of the two men, we have already discussed C. Trebonius, a hardened Caesarian loyalist who had been 'rewarded' with a truncated Consulship in 45 BC and had apparently already attempted one plot on Caesar's life.

The other man was D. Iunius Brutus Albinus.[41] Another member of the Gens Iunii Bruti, his father had been Consul of 77 BC under the Sullan regime. A staunch supporter of Caesar and another man who suffered gossip about whether Caesar was his natural father,[42] he served under Caesar in both the Romano-Gallic and Civil Wars, developing an expertise as a naval commander and commanding the naval portion of the siege of Massilia (with Trebonius commanding the land) in 49 BC. He was so trusted by Caesar that he was named amongst the next level of beneficiaries in his will. Given a Praetorship in 45 BC, he was named as Governor of Cisalpine Gaul for 44 BC.

Thus, whilst Brutus and Cassius represented the former Pompeian and Anti-Senatorial factions, Brutus Albinus and Trebonius (the only Consul amongst the conspirators), represented the disgruntled wing of the Caesarian faction, of which there were apparently many.

The Resurrection of a New Civil War Faction – The Members and the Plot

We need not dwell too long on the faction these men formed or the conspiracy itself as there has been a significant body of literature on the subject for the last 2,000 years.[43] The key factor was that it was composed of a number of mid-ranking oligarchs, mostly of Praetorian level, many of whom had been staunch Caesarian loyalists up to this point, not only Brutus Albinus and Trebonius, but men such as L. Minucius Basilus (Pr. 45 BC), L. Tillius Cimber (Pr. 45) and Ser. Sulpicius Galba (Pr. 54 BC). Yet as Epstein pointed out, many of the men had personal grievances against Caesar himself, rather than being inspired by more noble ideals of 'saving the Republic'.[44]

We will never know how many men (or women if we include Porcia) joined the conspiracy; but at its core lay frustrated long-term opponents of Caesar and embittered former allies. The faction's two (or four) leaders did seem to hold the idea that Caesar's death would save the Republic and remove a Tyrant, and hopefully ensure their own elevation as the 'saviours of the Republic' into the bargain. All would have been brought up with the cultural background of the Athenian Tyrant slayers, of Harmodius and Aristogeiton, not to mention the mythology of Brutus' own ancestor, the 'Founder of the Republic'. Cicero is the only surviving contemporary source for the conspirators:

Indeed, if leaders were wanted for the purpose of delivering the country, what need was there of my instigating the Brutuses, one of whom [Decimus] saw every day in his house the image of Lucius Brutus, and the other [Marcus] saw also the image of Ahala? Were these the men to seek counsel from the ancestors of others rather than from their own? and from elsewhere rather than at home? What? Caius Cassius, a man of that family which could not endure, I will not say the domination, but even the power of any individual, he, I suppose, was in need of me to instigate him? a man who even without the assistance of these other most illustrious men, would have accomplished this same deed in Cilicia, at the mouth of the River Cydnus, if Caesar had brought his ships to that bank of the river which he had intended, and not to the opposite one.

Was Cnaeus Domitius spurred on to seek to recover his dignity, not by the death of his father, a most illustrious man, nor by the death of his uncle, nor by the deprivation of his own dignity, but by my advice and authority? Did I persuade Caius Trebonius? a man whom I should not have ventured even to advise. On which account the Republic owes him even a larger debt of gratitude, because he preferred the liberty of the Roman People to the friendship of one man, and because he preferred overthrowing arbitrary power to sharing it. Was I the instigator whom Lucius Tillius Cimber followed? a man whom I admired for having performed that action, rather than ever expected that he would perform it; and I admired him on this account, that he was unmindful of the personal kindnesses which he had received, but mindful of his country. What shall I say of the two Servilii? Shall I call them Cascas, or Ahalas; and do you think that those men were instigated by my authority rather than by their affection for the Republic? It would take a long time to go through all the rest; and it is a glorious thing for the Republic that they were so numerous, and a most honourable thing also for themselves.[45]

Whilst Appian lists the following:

Each of them tested those of their own friends, and of Caesar's also, whom they considered the most courageous of either faction. Of their own friends they inveigled two brothers, Caecilius and Bucolianus, and besides these Rubrius Ruga, Quintus Ligarius, Marcus Spurius, Servilius Galba, Sextius Naso, and Pontius Aquila. These were of their own faction. Of Caesar's friends they secured Decimus Brutus, whom I have already mentioned, also Caius Casca, Trebonius, Tillius Cimber, and Minucius Basilius.[46]

Snatching Defeat – The Ides of March and Caesar's Failure

Subsequent Roman literature is naturally full of all sorts of warnings and prodigies of the impending event, but as the failed Sullan conspiracy of 63 BC showed, keeping a conspiracy a secret amongst such a tight-knit group of oligarchs, given how many people were involved, was a near impossible task and word was bound to have leaked. Given that, successfully assassinating the most powerful man in the Roman world in full view of the Senate, in the Theatre of Pompeius (a nice touch in itself), was a major achievement and one which changed the history of not just the Western World, but also the Eastern one as well (no doubt saving the Parthian Empire and its successors).

The Ides of March was the ultimate mark of Caesar's failure, both in the short term – allowing the conspiracy to succeed, the medium term – the failure of his five-month rule, and the long term – his failure to hold on to the power that he had won on the fields of Pharsalus, Thapsus, and Munda. Despite these battlefield victories he met the same fate as his long-time former allies, Pompeius and Crassus, being murdered, with the only consolation being that it was not at the hands of foreign enemies, on foreign shores. Held up against his First Civil War predecessors (including his uncle) Marius, as well as Sulla, who both died natural deaths, having achieved supreme power in Rome, his political failings can be seen. In comparison Caesar is more on a level of his former father-in-law, L. Cornelius Cinna, who held supreme power in Rome (between 87–84 BC) and was ignominiously murdered by his own side.

The fact that Caesar's myth endures owes more to his adopted son (C. Octavius, becoming C. Iulius Caesar Octavianus and finally Augustus), who learnt from Caesar's own failings, and probably learnt far more from Pompeius himself about the stealthy use of power in the Republic to establish a lasting dominance over Rome, which soon evolved from a Pompeian Principate to an un-Republican Emperor.

Caesar's career showed that victory on the battlefield did not translate into lasting political power, nor did they bring the Third Civil War to an end. As Caesar was marching to his destiny in the Theatre of Pompeius, the latter's son was still fighting in Spain, increasingly successfully, some five years after Caesar's first victory there (Ilerda in 49 BC). His planned attempt to resurrect the Romano-Parthian War in the East would be delayed by the fact that the Roman province of Syria was still held by the Pompeians, some three years after the Caesarian victory at Zela.

Thus, even at the point of his death, the civil war which he had helped to unleash some five years earlier was still raging across the Roman world. Though the Pompeian and Anti-Caesarian factions had been defeated on multiple occasions and had lost multiple leaders, new men rose to take up the challenge and the now-leaderless Caesarian faction faced the Pompeians under Sex. Pompeius and Anti-Caesarians under Brutus and Cassius. How Rome's ruling faction faced these challenges, and the vexed question of the succession, will be discussed in the next volume in this series; *The Battles of Forum Gallorum and Mutina (43 BC). Antony, Octavian, and Caesar's Legacy in the Third Roman Civil War.*

Appendix I

Civil War and Empire – The Illyrian Campaigns (45–44 BC)

Given the surviving sources' natural focus on events either in Spain or in Rome during this period, it is illuminating when we find a source that details military campaigns outside of the Civil War (or Caesar). One such comes from Appian and his work on the Illyrian Wars:

Caesar was preoccupied by the necessity of coming to a conclusion with Pompeius, and, after Pompeius' death, with the numerous parts of his faction still remaining. When he had settled everything, he returned to Rome and made preparations for war with the Getae and the Parthians.

The Illyrians began to fear lest he should attack them, as they were on his intended line of march. So they sent ambassadors to Rome to crave pardon for what they had done and to offer their friendship and alliance, vaunting themselves as a very brave race. Caesar was hastening his preparations against the Parthians; nevertheless, he gave them the dignified answer that he could not make friends of those who had done what they had, but that he would grant them pardon if they would subject themselves to tribute and give him hostages. They promised to do both, and accordingly he sent Vatinius thither with three legions and a large cavalry force to impose a light tribute on them and receive the hostages.

When Caesar was slain, the Dalmatians, thinking that the Roman power resided in him and had perished with him, would not listen to Vatinius on the subject of the tribute or anything else. When he attempted to use force, they attacked and destroyed five of his cohorts, including their commanding officer, Baebius, a man of Senatorial rank. Vatinius took refuge with the remainder of his force in Epidamnus [Dyrrhachium].

The Roman Senate transferred this army, together with the province of Macedonia and Roman Illyria, to Brutus Caepio, one of Caesar's murderers, and at the same time assigned Syria to Cassius, another of the assassins. But they also, being involved in war with Antonius and the second Caesar, surnamed Augustus, had no time to attend to the Illyrians.[1]

As we have seen, the Illyrian tribes, who at the best of times were only under nominal Roman control, had used the various civil war campaigns in the region to regain a greater degree of independence. In 47 BC, the Caesarian commander (and former Pompeian) A. Gabinius was defeated by the Illyrian tribes and had to retreat to the coastal city of Salonae.

Even with the wars in Spain and Syria and the impending Parthian expedition, Caesar deemed their threat so urgent that he dispatched his trusted lieutenant Vatinius, who had fought in Illyria during 47 BC against the Pompeians,[2] with three legions. Aside from Appian, we also have a contemporary source for these campaigns, as Vatinius was in correspondence with Cicero in Rome at the time and several of his letters survive.

> *Please support me if there is any need for it. Caesar still does me wrong. He is still not bringing forth a motion about my supplicationes and my achievements in Dalmatia, as if what I had done in Dalmatia was not most worthy of a Triumph! Or must I wait until I have finished the whole war, when there are twenty ancient towns in Dalmatia, and more than sixty which they lay claim to. If my supplicationes are not decreed unless I capture all of them, then I am a long way off from the situation of other generals.*[3]

It is interesting to see the difference in detail between the two sources, as Appian makes no reference to fighting before Caesar's death in 44 BC, yet Vatinius' letter (dated to January 44 BC) shows that he had been fighting through the latter stages of 45 BC and had done enough (in his mind at least) to earn a *supplicatio*, if not a full Triumph. It is also interesting that he believed that this was being blocked by Caesar himself, again highlighting tensions between Caesar and his 'loyal' commanders.

Despite his victories to date, if we return to Appian, the news of the death of Caesar impacted the campaign and a larger number of Illyrian tribes rose in revolt, inflicting a defeat on Vatinius' army, with five cohorts (nearly 2,500 men – half a legion) being commanded by a man named Baebius being destroyed, forcing Vatinius to vacate the Illyrian uplands and return to the safety of Dyrrhachium.

Thus the Caesarian campaign failed, and the Illyrian tribes maintained, and seemingly strengthened, their independence. This independence was further enhanced when Vatinius' remaining legions were transferred to M. Iunius Brutus later in 44 BC. Vatinius seemingly remained in Illyria until 43 BC, returning to Rome where, in 42 BC, he was awarded a Triumph for his campaigns. Either we have no record of subsequent activities, or this was a face-saving device. Given his lack of forces and the focus on the Civil War campaigns in Greece in this period, the latter seems more likely.

Thus we have a small window into the business-as-usual campaign the Romans were fighting in this period, and an insight into how the civil war events (such as Caesar's assignation) were undermining Roman control of supposedly long-conquered regions of their Empire. It was not until 35 BC, following Agrippa's defeat of Sex. Pompeius at the Battle of Naulochus, that Caesar Octavianus was able to focus on recovering control of the Illyrian tribes, which he achieved in 33 BC, finally recovering the Roman standards which Gabinius had lost.

Appendix II

Who's Who in the Third Roman Civil War (45 BC)

Given the continuous narrative of Caesar and the number of other surviving sources that comment on this period, we know the identities of a large number of Roman politicians and officers that were taking part in the conflict, in both major and minor roles. That being the case, the following is a brief Who's Who of those involved in the various campaigns of 45 BC, along with their subsequent fates.

The Main Protagonists

Cn. Pompeius 'Magnus'   Killed 45 BC
Eldest of the two sons of Pompeius Magnus and thus his political inheritor. Commanded a Pompeian fleet in 48 BC. Relocated to North Africa in the aftermath of both Pharsalus and his father's murder. Sent to Spain during the North African campaign, he successfully seized control of southern Spain ousting the Caesarian forces. Assuming command of the Pompeian faction following the suicide of Metellus Scipio, and aided by Labienus, he successfully rebuilt the Pompeian forces, raising thirteen legions to face Caesar. Chose to fight Caesar at the Battle of Munda and came close to defeating him. Took to the seas to escape Spain (for Syria) but lost his fleet in a skirmish and was hunted down and murdered, with his mantle being taken up by his younger brother.

T. Labienus   (Pr. c.59 BC)   Killed 45 BC
Senior Caesarian commander in Gaul but defected to join Pompeius when Caesar invaded Italy. Became a senior Pompeian commander, fighting at both Pharsalus in North Africa, and came close to defeating Caesar at the Battle of Ruspina in 46 BC. Retreating to Spain after Thapsus and (by default) found himself as joint leader of the Pompeian faction (along with Pompeius' sons). Helped Pompeius raise and train thirteen legions to fight Caesar and came close to defeating him at the Battle of Munda, choosing to die in battle rather than surrender or retreat. His son (Q. Labienus) took up his cause and briefly led a Parthian-sponsored Anti-Caesarian client state in Asia Minor.

C. Iulius Caesar   (Cos. 59, 48, 46, 45 BC)   Killed 44 BC
Nephew of the great C. Marius, who was a leading general in the First Civil War, and son-in-law of L. Cornelius Cinna, who ruled Rome between 87–84 BC. Came to notice in Roman politics in the 60s championing the Marian cause against the ruling Sullan faction, but still only a minor figure. Won the Consulship for 59 BC as an agent of Pompeius (and latterly Crassus) and was rewarded with a command in Gaul. Defied expectations by launching a war of conquest, backed by Pompeius and Crassus. Formed a fresh alliance with Pompeius and Crassus, whilst still being the junior member, remained in Gaul throughout the 50s BC. Identified by Pompeius as the last obstacle to his dominance in Rome and manipulated into invading Italy as an 'enemy of the state'.

Defeated at Dyrrhachium, he regrouped and won a major victory at the subsequent Battle of Pharsalus. Neither this victory nor the subsequent murder of Pompeius brought the war to a conclusion, and he fought the further Battles of Thapsus in 46 BC and Munda in 45 BC. Having finally secured the control of the bulk of the Roman Republic, he was preparing for a final civil war campaign against the Pompeians in Syria and then a renewal of the Romano-Parthian War when he was famously murdered in the Senate by a large group of Senators, composed of former enemies (Pompeians) and many of his own officers, to prevent him becoming sole ruler of Rome.

Notable Leading Figures

M. Aemilius Lepidus   (Cos. 46 and 42 BC)
Son of a First Civil War general. One of the Caesarian faction. Left by Caesar in charge of Rome during 49 BC. Proposed Caesar as Dictator. Became one of the main leaders of the faction after Caesar's death, but was politically outmanoeuvred by M. Antonius and Caesar Octavianus after the Battles of Philippi in 42 BC. Left alive by Octavianus (Augustus) as Princeps Maximus (Chief Priest). Died of natural causes in 13/12 BC.

C. Antistius Vetus   (Cos. 30 BC)
Caesarian commander, appointed to lead the campaign to capture Pompeian Syria in 45 BC, an act in which he ultimately failed, when Bassus was aided by the Parthians. Following Caesar's assassination, he joined the Anti-Caesarian forces but reconciled with the Caesarians in the aftermath of Philippi. Was raised to the Consulship with Octavianus in 30 BC and became part of the Augustan Aristocracy.

M. Antonius (Tr. 49, Cos. 44, 34, 31 BC) Suicide 30 BC

One of the two Tribunes who fled to Caesar at the beginning of 49 BC. Received an extraordinary Propraetorian command (which technically he could not hold as a serving Tribune). Held command in Italy during 49 BC and led the defence of Brundisium in early 48 BC. Took command of the Caesarian relief army which crossed into Illyria in early 48. Present at the Battles of Dyrrhachium and Pharsalus. Was Caesar's deputy during his Dictatorship and became one of the leaders of the Caesarian faction following Caesar's murder in 44 BC. Seized control of the Republic as one of the Second Triumvirate and took control of the Eastern Republic. Took command of the Second Romano-Parthian War and attempted to carve out his own familial empire in the east. Defeated by Caesar Octavianus at the Battle of Actium in 31 BC. Committed suicide following Octavianus' invasion of Egypt.

C. Asinius Pollio (Cos. 40 BC) Died AD 4

Caesarian commander who survived the disastrous Caesarian invasion of Africa in 49 BC. Was with Caesar at the Battle of Pharsalus in 48 BC and in North Africa in 46 BC and possibly Spain in 45 BC. Appointed Governor of Farther Spain in 44 BC to fight Sex. Pompeius but was defeated and fled. Supported Antonius in the aftermath of Caesar's assassination and was made Consul in 40 BC, celebrating a Triumph in 39 BC for fighting in Illyria. He remained in Rome and made peace with Octavianus and became a celebrated historian of the period.

P. Attius Varus (Pr. c.53 BC) Killed 45 BC

Pompeian commander. Briefly fought Caesar's men in Italy before withdrawing. Seized command of Roman Africa and defeated the Caesarian invasion (with Numidian help). Created a Pompeian stronghold and quasi-independent fiefdom in North Africa. Became one of the Pompeian faction leaders in the aftermath of Pharsalus. Fled from Africa to Spain after the defeat at Thapsus. Killed during the final battle of Munda.

C. Caninus Rebilus (Cos. 45 BC)

Long standing Caesarian officer who fought under Caesar (and Labienus) in Gaul. One of the few survivors of the defeated Caesaria invasion of Africa in 49 BC. Fought with Caesar in North Africa in 46 BC and in Spain, and most likely present at the Battle of Munda. He was made Consul for one day, on the last day of 45 BC, when Fabus Maximus died unexpectedly. Subsequent career and fate unknown.

C. Carrinas (Cos. 43 BC)

Son of a Marian First Civil War general. Caesarian commander appointed by Caesar in 45 BC to subdue Sex. Pompeius, a task he failed in. Supported the Caesarian Triumvirate after Caesar's assassination and gained a Suffect Consulship. Continued to fight for the Caesarian faction throughout the Civil War, in Spain, Sicily and finally Gaul, winning a Triumph under the Augustan Republic. Date of death is unknown.

C. Cassius Longinus (Pr. 44 BC) Killed 42 BC

Former supporter of Crassus who took over the defence of the Roman East in the aftermath of the Battle of Carrhae. Pompeian naval commander in 48 BC who led an abortive attack on Sicily. Took his navy to the east in the aftermath of Pharsalus but rather than defeat Caesar as he crossed the Bosphorus, defected, providing Caesar with an effective navy, and quickening his pursuit of Pompeius. Pardoned and promoted by Caesar, he was famously one of the co-leaders of the conspiracy that murdered Caesar in 44 BC and co-leaders of the 'Anti-Caesarian' faction in the subsequent civil war. Killed in 42 BC after the Battles of Philippi.

Q. Caecilius Bassus Killed 42 BC?

Middle-ranking Roman knight who supported Pompeius and fought at the Battle of Pharsalus, retreating to the province of Syria. Led the conspiracy that saw the murder of Sex. Iulius Caesar in a Pompeian inspired revolt and ruled the province in the name of the Pompeian government. Defended Syria against the Caesarian invasions of Antistius Vetus and Staius Murcus in 45 and 44 BC respectively, negotiating with the Parthians who sent a force to relieve him. Surrendered to C. Cassius in 43 BC and subsequently disappears from the sources, possibly killed at the Battles of Philippi.

M. Claudius Marcellus (Cos. 51 BC) Killed 45 BC

Prominent Pompeian supporter who was present in Greece for the battles of 48 BC. Fled to the island of Mitylene after the Battle of Pharsalus. Was pardoned by Caesar but murdered in Athens by one of his retinue as he made his way back to Rome. Suspicions were raised about Caesar's sponsorship of this act.

M. Claudius Marcellus Aeserninus (Cos. 22 BC)

Caesarian Quaestor in Spain, who led the rebellion against Q. Cassius. Surrendered his force to the Caesarian Governor, Lepidus, and was pardoned. Later became a Consul under Augustus.

P. Cornelius Dolabella   (Cos. 44 BC)   Suicide 43 BC
Caesarian legate in charge of the Adriatic fleet in 49 BC, defeated by the Pompeians and withdrew. Clashed with M. Antonius, as Tribune in 47 BC but took Caesar's place in the Consulship of 44 BC and command of the proposed Parthian War. Clashed with C. Trebonius and C. Cassius in the east, committed suicide in Syria in 43 BC.

Q. Cornificius   (Pr. 45 BC)   Killed 42 BC
Caesarian Governor of Illyria, who re-secured the province for the Caesarian faction defeating the Pompeian commander M. Octavius. Appointed by Caesar to command in Syria in 46 BC and attempted to recover the province from the Pompeians. Later became Caesarian Governor of Africa but was proscribed by the Triumvirate. Killed in battle with his Triumviral successor.

C. Didius   Killed 45 BC
Caesarian commander in Spain, who led a naval victory over Attius Varus in 46 BC and later intercepted Cn. Pompeius after the Battle of Munda. Sent Pompeius' head to Caesar but was killed in a battle with the Lusitanians shortly afterwards.

Cn. Domitius Calvinus   (Cos. 53 and 40 BC)
Caesarian commander dispatched to face Metellus Scipio in 48 BC in Greece and later took part in the Battle of Pharsalus. Became Governor of Asia but was defeated by Pharnaces II later in 48 BC. Designated as Master of the Horse for 43 BC. He became an ally of Octavianus, following Caesar's murder and remained a key member of Octavianus' circle of supporters. His date of death is unknown.

Q. Fabius Maximus   (Cos. 45 BC)   Died 45 BC
Scion of one of the Republic's most famous families, but having achieved little of note to date, threw in his lot with Caesar (unlike the bulk of the other noble families). There is no record of any civil war activities prior to 46 BC, when he was sent to Spain to command the remaining Caesarian forces. Again, there is no record of any notable activities, but was granted a Triumph by Caesar (illegally) for his Spanish campaign and made Consul for the remainder of 45 BC. Died on the last day of the year, presumably of natural causes.

Q. Fufius Calenus   (Cos. 47 BC)   Died 40 BC
Caesarian commander in Spain and Greece. Commanded the Caesarian forces which recovered Greece in the aftermath of Pharsalus. Became Consul in 47 BC and joined M. Antonius in the aftermath of Caesar's murder. Died of (presumed)

natural causes, in 40 BC, whilst commanding forces in Transalpine Gaul against Caesar Octavianus.

Sex. Iulius Caesar   Killed 46 BC
Cousin of Caesar and one of his junior officers in Spain. Appointed Governor of Syria in 47 BC. He was subsequently murdered in a Pompeian-sponsored revolt, denying Caesar both the province and a possible heir.

D. Iunius Brutus Albinus   (Pr. 45 BC)   Killed 43 BC
Caesarian loyalist (and rumoured illegitimate son). Fought with Caesar in the Romano-Gallic and Civil Wars and was appointed Governor of Cisalpine Gaul for 44 BC. Was one of the leading Caesarians in the conspiracy to murder Caesar. Held Cisalpine Gaul against Antonius in 44/43 BC, but fled the Triumvirate and was murdered by a Tribal Chieftain on Antonius' orders.

M. Iunius Brutus   (Pr. 44 BC)   Suicide 42 BC
Scion from a family that claimed to be descended from the Bruttii who helped (perhaps inadvertently) to found the Republic. Rumoured to be the bastard son of Caesar himself. Supported Pompeius in 48 BC, was present at the Battle of Pharsalus and reconciled with Caesar after the battle. Famously was one of the co-leaders of the conspiracy that murdered Caesar in 44 BC and co-leaders of the 'Anti-Caesarian' faction in the subsequent civil war. Committed suicide in 42 BC after the Battles of Philippi.

C. Marius   Killed 44 BC
An individual who claimed to be the son of C. Marius (Cos. 82 BC) and grandson of the Roman General C. Marius. Appeared in Rome in 45 BC and was banished by Caesar, as a political rival. Re-appeared after Caesar's death and tried to seize power as Caesar's heir. Murdered by M. Antonius.

L. Minucius Basilus   (Pr. 45 BC)   Killed 43 BC
Caesarian commander who took part in the assassination of Caesar. Murdered by his own slaves in 43 BC.

L. Munatius Plancus   (Cos. 42 BC)   Died c. 15 BC
Caesarian commander in Spain in 49 BC. Supported the Triumvirate in the aftermath of Caesar's assassination and became Consul in 42 BC, along with Lepidus. Proconsul of Syria during the Second Romano-Parthian War, he defected to Caesar Octavianus before the latter's war with M. Antonius. Was

appointed one of the last two ever Censors in 22 BC, before it became part of imperial power. Died of natural causes in c.15 BC.

C. Octavius   (Cos. 43, 33, 31–23 BC)   Died AD 14

Caesar's great nephew (via his sister) and by 44 BC, his Roman heir. Joined Caesar on the Mundan campaign, but after the battle, designated as Master of the Horse for 44 BC. In the aftermath of Caesar's assassination, he sided with the Senate against Antonius and then formed the Caesarian Triumvirate, which seized power in Rome. Sided with Antonius against Lepidus after their victories at the Battles of Philippi and fought Sex. Pompeius for control the Western Republic. His (Agrippa's) victories at the Battles of Naulochus and Actium gave him control of the whole Roman world. His subsequent political settlement and longevity turned the Republic into an Empire.

M. Octavius

Pompeian naval commander in Illyria, who helped to defeat the Caesarian forces there in 49 BC. Defeated by Cornificius in 48 BC in the aftermath of Pharsalus. Continued his naval command in Africa in 47–46 BC. Subsequent career and fate unknown.

Q. Pedius   (Cos. 43 BC)   Died 43 BC

Caesarian commander, who served in Gaul and was a nephew of Caesar. Crushed Milo's rebellion in 48 BC. Fought in Spain in 45 BC. Named an heir in Caesar's will, along with his cousin Caesar Octavianus. Supported the Triumvirate and made Consul in 43 BC along with Octavianus but died in office.

Sex. Pompeius   Killed 35 BC

Youngest of the two sons of Pompeius Magnus and an accomplished naval commander. He became joint leader of the Pompeian faction after the Battle of Thapsus and faced Caesar in Spain at the Battle of Munda in 45 BC. Escaping the battle, he rallied the Pompeian faction in Spain, winning victories over Caesarian armies, until recalled by the Senate in the aftermath of Caesar's assassination. Annexing Sicily, he fought a civil war campaign against Caesar Octavianus and was ultimately defeated, before fleeing east to fight civil war campaigns against Antonius' forces. Captured and murdered in 35 BC by the Antonine general M. Titius.

T. Quintius Scapula   Suicide 45 BC

Pompeian commander, appears to have been a Spanish native who helped organise the 'Pompeian' revolt against the Caesarian control of Spain in 47 BC.

Seems to have accompanied Cn. Pompeius to Spain in 46 BC and again was a leader of the Pompeian revolt in 46 BC which drove Trebonius from Spain. He was present at (and survived) the initial Battle of Munda only to commit suicide at the subsequent fall of the city.

P. Servilius Isauricus   (Cos. 48 and 41 BC)
Son of a First Civil War general (Sullan faction). Caesar's fellow Consul in 48 BC. Defended Rome against Caelius and Milo. Named Caesar as Dictator after the Battle of Pharsalus. Governor in Asia during Bassus' Syrian rebellion. Sided with Caesar Octavianus after Caesar's murder and remained loyal throughout the subsequent civil war, earning another Consulship in 41 BC. Date and cause of death unknown.

L. Staius Murcus   (Pr. 45 BC)   Killed 40/39 BC
Caesarian commander appointed to lead the campaign against Bassus in Syria in 44 BC. Took part in the assassination of Caesar and then left for the eastern command. Became an Anti-Caesarian faction general in the Civil Wars which followed and successfully led a naval force. He later joined Sex. Pompeius but was murdered by the latter.

Ser. Sulpicius Galba   (Pr. 54 BC)   Killed 43 BC
Caesarian commander of the Romano-Gallic Wars, he joined the conspiracy to assassinate Caesar. Proscribed by the Caesarian Triumvirate in 43 BC, he was the great-grandfather of the first non-Julio-Claudian Emperor of Rome.

L. Tillius Cimber   (Pr. 45 BC)   Killed 42 BC?
Caesarian commander who played a key role in Caesar's assassination, being the man who distracted Caesar, allowing the assassins to strike. Was appointed Governor to Bithynia-Pontus. Supported the Anti-Caesarian faction in their war with the Caesarians, but disappears from the surviving sources in 42 BC and is presumed to have been killed at the Battles of Phillipi.

C. Trebonius   (Cos. 45 BC)   Killed 43 BC
Caesarian commander, who had served with him in Gaul and was placed in charge of the siege of Massilia. As Praetor in 48 BC, opposed Caelius' measure on debt alleviation. Served in Spain as a Provincial Governor and was driven out by the Pompeians in 46 BC. He went on to hold a Consulship in 45 BC. Became one of the conspirators in the murder of Caesar in 44 BC. Took up command in Asia where he fought against P. Cornelius Dolabella in 43 BC, but was captured and murdered.

M. Tullius Cicero   (Cos. 63 BC)   Killed 43 BC

Famous political commentator and lawyer who held the Consulship in 63 BC and was central in the events of the Second Civil War. Remained in Italy during Caesar's invasion and only latterly joined Pompeius in Greece. Returned to Italy after the Battle of Pharsalus and was pardoned by Caesar. Murdered in 43 BC on the order of M. Antonius.

P. Vatinius   (Cos. 47 BC)   Died c.42 BC

A long time Caesarian ally and the commander in charge of the defence of Brundisium in 49 and 48 BC. He campaigned in Illyria during 47 BC and defeated the Pompeian commander M. Octavius, recovering the province. Was rewarded with a Consulship in late-47 BC. Sent back to Illyria again in 45–44, he campaigned to restore Roman control of the region, eventually celebrating a Triumph in 42 BC. He is presumed to have died shortly afterwards.

L. Volcatius Tullus   (Cos. 33 BC)

Son of a Consul. Caesarian commander in Cilicia in 45 BC, who took part in the Civil War campaign against Caecilius Bassus. Supported the Caesarians in the aftermath of Caesar's assassination and became part of the Augustan regime.

Non-Romans

Alchaudonius

Arabian chieftain who led a mercenary force to assist Caecilius Bassus in defending Apamea from the Caesarians in 45 and presumably 44 BC. Had previously fought both with the Romans (in the Great Eastern War) and against them (during the First Romano-Parthian War), both times on the winning side.

Antipater   Killed 43 BC

Roman Procurator of Judea under the native Hasmonean Dynasty. Sent Judean forces to support the attempted Caesarian re-conquest of Syria in 45 BC. Was poisoned by a Judean rival in 43 BC, but his son Herod went on to become King of Judea and found a new ruling dynasty.

Arabio   Killed 40 BC

Numidian Prince who fled to Pompeian Spain after the fall of Numidia, where he fought with Sex. Pompeius. Led a Pompeian-sponsored invasion of Numidia in 44 BC, recovering two-thirds of Juba's kingdom and killing P. Sittius. Sided with the Caesarian Triumvirate after Caesar's death and took part in the campaigns for the North Africa, between Cornificius and Sextius and then Sextius and Fuficius Fango, but was later murdered by his ally Sextius.

Bocchus II (King of the Eastern Mauri 49–33 BC)   Died 33 BC
King of the Eastern Mauri, who had initially supported Caesar, both in helping to stamp out the pro-Pompeian Spanish rebellion in 48–47 BC and invading Western Numidia during Caesar's African campaign of 46 BC. Having been well rewarded by Caesar after his victory, he seems to have fallen out with his brother and sided with the Pompeians, sending a contingent to fight at the Battle of Munda. In the subsequent civil war between Antonius and Octavianus the two brothers again took opposing sides, with Bocchus deposing his brother, but dying in 33 BC.

Bogud (King of the Western Mauri 49–31 BC)   Killed 31 BC
King of the Western Mauri, who had initially supported Caesar, both in helping to stamp out the pro-Pompeian Spanish rebellion in 48–47 BC and supporting the invasion of Western Numidia during Caesar's African campaign of 46 BC. Having been well rewarded by Caesar after his victory, he seems to have fallen out with his brother and sided with Caesar, personally leading a Mauri contingent at the Battle of Munda. In the subsequent civil war between Antonius and Octavianus the two brothers again took opposing sides, with Bogud being deposed and dying during the prelude to the Battle of Actium.

Pacorus   Killed 38 BC
Eldest son of King Orodes II, the Parthian Emperor. He led a Parthian force into Syria in 45 BC, this time at the request of its Pompeian Governor Caecilius Bassus and relieved the siege of Apamea. This was the first Parthian intervention in the Third Civil War. Seems to have returned to Parthia in late-45 BC. Led the massive Parthian invasion of the Roman East, which heralded the start of the Second Romano-Parthian War in 40 BC, allied to none other than Q. Labienus, whom he set up as a client ruler of a Pompeian-Parthian state. Killed in the Battle of Gindarus int 38 BC by the Roman general Ventidius Bassus.

Lesser Figures

Q. Aponius
A Pompeian commander who led the revolt of the Spanish legions in 46 BC.

M. Appuleius
Caesarian Governor of Asia in 44 BC.

Arguetius
Caesarian officer who brought cavalry reinforcements to Caesar in Spain.

Caecilius Niger
A Spaniard who commanded a force of Lusitanians, who captured the city of Hispalis in the aftermath of the Battle of Munda, massacring the Caesarian garrison.

Caesennius Lento
Caesarian officer in Spain who is named as the killer of Cnaeus Pompeius.

Q. Marcius
Pompeian Military Tribune who deserted to Caesar during the Spanish campaign.

Q. Marcius Crispus   (Pr. 46 BC)
Caesarian Governor of Bithynia and Pontus in 45 BC, commanded legions in the attempt to recover Pompeian Syria.

L. Munatius Flaccus
Pompeian commander of the Siege of Ategua.

Philo
A pro-Pompeian citizen of the city of Hispalis who secured a force of Lusitanians to seize the city back, massacring the Caesarian garrison.

L. Vibius Paciaecus
Caesarian commander who fought under Caesar in Spain in 46/45 BC.

Appendix III

How Many Civil Wars?[1]

As readers will note, I have deliberately chosen to include the provocative sub-title of the Third Roman Civil War for this series of books. This deliberately challenges the cosy status quo that has emerged in modern historiography of the Roman civil war period, and which ignores a fundamental question for anyone studying this period of Roman history; namely, when is a civil war not a civil war? The short answer seems to be when it is a rebellion, revolt or even a conspiracy. There seems to have developed a very narrow and illogical definition of when a Roman army fighting a Roman army constitutes a civil war and when one does not.

Thus we have absurdity of a Consul marching his army on Rome itself in 88 and 87 BC constitutes a Civil War, whilst a Proconsul doing so just ten years later (in 77 BC) does not.

Throughout my various works I have sought to challenge this cosy and somewhat lazy consensus that has emerged, first by lengthening the duration of the First Civil War from its traditional 88–82 BC to 91–70 BC, which allows us to include the Lepidian, Sertorian and Marian campaigns, where again Roman fought Roman, as sequels to the events of the 80s BC.[2] Under this schema, the war only ended in 70 BC (with the last military campaign being fought in 71 BC) with the Consulships of Pompeius and Crassus and their political reform and general amnesty. This approach owes more to Appian, with his work on the civil wars covering 133–31 BC, than to Florus, with each campaign being a separate war.

All too often modern historiography ignores this question and seems to follow the Florine route and wants to separate these various conflicts into nice self-contained wars. This is not just a problem with Roman history. Modern historiography seems to demand that civil wars be clearly defined between two opposing sides, each with a different ideological standpoint. Thus, English history only has one Civil War (1642–1651), with two clearly defined sides, each with separate ideological stand points (monarchy vs parliament) and even clearly defined costumes. Yet this war was at least the seventh fought between the English in the last thousand years. We have the civil war between Stephen and Maud for the crowns of England and Normandy (1135–1153), the two civil wars fought between Kings John and Henry III and their rebellious nobles

(1215–1217 and 1264–1267), another in the reign of Edward II (1312–1322), and the two wars fought for the English crown between the various branches of the Plantagenet dynasty between 1399 to 1403 and 1455 to 1487 (the latter of which being dubbed the War of the Roses).

Thus, English history has at least seven civil wars in the last thousand years, yet only one makes the cut as an 'official' Civil War. The obvious question is: why are the others ignored and downgraded into non-civil wars, each with a meaningless title (Baron Wars, Wars of the Roses)? Is it because they do not fit into a nice ideological framework, or an unwillingness to admit that societies collapse more often that we would like to admit?

If we look at history, we can discern two broad types of civil war. One is the 'modern' version, where we have a clash between two clear sides each with an ideological standpoint, usually centred on a question of governance. Thus, we have the classic English, American, Spanish and Chinese Civil Wars. Yet the second type is where there is a complete breakdown of government, and a society collapses into anarchy, with various competing warlords emerging and fighting for supremacy. These types can most commonly be seen in modern Africa.

Yet returning to Rome, which type of civil wars can we see? All too often modern historians want them to be the clear cut, ideological civil wars between *optimates* and *populares* (terms which have been grossly distorted). Thus, our two official civil wars of the period – Sulla vs Marius and Caesar vs Pompeius – are often painted in these terms. Yet having reviewed these events, such terms are meaningless. The various protagonists did not go to war over differing views of how to govern, but turned to their armies to defend their own positions from the attacks of their enemies. The events of the 80s and 40s both snowballed out of everyone's control, with the Republican system collapsing and leading to periods of anarchy where various Roman generals fought for supremacy amongst themselves until a victorious individual emerged who could rebuild central authority and 'calm the bloodshed' i.e. dominate without looking like they were doing so; Pompeius and Crassus in 71–70 BC and Octavianus in 30–27 BC.

Thus, modern Roman historiography leaves us with a Florine-like patchwork of different wars:

Social War	(91–88 BC)
First Civil War	(88–81 BC)
Sertorian Rebellion	(81–72 BC)
Lepidian Revolt	(78–77 BC)
Catiline Conspiracy	(63–62 BC)
Second Civil War	(49–31 BC)

The clear danger of following such an approach, of course, is that it shifts focus away from the underlying causes of these conflicts and onto the individuals, and thus blurs the line between symptom and cause. Should we be focusing on Sulla, Lepidus, Catilina or Caesar, or the underlying issues that were at work behind them? Clearly, having read this volume, the reader will understand that focussing on the individuals at the expense of the wider picture is not a method I chose to pursue. Not one of these men woke up one morning and thought that they would like to march their army against their own state simply to gain power for themselves, but Republican politics had forced them to believe that they had no alternative and that what they were doing was for the benefit of the Republic.

Ultimately, as these events proved, the Republican system did not provide a robust-enough framework to keep the various tensions between the Senatorial oligarchy from spilling over into violence and civil war. Various attempts were made to modify the Republic, be it Triumvirate (official or unofficial) or sole rule (subtle or obvious). The one version that emerged victorious from this period was sole rule, with one figure guiding and overseeing the smooth running of the Republic and acting as arbiter to keep the others in check. Yet this too was flawed and laid the foundations for the role of Emperor, first on a hereditary basis, later merit or armed force.

Yet, if we are to reject the Florine version of the wars in this period, what are we to replace it with? Do we simply follow the Appianic version and state that all this period was one giant civil war, or do we reject the notion of a civil war in a society such as Rome altogether? I have and will continue to argue that within this period of Roman history there were distinct periods of civil wars, when the clashes and tensions within the Republican system boiled over into full blown military conflict and in two out of the three cases, total system-wide (and empire-wide) collapse.

Civil war within a country is one thing, but civil war in a society that had a full-blown empire is another matter altogether and magnified the chaos and fighting on a Mediterranean-wide level. As we have seen, in two out of three cases Rome's empire became a battleground for the various parties of the civil war and led to the extinction of several independent kingdoms who became too closely associated with a losing side (namely Numidia and Egypt).

Having rejected the modern Florine notion of multiple separate wars, I would like to offer up a fresh scheme for the civil wars within this period, if only to stimulate further debate on a subject that can never have a right answer.

The First Civil War 91–70 BC

All too often, discussions of the First Civil War ignore the fact that Italy had been riven by civil warfare for three years, with two rebel factions fighting the Republican government. This is the very reason that Sulla had an army of battle-hardened veterans in Italy within marching distance of Rome and citizen distribution was at the heart of the political manoeuvring which led to Sulla's loss of command. Thus, the war that broke out in 91 BC between the various societies that made up the Roman system must be classed as a civil war, with neighbour fighting neighbour and, if we are to believe the more dramatic sources, brother fighting brother.

Thus, the First Civil War period saw a number of different phases, which were not neatly separate conflicts but were all intertwined. The war in Italy led to the Consular attack on Rome in 88 BC, both of which mixed together to spark off the war of 87 BC. There then followed a lull, whilst at least two different Roman armies separately fought off a foreign invasion. When that invasion had been dealt with, all sides then engaged in a fight for supremacy which brought about another lull as Sulla consolidated his control of Italy and the western empire. Some regions were forcibly reunited (Sicily, Africa), whilst others (Spain and Gaul) were reclaimed through negotiation between warlords. Yet the faction that lost Italy soon stoked a rebellion in Spain, where the civil war continued (mixed in with a native rebellion, as it had done in Italy) for another nine years. Whilst the civil war continued in the Western Republic (Spain), other elements of the faction that lost Italy spearheaded another foreign invasion of Rome's empire, again blurring the lines between civil war and foreign war.

Thus, we can see that during this period there were no neat delineations between civil war, native rebellion and foreign wars, but all became inexorably interlinked in one great collapse of the Republican system. It is also not a coincidence that the largest slave rebellion in Roman history happened during this period of chaos, when a certain slave named Spartacus took advantage of the devastation in Italy, disaffection with Rome, and overseas wars to launch his rebellion.

By 71 BC there emerged another lull, with the fighting ended in Spain, Italy and Asia. Yet it took the actions of Pompeius and Crassus, who chose to unite Rome (rather than continue the division (and personally benefit from it). Their Consulship not only set an example that two oligarchs could work in a peaceful manner, especially if they cooperated by the constitutional settlement, but they introduced a number of tension points (though some would say reintroduced them) and saw a very public recall of all Romans exiled during the previous twenty years of tumult. Thus, it can be argued that a lull became a definite end.

The Second Civil War 63–62 BC

That the events of 63/62 BC constitute a civil war should not be difficult to argue. Although the ancient sources and modern historiography choose to focus on events in Rome, the key facts are that there were wide-scale rebellions against Rome throughout Italy and native rebellions in Gaul (again mixing the two) and two Romano-Italian armies fought one another in a set piece battle. That there was only one set piece battle, and that it was over relatively quickly, should not disqualify this from being classed as a civil war. In fact, the surviving sources paint a picture of wider military action across Italy, but we only have the barest of detail for it. Had we fuller sources for this fighting then we would be able to see the true scale of the civil war in Italy.

The other argument is that if this was a civil war, was it a continuation of the first war and thus can we extend the First Civil War down to 62 BC? As we have reviewed, the causes of this war did have its roots in the first war, be they disgruntled Sullan politicians and veterans or displaced Italian communities. Yet I would argue that it was a separate conflict from that of 91–70 BC, and that the years 69–64 BC were not merely a lull in the first war, but that the Pompeian-Crassan Consulships did end the First Civil War. That a war can be finished but still leave matters unsettled can be seen frequently throughout history; most recently in the First and Second World Wars (at least in Europe). So, although the Second Civil War had its roots in the First, they were, I believe, separate conflicts. This can also be seen by the fact that the New Republic reconstituted out of the ashes of the First Civil War did not collapse, as it had done in 91–70 or 49–30 BC.

The Third Civil War 49–27 BC

This is perhaps the most uncontentious of the three, with it being widely accepted that the events between the crossing of the Rubicon in 49 BC and the victory of Octavianus constitute another period of a single civil war, which again saw a total collapse of the Republican system and the emergence of various factions and warlords. It too saw the blurring between civil war and foreign war, again most easily seen in the east with the attack of the Parthian Empire being spearheaded by Roman generals. This period too saw lulls in the fighting between the various overlapping conflicts. There was no certainty that Octavianus' victory at Actium in 31 BC would be the final major battle of the war, any more than the Battle of Pharsalus in 48 BC or Philippi in 42 BC.

If there is one contentious issue, then it must be the end date of this civil war. It clearly did not end with the Battle of Actium in 31 BC as Antonius still fought on with his defence of Egypt, which only fell in 30 BC. Yet, as we have explored above, winning a campaign did not bring about victory, especially in a civil war; it was winning the peace. This is where both Sulla and Caesar failed when they had military control of the Republic. Roman civil wars did not seem to end when one side was victorious in battle, as new opponents soon emerged. Roman Civil Wars only ended when everyone agreed that there was no more need to fight and that the imbalances in the Republican system that they had believed were there, had been righted. For that reason, I would argue that the Third Civil War did not end until the First Constitutional Settlement of the newly-renamed Augustus in 27 BC; with the intervening years 30–27 BC being merely a lull in the fighting. Thus, Republican politics was both the cause of the civil wars and the solution (however temporary).

Notes

Chapter One
1. See G. Sampson: (2022). *The Battle of Dyrrhachium (48 BC). Caesar, Pompey, and the Early Campaigns of the Third Roman Civil War* (Barnsley); (2023). *The Battle of Pharsalus (48 BC). Caesar, Pompey, and their Final Clash in the Third Roman Civil War* (Barnsley); (2024). *The Battle of Thapsus (46 BC): Caesar, Metellus Scipio, and the Renewal of the Third Roman Civil War* (Barnsley).
2. Named after the Second Romano-Punic War Roman general; Q. Fabius Maximus Verrucosus, who successfully contained Hannibal, during his invasion of Italy, by avoiding battle.
3. See T. Broughton. (1952). *The Magistrates of the Roman Republic* 2, p. 283.

Chapter Two
1. See P. Matyszak. (2023). *Julius Caesar in Egypt: Cleopatra and the War in Alexandria* (Barnsley).
2. See G. Sampson. (2023).
3. See G. Sampson. (2013). *The Collapse of Rome, Marius, Sulla, and The First Civil War 91–70 BC* (Barnsley).
4. See R. Billows. (1982). 'The Last of the Scipios', *American Journal of Ancient History* 7, pp.53–68 and J. Linderski, (1996). 'Q. Scipio Imperator', in J. Linderski (ed.). *Imperium Sine Fine: T. Robert S. Broughton and the Roman Republic* (Stuttgart), pp.145–185.
5. *de. bell. afr.* 87 and 90.
6. Appian mentions them in passing. App. *BC.* 2.100.
7. See Plut. *Caes.* 11.6.
8. See G. Sampson. (2022).
9. *de. bell. alex.* 43, App. *Ill.* 12 and 27–28.
10. See also Cic. *Att.* 11.16.1.
11. App. *Ill.*12.
12. *de. bell. alex.* 44.
13. Dio. 42.14.1 and 3. See L. Amela. (2008). 'The Campaign of Quintus Fufius Calenus in Greece During the Year 48 B.C. and the City of Megara. The Consequences of the War'. *Athenaeum* 96, pp.279–291.
14. See G. Sampson. (2023).
15. Dio. 43.1.2.
16. See G. Sampson. (2023).
17. Dio 42.56.3, *de. bell. Afr.* 98. Also see a reference to Nasidius in *de. bell. afr.* 64.
18. Dio. 42.56.4.
19. See Sampson (2024).
20. See Dio. 42.52–54, App. *BC.* 2.93–94, Plut. *Caes.* 51, Suet. *Caes.* 40.1, Frontin. *Str.* 1.9.4.
21. *de. bell. afr.* 3.

22. Ibid.
23. *de. bell. afr.* 5.
24. The *de bello africo* (5) states that 'the rest of Caesar's forces failed to arrive to reinforce him'.
25. *de. bell. afr.* 9–11.
26. Ibid. 19.
27. *de. bell. afr.* 17.
28. Ibid. 18.
29. G. Sampson. (2024).

Chapter Three
1. See M. Deutsch. (1926). 'Caesar's Triumphs', *Classical Weekly* 19, pp.101–106.
2. See P. Matyszak. (2023).
3. App. *BC.* 2.101.
4. Ibid.
5. See P. Berdowski. (2012). 'Cn. Pompeius, the son of Pompey the Great: an embarrassing ally in the African War? (48–46 BC)', *Palamedes* 7, pp.117–142.
6. See F. Abbott. (1917). 'Titus Labienus', *Classical Journal* 13, pp.4–13, R. Syme. (1938). 'The Allegiance of Labienus', *Journal of Roman Studies* 28, pp.113–125.
7. Caes. *BG.* 2.2, 2.26, 5.57, 6.8, 7.61, 7.62, 8.52.
8. See W. Tyrrell. (1972). 'Labienus' Departure from Caesar in January 49 BC', *Historia* 21, pp.424–440 and G. Wylie. (1989). 'Why Did Labienus Defect From Caesar in 49 BC?', *Ancient History Bulletin* 3, pp.123–127.
9. Plut. *Pomp.* 68.1.
10. Val. Max. 8.14.5.
11. Dio. 43.29.1.
12. Ibid. 43.29.2.
13. Dio. 43.29.3–30.5.
14. Ibid. 43.29.3.
15. *de. bell. hisp.* 7.4.
16. See P. Berdowski. (2019). 'Was Carthago Nova Captured by Gnaeus Pompeius in 46 BC and Sextus Pompeius in 44 BC?', *Aevum* 93, pp.175–190.
17. Dio. 43.30.5.
18. Ibid. 43.30.4.
19. *de. bell. hisp.* 7.4.
20. App. *BC.* 103.
21. Dio. 43.28.1.
22. Ibid. 43.31.1.
23. See. G. Sampson. (2021).
24. App. *BC.* 3.77. Also see App. *BC.* 4.58, Dio, 47.26.4–7, Strab. 16.752, Joseph. *BJ.* 1.216, and *AJ.*14.268, Liv. *Per.* 114.
25. Dio. 47.26.4–7.
26. Strab. 16.752–753.
27. Dio. 42.27.1–2.
28. App. *BC.* 4.58.
29. Cic. *Fam.* 12.18.
30. Ibid. 12.19.

Chapter Four

1. Dio. 43.14.3.
2. Ibid. 43.28.2.
3. Nic. Dam. 10.
4. Oros. 6.16.6.
5. App. *BC.* 2.103, Strab. 3.160.
6. See G. Sampson. (2022).
7. *de. bell. hisp.* 2.
8. Dio. 43.21.3.
9. Flor. 2.13.75–76.
10. *de. bell hisp.* 3.
11. Ibid 18.
12. *de. bell hisp.* 4.
13. Ibid. 5.
14. *de. bell hisp.* 6.
15. Ibid. 8.
16. *de. bell hisp.* 9.
17. Ibid.10.
18. *de. bell hisp.* 11.
19. Ibid. 12.
20. Ibid.
21. *de. bell hisp.* 13.
22. Dio. 43.33.2.
23. *de. bell hisp.* 14.
24. Frontin. *Str.* 3.14.1.
25. *de. bell hisp.*15.
26. Ibid.16.
27. Dio. 43.33.3–34.3.
28. *de. bell hisp.* 18.
29. Ibid. 15 and 16.
30. Val. Max. 9.2.4.
31. Dio. 43.34.3–5.
32. *de. bell hisp.* 21.
33. Ibid. 23.
34. *de. bell hisp.* 24.
35. See R. Storch. (1973). 'The Author of the De bello Hispaniensi: A Cavalry Officer?', *Classical Journal* 68, pp.381–383.
36. Ibid. 25.
37. *de. bell hisp.* 27.
38. Ibid. 27.
39. *de. bell hisp.* 28.
40. Dio. 33.35.1–4.

Chapter Five

1. *de. bell hisp.* 29.
2. Ibid. 7.
3. *de. bell hisp.* 30.
4. Dio. 43.36.1.

5. Ibid. 43.36.2–3.
6. *de. bell hisp.* 18.
7. Ibid. 30.
8. Dio. 43.36.1.
9. *de. bell hisp.* 30.
10. Ibid. 29.
11. *de. bell hisp.* 30–31.
12. App. *BC.* 2.104.
13. Dio. 43.37–38.
14. *de. bell hisp.* 31.
15. Dio. 43.38.2–4.
16. Though Dio does not mention Labienus being on a wing, he clearly could not detach from the centre.
17. Oros. 6.16.7.
18. Flor. 2.13.78–84.
19. Plut. *Caes.* 56.2–4.
20. Vell. 2.55.3–4.
21. Suet. *Caes.* 36.
22. Eutrop. 6.24.
23. Frontin. *Str.* 2.8.13.
24. Polyn. 8.23.16.
25. Plut. *Caes.* 56.4.
26. Liv. *Per.* 115.5.
27. *de. bell hisp.* 31.
28. App. *BC.* 2.105.
29. Plut. *Caes.* 56.3.
30. Dio. 43.38.4.
31. *de. bell hisp.* 31.
32. Ibid. 32.
33. Dio. 43.38.4.
34. App. *BC.* 2.105.

Chapter Six
1. *de. bell hisp.* 32.
2. Ibid.
3. *de bell. alex.* 55. Named as Annius Scapula.
4. App. *BC.* 2.87.
5. Dio. 43.29.3.
6. Ibid. 43.30.2.
7. *de. bell hisp.* 33. Also see App. *BC.* 2.105.
8. Ibid. 34.
9. Ibid.
10. Ibid.
11. *de. bell hisp.* 35.
12. Ibid. 36.
13. Dio. 43.38.3.
14. *de. bell hisp.* 37.
15. Ibid.

16. *de. bell hisp.* 38.
17. Ibid.
18. *de. bell hisp.* 39.
19. App. *BC.* 2.105.
20. Nothing more is known about Caesennius Lento, other than a reference to a man of the same name by Cicero in his *Philippics* when he refers to him as taking a life. (Cic. *Phil.* 12.23).
21. Flor. 2.13.86. Also see. Oros. 6.16.
22. Dio. 43.40.2.
23. Ibid.
24. *de. bell hisp.* 40.
25. The men responsible for the elder Pompeius' death did not live long either.
26. *de. bell hisp.* 32.
27. Flor. 2.13.85.
28. Val. Max. 7.6.5.
29. *de. bell hisp.* 34.
30. Ibid. 36.
31. *de. bell hisp.* 41.
32. Oros. 6.16.
33. *de. bell hisp.* 41.
34. See the Caesarian inscription CIL.1.594, ARS. 114.
35. Cic. *Att.* 12.37.4.
36. App. *BC.* 2.106.
37. Ibid. 4.83.
38. Dio. 45.10.1.
39. Vell. 2.56.3.
40. See Cic. *Att.* 16.4.2.
41. App. *BC.* 4.83–84.
42. Dio. 45.10.2–6.
43. Cic. *Att.* 15.20.3.
44. Ibid. 16.4.2.
45. App. *BC.* 4.83.
46. Ibid. 4.84.
47. Dio. 45.10.3–5. Also see P. Berdowski. (2019).
48. See G. Sampson. (2024).
49. App. *BC.* 4.54.

Chapter Seven
1. See G. Sampson. (2021).
2. G. Sampson. (2008). *The Defeat of Rome. Crassus, Carrhae and the Invasion of the East* (Barnsley).
3. See G. Sampson. (2024).
4. Dio. 47.27.1–5.
5. Cic. *Att.* 14.9.3.
6. Joseph. *BJ.* 216–217.
7. Joseph. *AJ.* 268–269.
8. App. *BC.* 3.77.
9. Dio. 47.27.4–5.

10. Dio. 47.27.5, Cic. *Att.* 14.9.3.
11. Caes. *BC.* 3.15.
12. Cic. *Att.* 12.2.1.
13. App. *BC.* 2.119.
14. Dio 47.27.5.
15. App. *BC.* 3.77.
16. Ibid 4.58.
17. Vell. 2.69.
18. See G. Sampson. (2020). *Rome and Parthia: Empires at War: Ventidius, Antony and the Second Romano-Parthian War, 40–20 BC* (Barnsley).
19. See A. Powell and K. Welch (2002). *Sextus Pompeius* (London) and K. Welsch. (2012). *Magnus Pius. Sextus Pompeius and the Transformation of the Roman Republic* (Swansea).

Chapter Eight
1. Vell. 2.56.
2. See B. Marshall. (1985). 'Catilina and the Execution of M. Marius Gratidianus', *Classical Quarterly* 35, pp.124–133.
3. See F. Meijer. (1986). 'Marius' Grandson', *Mnemosyne* 39 pp.112–121.
4. Cic. *Att.* 12.49.
5. Cic. *Phil.* 1.2.
6. Val. Max. 9.15.2.
7. App. *BC.* 3.2.3.
8. Liv. *Per.* 116.
9. See G. Sampson. (2024).
10. See R. Syme. (1980).
11. Again as with Brutus and Cassius, Lepidus comes off poorly in relation to Antonius in terms of modern historiography. See R. Weigel. (1974). 'Lepidus Reconsidered', *Acta Classica* 17, 67–73 and (1992). *Lepidus: the Tarnished Triumvir* (London). Also T. Broughton. (1989). 'M. Aemilius Lepidus: His Youthful Career', in R. Curtis (ed.). *Studio Pompeiana & Classica in Honour of Wilhelmina F. Jashemski, Volume. II*: (New York), pp.13–23, K. Welsh. (1995). 'The Career of M. Aemilius Lepidus 49–44 BC', *Hermes* 123, pp.443–454.
12. Cic. *Fam.* 4.12.
13. Cic. *Att.* 13.10.
14. See M. Deutsch. (1926) and C. Lange. (2013). 'Triumph and Civil War in the Late Republic', *Papers of the British School at Rome* 81, pp.67–90 and (2018). *Triumphs in the Age of Civil War: The Late Republic and the Adaptability of Triumphal Tradition* (London).
15. Plut. *Caes.* 56.7.
16. Dio. 43.42.
17. Plut. *Ant.* 11.2–3 . Also see Cic. *Phil.* 1.31, 2.79, 82–83, 88,99, 3.9, 5.9; Plut. *Caes.* 62.5.
18. Plut. *Caes.* 57. See M. Pucci Ben Zeev. (1996). 'When was the title «Dictator perpetuus» given to Caesar?' *L'antiquité classique* 65, pp.251–253.
19. Ibid.
20. Dio. 44.9.
21. Plut. *Caes.* 60.1–3.
22. Suet. *Caes.* 79.
23. Caes. *BC.* 1.7.
24. Liv. *Per.* 116.

25. See J. Collins. (1955). 'Caesar and the Corruption of Power', *Historia* 4, pp.445–465 and R. Carson. (1957). 'Caesar and the Monarchy', *Greece & Rome* 4, pp.46–53.
26. Plut. *Caes.* 57.4–5.
27. Dio. 43.50.1.
28. App. *BC.* 2.107.
29. See B. Jordan. (2017). 'The Consular Provinciae of 44 BC and the Collapse of the Restored Republic', *Hermes* 145, pp.174–194.
30. Plut. *Caes.* 57.6.
31. Polyn. 8.23.3.
32. See C. Jones. (1970). 'Cicero's Cato', *Rheinisches Museum für Philologie* 113, pp.188–196.
33. Plut. *Caes.* 54.5–6.
34. Cic. *Phil.* 2.74.
35. Plut. *Ant.* 13.1.
36. See the continuing release of biographies on Brutus but not Cassius, K. Corrigan. (2015). *Brutus: Caesar's Assassin* (Barnsley) and K. Tempest. (2017). *Brutus: The Noble Conspirator* (Yale).
37. 171, 164, 127, 107, 96 BC respectively.
38. Cic. *Phil.* 2.26.
39. See J. Balsdon. (1958). 'The Ides of March', *Historia* 7, p. 82.
40. Aside from cadet branches holding Consulships in 325, 317, 292 and 291 there are no recorded Iunii Bruti holding office between the 490s and the 190s BC.
41. See B. Bondurant. (1907). *Decimus Junius Brutus Albinus: A Historical Study* (Chicago).
42. See R. Syme. (1980). 'No Son for Caesar?', *Historia* 29, pp.422–437. Also G. Duval. (1991). 'D. Junius Brutus: mari ou fils de Sempronia?', *Latomus* 50, pp.608–615.
43. See R. Miola. (1985). 'Julius Caesar and the Tyrannicide Debate', *Renaissance Quarterly* 38, pp. 271–289. Some of the most recent being G. Woolf. (2007). *Et Tu Brute? The Murder of Caesar and Political Assassination* (Cambridge) and P. Stothard. (2020). *The Last Assassin: The Hunt for the Killers of Julius Caesar* (London).
44. See D. Epstein. (1987). 'Caesar's Personal Enemies on the Ides of March', *Latomus* 46, pp.566–570.
45. Cic. *Phil.* 2.27.
46. App. *BC.* 2.113.

Appendix One
1. App. *Ill.* 13.
2. *de. Bell. Alex.* 43.4–47.5.
3. Cic. *Ad Fam.* 5.10.

Appendix Three
1. This is a variation of the appendix found in G. Sampson (2019), pp.307–313.
2. See G. Sampson (2013).

Bibliography

Abbott, F. (1917). 'Titus Labienus', *Classical Journal* 13, 4–13.
Amela, L. (2003). *Cneo Pompeyo Magno. El defensor de la República Romana* (Madrid).
——. (2008). 'The Campaign of Quintus Fufius Calenus in Greece During the Year 48 B.C. and the City of Megara. The Consequences of the War'. *Athenaeum* 96, 279–291.
Anders. A. (2015). 'The Face of Roman Skirmishing', *Historia* 64, 263–300.
Appel, H. (2012). 'Pompeius Magnus: his Third Consulate and the senatus consultum ultimum', *Biuletyn Polskiej Misji Historycznej* 7, 341–360.
Badian, E. (1974). 'The Attempt to Try Caesar,' in J. Evans (ed.), *Polis and Imperium: Studies in Honour of Edward Togo Salmon* (Toronto), 145–166.
——. (1996). 'Tribuni Plebis and Res Publica', in J. Linderski (ed.) *Imperium Sine Fine* (Stuttgart), 187–214.
Balsdon, J. (1957). 'The Veracity of Caesar', *Greece & Rome* 4, 19–28.
——. (1958). 'The Ides of March', *Historia* 7, 80–94.
Barrett, A. (1972). 'Catullus 52 and the Consulship of Vatinius', *Transactions and Proceedings of the American Philological Association* 103, 23–38.
Bartsch, S. (1997). *Ideology in Cold Blood. A Reading of Lucan's Civil War* (Cambridge).
Batstone, W. and Damon, C. (2006). *Caesar's Civil War* (Oxford).
Bell, A. (1994). 'Fact and "Exemplum" in Accounts of the Deaths of Pompey and Caesar', *Latomus* 53, 824–836.
Beneker, J. (2011). 'The Crossing of the Rubicon and the Outbreak of Civil War in Cicero, Lucan, Plutarch and Suetonius', *Phoenix* 65, 74–99.
Berdowski, P. (2012). 'Cn. Pompeius, the son of Pompey the Great: an embarrassing ally in the African War? (48–46 BC)', *Palamedes* 7, 117–142.
——. (2019). Was Carthago Nova Captured by Gnaeus Pompeius in 46 BC and Sextus Pompeius in 44 BC?', *Aevum* 93, 175–190.
Billows, R. (1982). 'The Last of the Scipios', *American Journal of Ancient History* 7, 53–68.
——. (2008). *Julius Caesar: The Colossus of Rome* (London).
Boak, A. (1918). 'The Extraordinary Commands from 80 to 48 BC: A Study in the Origins of the Principate', *American Historical Review* 24, 1–25.
Boatwright, M. (1988). 'Caesar's Second Consulship and the Completion and Date of the "Bellum Civile"', *Classical Journal* 84, 31–40.
Bondurant, B. (1907). *Decimus Junius Brutus Albinus: A Historical Study* (Chicago).
Börm, H. Gotter, U. and Havener, W. (eds.). *A Culture of Civil War? Bellum Civile and Political Communication in Late Republican Rome* (Stuttgart).
Brown, R. (1999). 'Two Caesarian Battle-Descriptions: A Study in Contrast', *Classical Journal* 94, 329–357.
Broughton, T. (1951/2). *The Magistrates of the Roman Republic, Volumes 1 and 2* (New York).
——. (1960). *Supplement to the Magistrates of the Roman Republic* (New York).
——. (1986). *Supplement to the Magistrates of the Roman Republic* (New York).

——. (1989). 'M. Aemilius Lepidus: His Youthful Career', in R. Curtis (ed.). *Studio Pompeiana & Classica in Honour of Wilhelmina F. Jashemski, Volume II* (New York), 13–23.
Brunt, P. (1971). *Social Conflicts in the Roman Republic* (London).
——. (1988). *The Fall of the Roman Republic* (Oxford).
Canfora, L. (2007). *Julius Caesar: The Life and Times of the People's Dictator* (Edinburgh).
Carson, R. (1957). 'Caesar and the Monarchy', *Greece & Rome* 4, 46–53.
Chrystal, P. (2019). *Rome: Republic into Empire: The Civil Wars of the First Century BC* (Barnsley).
Collins, H. (1953). 'The Decline and Fall of Pompey the Great', *Greece & Rome* 22, 98–106.
Collins J. (1955). 'Caesar and the Corruption of Power', *Historia* 4, 445–465.
Cornwell, H. (2014). 'The Construction of One's Enemies in Civil War (49–30 BC)', *Hermathena* 196/197, 41–68.
Corrigan, K. (2015). *Brutus: Caesar's Assassin* (Barnsley).
Coulter, C. (1952). 'Pollio's History of the Civil War', *Classical Weekly* 46, 33–36.
Damon, C. (1994). 'Caesar's Practical Prose', *Classical Journal* 89, 183–195.
De Méritens De Villeneuve, (2023). *Les fils de Pompée et l'opposition à César et au Triumvirat (46–35 av. J.-C.)* (Rome).
De Ruggiero, P. (2013). *Mark Antony. A Plain Blunt Man* (Barnsley).
Deutsch, M. (1926). 'Caesar's Triumphs', *Classical Weekly* 19, 101–106.
Dijcks, N. (2019). 'Wavering Loyalties: Ideology, Opportunism, and 'Changing Sides' in the Late Republican Civil Wars', *Latomus* 78, 591–620.
Drogula, F. (2019). *Cato the Younger: Life and Death at the End of the Roman Republic* (Oxford).
Duncan, M. (2017). *The Storm Before the Storm: The Beginning of the End of the Roman Republic* (London).
Duval, G. (1991). 'D. Junius Brutus: mari ou fils de Sempronia?', *Latomus* 50, 608–615.
Eden, P. (1962). 'Caesar's Style: Inheritance versus Intelligence', *Glotta* 40, 74–117.
Ehrhardt, C. (1995). 'Crossing the Rubicon', *Antichthon* 29, 37–41.
Epstein, D. (1987). *Personal Enmity in Roman Politics 218–43 BC* (London).
——. (1987). 'Caesar's Personal Enemies on the Ides of March', *Latomus* 46, 566–570.
Étienne, R. (1973). *Les Ides de Mars. L'assassinat de César ou de la dictature?* (Paris).
Evans, R. (2004). 'Caesar's use of the tribuni plebis', *Questioning Reputations* (Pretoria), 65–92.
——. (2016). Pompey's Three Consulships: The End of Electoral Competition in the Late Roman Republic', *Acta Classica* 59, 80–100.
Ezov, A. (1996). 'The "Missing Dimension" of C. Julius Caesar', *Historia* 45, 64–94.
Fezzi, L. (2019). *Crossing the Rubicon: Caesar's Decision and the Fate of Rome* (London).
Field, N. (2009). *Warlords of Republican Rome: Caesar Versus Pompey* (Barnsley).
Flower, H. (2010). *Roman Republics* (Princeton).
Frank, T. (1907). 'Caesar at the Rubicon', *Classical Quarterly* 1, 223–225.
Fuller, J. (1965). *Julius Caesar: Man, Soldier, and Tyrant* (London).
Gelzer, M. (1980). *Caesar: Politician and Statesman* (London).
Gerrish, J. (2019). *Sallust's Histories and Triumviral Historiography. Confronting the End of History* (London).
Golden, G. (2013). *Crisis Management during the Roman Republic: The Role of Political Institutions in Emergencies* (Cambridge).
Goldsworthy, A. (2006). *Caesar: Life of a Colossus* (Yale).
——. (2023). *Caesar's Civil War: 49–44 BC* (London).
Goodman, R and Soni, J. (2012). *Rome's Last Citizen. The Life and Legacy of Cato, Mortal Enemy of Caesar* (New York).
Greenhalgh, P. (1980). *Pompey. The Roman Alexander* (London).

———. (1981). *Pompey. The Republican Prince* (London).
Grillo, L. (2012). *The Art of Caesar's Bellum Civile: Literature, Ideology, and Community* (Cambridge).
Gruen. E. (1974). *The Last Generation of the Roman Republic* (Berkeley).
Haley, S. (1985). 'The Five Wives of Pompey the Great', *Greece & Rome* 32, 49–59.
Hillman, T. (1996). 'Pompeius ad Parthos?' *Klio* 78, 380–399.
Holland, T. (2003). *Rubicon: The Triumph and Tragedy of the Roman Republic* (London).
Holliday, V. (1969). *Pompey in Cicero's Correspondence and Lucan's Civil War* (Hague).
Holzapfel, L. (1904). 'Die Anfänge des Bürgerkrieges zwischen Cäsar und Pompejus', *Klio* 4 327–382.
Horsfall, N. (1974). 'The Ides of March: Some New Problems', *Greece & Rome* 21, 191–199.
Huzar, E. (1978). *Mark Antony; A Biography* (Minneapolis).
Isayev, E. (2007). 'Unruly Youth? The Myth of Generation Conflict in Late Republican Rome', *Historia* 56, 1–13.
Jal, P. (1962). 'Le rôle des Barbares dans les guerres civiles de Rome, de Sylla à Vespasien', *Latomus* 21, pp. 8–48.
———. (1963). *La guerre civile à Rome* (Paris).
Jehne, M. (2015). From Patronus to Pater. The Changing Role of Patronage in the Period of Transition from Pompey to Augustus, in M. Jehne and F. Pina Polo (eds.) *Foreign Clientelae in the Roman Empire. A Reconsideration* (Stuttgart), 297–320.
Jones, C. (1970). 'Cicero's Cato', *Rheinisches Museum für Philologie* 113, 188–196.
Jordan, B. (2017). 'The Consular Provinciae of 44 BC and the Collapse of the Restored Republic', *Hermes* 145, 174–194.
Keaveney, A. (1982) *Sulla. The Last Republican* (London).
———. (2007). *The Army in the Roman Revolution* (London).
Knight, D. (1968). 'Pompey's Concern with Pre-eminence After 60 BC', *Latomus* 27, 878–883.
Konrad, C. (1996). 'Notes on Roman Also Rans', in J. Linderski (ed.). *Imperium Sine Fine: T. Robert S. Broughton and the Roman Republic* (Stuttgart), 103–143.
Lange, C. (2013). 'Triumph and Civil War in the Late Republic', *Papers of the British School at Rome* 81, 67–90.
———. (2018). *Triumphs in the Age of Civil War: The Late Republic and the Adaptability of Triumphal Tradition* (London).
Lange, C. and Scott, A. (2020). *Cassius Dio: The Impact of Violence, War, and Civil War* (Leiden).
Lange, C. and Vervaet, F. (2019) *The Historiography of Late Republican Civil War* (Leiden).
Leach, J. (1978). *Pompey the Great* (London).
Linderski, J. (1996). Q. Scipio Imperator', in J. Linderski (ed.). *Imperium Sine Fine: T. Robert S. Broughton and the Roman Republic* (Stuttgart), 145–185.
Lintott, A. (1968). *Violence in Republican Rome* (Oxford).
———. (1971). 'Lucan and the History of the Civil War', *Classical Quarterly* 21, 488–505.
———. (1974). 'Cicero and Milo', *Journal of Roman Studies* 64, 62–78.
———. (1999). *The Constitution of the Roman Republic* (Oxford).
Liubimova, O. (2021). 'The Mother of Decimus Brutus and the Wife of Gaius Gracchus', *Mnemosyne* 74, 825–850.
Long, G. (1864). *The Decline of the Roman Republic, Volumes 1–5* (London).
López Barja de Quiroga, P. (2019). 'The Bellum Civile Pompeianum: The War of Words', *Classical Quarterly* 69, 700–714.
Lord, L. (1938). 'The Date of Julius Caesar's Departure from Alexandria', *Journal Roman Studies* 28, 19–40.

Lounsbury, R. (1976). 'History and Motive in Book Seven of Lucan's Pharsalia', *Hermes*, 104, 210–239.
MacKay, L. (1952). 'Pharsalus and the Roman Fate', *Phoenix* 6, 147–150.
Marin, P. (2009). *Blood in the Forum. The Struggle for the Roman Republic* (London).
Marshall B. (1985). 'Catilina and the Execution of M. Marius Gratidianus', *Classical Quarterly* 35, 124–133.
Masters, J. (1992). *Poetry and Civil War in Lucan's Bellum Civile* (Cambridge).
Matyszak, P. (2023). *Julius Caesar in Egypt: Cleopatra and the War in Alexandria* (Barnsley).
Meier, C. (1995). *Caesar. A Biography* (London).
Meyer, E. (1919). *Caesars Monarchie und das Prinzipat des Pompejus* (Stuttgart).
Miączewska, A. (2014). 'Quintus Fufius Calenus: A Forgotten Career', *Hermathena* 196/197, 163–204.
Meijer, F. (1986). 'Marius' Grandson', *Mnemosyne* 39, 112–121.
Melchior, A. (2009). 'What Would Pompey Do? Exempla and Pompeian Failure in the "Bellum Africum"', *Classical Journal* 104, 241–257.
Millar, F. (1994). 'Popular Politics at Rome in the Late Republic', in I. Malkin and Z. Rubinsohn (eds.) *Leaders and Masses in the Roman World: Studies in Honor of Zvi Yavetz* (Leiden), 91–113.
Miola, R. (1985). 'Julius Caesar and the Tyrannicide Debate', *Renaissance Quarterly* 38, 271–289.
Mitchell, H. (2023). 'On Not Joining Either Side: The Discourse of Elite Neutrality in Roman Civil War' in H. Börm, U. Gotter, and W. Havener. (eds.). *A Culture of Civil War? Bellum Civile and Political Communication in Late Republican Rome* (Stuttgart), 31–64.
Morgan, L. (1997). 'Levi Quidem de re...': Julius Caesar as Tyrant and Pedant', *Journal of Roman Studies* 87, 23–40.
———. (2000). 'The Autopsy of C. Asinius Pollio', *Journal of Roman Studies* 90, 51–69.
Morrell, K. (2017). *Pompey, Cato, and the Governance of the Roman Empire* (Oxford).
Morstein-Marx, R. (2007). 'Caesar's Alleged Fear of Prosecution and His "Ratio Absentis" in the Approach to the Civil War', *Historia* 56, 159–178.
Niccolini, G. (1934). *I fasti dei tribuni della plebe* (Milan).
Osgood, J. (2006). *Caesar's Legacy: Civil War and the Emergence of the Roman Empire* (London).
———. (2015). 'Ending Civil War at Rome: Rhetoric and Reality, 88 BC–197 AD', *American Historical Review* 120, 1683–1695.
———. (2022). *Uncommon Wrath: How Caesar and Cato's Deadly Rivalry Destroyed the Roman Republic* (Oxford).
Östenberg, I. (2013) '"Veni Vidi Vici" Ano Caesar's Triumph', *Classical Quarterly* 63, 813–27.
———. (2014). 'Triumph and Spectacle. Victory Celebrations in the Late Republican Civil Wars', in C. Lange and F. Vervaet (eds), *The Roman Republican Triumph. Beyond the Spectacle* (Rome), 181–193.
Peaks, M. (1903). 'Caesar's Movements, January 21 to February 14, 49 BC', *Classical Review* 18, 346–349.
Peer, A. (2015). *Julius Caesar's Bellum Civile and the Composition of a New Reality* (London).
Pelling, C. (1973). 'Pharsalus', *Historia* 22, 249–259.
Pina Polo, F. (2006). The Tyrant Must Die. Preventative Tyrannicide in Roman Political Thought', in F. Simon, F. Pina Polo and J. Rodirguez (eds). *Republicas y Ciudadanos: Modelos De Participacion Civica en el Mundo Antiguo* (Barcelona), 71–101.
———. (2008) 'Hispania of Caesar and Pompey: A Conflict of Clientelae?', in M. García-Bellido, A. Mostalac, A. Jiménez (eds.) *Del Imperium de Pompeyo a la Auctoritas de Augusto. Home-naje a Michael Grant* (Madrid), 41–48.

——. (2017). 'Pompey's Clientelae in Hispania: A Reappraisal', in M. Haake and A. Harders (eds.), *Politische Kultur und soziale Struktur der Römischen Republik* (Stuttgart), 269–285.

——. (2019). 'Losers in the Civil War between Caesarians and Pompeians. Punishment and Survival', in K-J Hölkeskamp and H. Beck (eds.) *Verlierer und Aussteiger in der Konkurrenz unter Anwesenden. Agonalität in der politischen Kultur des antiken Rom* (Stuttgart), 147–168.

Pocock, L. (1959). 'What Made Pompeius Fight in 49 BC?', *Greece & Rome* 6, 68–81.

Postgate, J. (1905). 'Pharsalia Nostra', *Classical Review* 19, 257–260.

Powell, A. and Welch, K. (1998). *Julius Caesar as Artful Reporter: The War Commentaries as Political Instruments* (Swansea).

——. (2002). *Sextus Pompeius* (London).

Pucci Ben Zeev, M. (1996). 'When was the title "Dictator perpetuus" given to Caesar?' *L'antiquité classique* 65, 251–253.

Raaflaub, K. (2003). 'Caesar the Liberator? Factional Politics, Civil War, and Ideology.' In F. Cairns and E. Fantham (eds.). *Caesar Against Liberty? Perspectives on his Autocracy* (Cambridge). 35–67.

Ramsey, H. and Raaflaub, K. (2017). 'Chronological Tables for Caesar's Wars (58–45 BC)', *Histos* 11, 162–217.

Rawson, E. (1978). 'The Identity Problems of Q. Cornificius', *Classical Quarterly* 28, 188–201.

Reubel, J. (1994). *Caesar and the Crisis of the Roman Aristocracy. A Civil War Reader* (Oklahoma).

Ridley, R. (1981). 'The Extraordinary Commands of the Late Republic: A Matter of Definition', *Historia* 30, 280–297.

——. (1983). 'Pompey's Commands in the 50's: How Cumulative?' *Rheinisches Museum für Philologie* 126, 136–148.

——. (2000). 'The Dictator's Mistake: Caesar's Escape from Sulla', *Historia* 49, 211–229.

——. (2004). 'Attacking the World with Five Cohorts; Caesar in January 49', *Ancient Society* 34, 127–152.

Riggsby, A. (2006). *Caesar in Gaul and Rome: War in Words* (Austin).

Rondholz, A. (2009). 'Crossing the Rubicon: A Historiographical Study', *Mnemosyne* 62, 432–450.

Rossi, A. (2000). 'The Camp of Pompey: Strategy of Representation in Caesar's Bellum Civile', *Classical Journal* 95, 239–256.

Rowe, G. (1967). 'Dramatic Structures in Caesar's Bellum Civile', *Transactions of the American Philological Association* 98, 399–414

Ryan, F. (1994). 'The Quaestorship of Favonius and the Tribunate of Metellus Scipio', *Athenaeum* 82, 505–521.

Sabin, P. (2000). 'The Face of Roman Battle', *Journal of Roman Studies* 90, 1–17.

Sage, E. (1920). 'The Senatus Consultum Ultimum', *Classical Weekly* 13, 185–189.

Sampson. G. (2005). *A re-examination of the office of the Tribunate of the Plebs in the Roman Republic (494 – 23 BC)* (Unpublished Thesis).

——. (2008). *The Defeat of Rome. Crassus, Carrhae and the Invasion of the East* (Barnsley).

——. (2010). *The Crisis of Rome. The Jugurthine and Northern Wars and the Rise of Marius* (Barnsley).

——. (2013). *The Collapse of Rome, Marius, Sulla, and The First Civil War 91–70 BC* (Barnsley).

——. (2017). *Rome, Blood, and Politics. Reform, Murder and Popular Politics in the Late Republic 146–70 BC* (Barnsley).

——. (2019). *Rome, Blood and Power: Reform, Murder and Popular Politics in the Late Republic 70–27 BC* (Barnsley).

——. (2020). *Rome and Parthia: Empires at War: Ventidius, Antony and the Second Romano-Parthian War, 40–20 BC* (Barnsley).

———. (2021). *Rome's Great Eastern War: Lucullus, Pompey, and the Conquest of the East, 74–62 BC* (Barnsley).
———. (2022). *The Battle of Dyrrhachium (48 BC). Caesar, Pompey, and the Early Campaigns of the Third Roman Civil War* (Barnsley).
———. (2023). *The Battle of Pharsalus (48 BC). Caesar, Pompey, and their Final Clash in the Third Roman Civil War* (Barnsley).
———. (2024). *The Battle of Thapsus (46 BC): Caesar, Metellus Scipio, and the Renewal of the Third Roman Civil War* (Barnsley).
Seager, R. (1979). *Pompey. A Political Biography* (Oxford).
Shackleton-Bailey, D. (1960). 'The Roman Nobility in the Second Civil War', *Classical Quarterly* 10, 253–26.
Sirianni, F. (1979). Caesar's Decision to Cross the Rubicon', *L'Antiquité Classique* 48, 636–638.
———. (1993). 'Caesar's Peace Overtures to Pompey', *L'Antiquité Classique* 62 (1993), 219–237.
Smith, R. (1957). 'The Conspiracy and the Conspirators', *Greece & Rome* 4, 58–57.
Southern, P. (1998). *Mark Antony* (Stroud).
———. (2002). *Pompey the Great* (Stroud).
Stanton, G. (2003). 'Why Did Caesar Cross the Rubicon?', *Historia* 52, 67–94.
Stem, S. (1999). *Cicero and the Legacy of Cato Uticensis* (Unpublished).
———. (2005). 'The First Eloquent Stoic: Cicero on Cato the Younger', *Classical Journal* 101, 37–49.
Sternkopf, W. (1912). 'Die Verteilung der Römischen Provinzen vor dem Mutinensischen Kriege', *Hermes* 47, 321–401.
Stevenson, T. (2015). 'Appian on the Pharsalus Campaign: Civil Wars 2.48–91.' in K. Welch (ed.), *Appian's Roman History. Empire and Civil War* (Swansea), 257–275.
Storch, R. (1973). 'The Author of the De bello Hispaniensi: A Cavalry Officer?', *Classical Journal* 68, 381–383.
Stothard, P. (2020). *The Last Assassin: The Hunt for the Killers of Julius Caesar* (London).
Sumner, G. (1977). 'The Pompeii in their Families', *American Journal of Ancient History* 2, 8–25.
Syme, R. (1938). 'The Allegiance of Labienus', *Journal of Roman Studies* 28, 113–125.
———. (1939). *The Roman Revolution* (Oxford).
———. (1980). 'No Son for Caesar?', *Historia* 29, 422–437.
Tatum, W. (2008). *Always I Am Caesar* (Oxford).
———. (2024). *A Noble Ruin: Mark Antony, Civil War, and the Collapse of the Roman Republic* (Oxford).
Taylor, L. (1941). 'Caesar's Early Career', *Classical Philology* 36, 113–132.
———. (1957). 'The Rise of Julius Caesar', *Greece & Rome* 4, 10–18.
———. (1949). *Party Politics in the Age of Caesar* (Berkeley).
Tempest, K. (2017). *Brutus: The Noble Conspirator* (Yale).
Treggiari, S. (1969). 'Pompeius' freedman biographer again', *Classical Review* 19, 264–266.
Tucker, R. (1988). 'What Actually Happened at the Rubicon?' *Historia* 37, 245–248.
Tyrrell, W. (1972). 'Labienus' Departure from Caesar in January 49 BC', *Historia* 21, 424–440.
van Ooteghem, J. (1954). *Pompee le Grand. Batisseur d' Empire* (Bruxelles).
Veith, G. (1920). *Der Feldzug von Dyrrhachium zwischen Caesar und Pompeius* (Wien).
Vervaet, F. (2006). 'The Official Position of Cn. Pompeius in 49 and 48 BC', *Latomus* 65, 928–953.
von Fritz, K. (1942). 'Pompey's Policy before and after the Outbreak of the Civil War of 49 BC', *Transactions and Proceedings of the American Philological Association* 73, 145–180.
von Ravensburg, A. (1961). *Burgerkrieg Zwischen Casar Und Pompejus, Im Jahre 50/49 V. Chr. Und Die Kampfe Dei Dyrrhachium Und Pharsalus.*

Watts, E. (2019). *Mortal Republic: How Rome Fell into Tyranny* (London).
Weigel, R. (1974). 'Lepidus Reconsidered', *Acta Classica* 17, 67–73.
——. (1992). *Lepidus: the Tarnished Triumvir* (London).
Welsh, K. (1995). 'Antony, Fulvia, and the Ghost of Clodius in 47 BC', *Greece & Rome* 42, 182–201.
——. (1995). 'The Career of M. Aemilius Lepidus 49–44 BC', *Hermes* 123, 443–454.
——. (1998). *Julius Caesar as Artful Reporter: The War Commentaries as Political* (London).
——. (2012). *Magnus Pius. Sextus Pompeius and the Transformation of the Roman Republic* (Swansea).
——. (2015). *Appian's Roman History: Empire and Civil War* (Swansea).
Westall, R. (2013). 'The Relationship of Appian to Pollio.' *Analecta Romana Instituti Danici* 38, 7–34.
——. (2015). 'The Sources for the Civil Wars of Appian of Alexandria', in K. Welch (ed.). *Appian's Roman History. Empire and Civil War* (Swansea), 125–167.
——. (2016). 'The Sources of Cassius Dio for the Roman Civil Wars of 49–30 BC', in C. Lange and J. Madsen (eds.) *Cassius Dio. Greek Intellectual and Roman Politician* (Leiden), 51–75.
——. (2017). *Caesar's Civil War. Historical Reality and Fabrication* (Leiden).
Wiseman, T. (1996). 'Crossing the Rubicon, and Other Dramas', *Scripta Classica Israelica* 15, 152–158.
——. (2010). 'The Two-Headed State: How Romans Explained Civil War', in B. W. Breed, C. Damon, and A. Rossi (eds.). *Citizens of Discord. Rome and its Civil Wars* (Oxford). 25–44.
Wylie, G. (1989). 'Why Did Labienus Defect From Caesar in 49 BC?', *Ancient History Bulletin* 3, 123–127.
——. (1992). 'The Road to Pharsalus', *Latomus* 51, 557–565.
Woolf, G. (2007). *Et Tu Brute? The Murder of Caesar and Political Assassination* (Cambridge).
Yarrow, L. (2006). *Historiography at the End of the Republic: Provincial Perspectives on Roman Rule* (Oxford).
Yates, D. (2011). 'The Role of Cato the Younger in Caesar's "Bellum Civile"', *Classical World* 104, 161–174.
Yavetz, Z. (1971). 'Caesar, Caesarism, and the Historians', *Journal of Contemporary History* 6, 184–201.

Index

Adriatic, 6–7, 10–12, 14, 25, 44
Aemilius Lepidus, M. (Cos. 78 BC), 16, 148
Aemilius Lepidus, M. (Cos. 46 & 42 BC), 27, 43, 49, 63, 114, 117, 122, 134, 138, 143
Afranius, L. (Cos. 60 BC), 8–9, 22, 35–6, 43, 50–1, 81–2, 117
Africa, 4, 6–8, 10–11, 14, 16, 21–33, 35–6, 41–48, 50–2, 54, 56–8, 61, 63, 67, 70, 71, 81, 83–4, 88, 102–103, 105, 144, 116–18, 121, 142, 148
Alexander III (Macedonian King), 20, 24, 41–2, 135, 142
Alia, Battle of (48 BC), 27
Alchaudonius, 123–4
Allobroges, 49
Annius Milo, T. (Tr. 57 BC), 53, 122
Antipater, 123–4
Antistius Vetus, C. (Cos. 30 BC), 60, 122–4
Antonius, C. (Pr. 44 BC), 11
Antonius, M. (Cos. 44, 34 & 31 BC), 11, 23, 25, 29, 43, 62, 114, 117, 122, 127, 134, 137–8, 140, 142–3, 146, 153
Apamea, 58, 122–6
Aponius, Q., 49, 61
Appuleius Saturninus, L. (Tr. 103, 100 & 99 BC), 141
Arabio, 114, 117–18
Aristogeiton, 150
Armenia, 124
Ascurum, Battle of (46 BC), 45
Asia, 4, 11, 23–4, 55, 58–60, 120–2, 124–6
Asinius Pollio, C. (Cos 40 BC), 114–16
Ategua, 66–8, 71–4, 77, 82
Athens, 26, 134
Atia, 64
Attius Varus, P. (Pr. c.53 BC), 8, 22, 35–7, 44, 46–8, 50, 65, 76, 82–3, 95

Baebius, 153–4
Baetis, River, 66, 104
Balearic Islands, 35, 45–9, 52
Bagradas River, Battle of (49 BC), 42, 47, 83
Bithynia, 59–60, 122, 124–6
Bocchus II (Maurian King 49–33 BC), 27, 81, 83, 117–18
Bogud (Maurian King 49–31 BC), 27, 81, 83, 87–8, 90
Bosporan Kingdom, 15, 41, 55, 121, 124, 143
Brundisium, 6, 11, 25
Brundisium, Battle of (49 BC), 6

Caecilius Bassus, 56–61, 105, 121–7, 135, 157, 163–5
Caecilius Metellus, L. (Tr. 49 BC), 142
Caecilius Metellus Pius Scipio Nasica, Q. (Cos. 52 BC), 11–13, 21–2, 31–2, 34–6, 43–8, 54, 58, 61–2, 77–8, 105, 121, 136
Caecilius Niger, 103
Caelius Rufus, M. (Pr. 48 BC), 27
Caesennius Lento, 107–108
Caesetius Flavius, L. (Tr. 44 BC), 139–40, 142
Calpurnius Bibulus, M. (Cos. 59 BC), 60
Camp Postumius, Battle of (45 BC), 68
Carrinas, C. (Cos. 43 BC), 114–15
Carruca, 76
Carteia, 95, 101, 105–106, 108, 114
Carteia, Battle of (46/45 BC), 65
Carrhae, Battle of (53 BC), 4, 33, 54, 60, 120, 135, 147
Cassius Longinus, C. (Pr. 44 BC), 15, 20, 56, 106, 108, 125–7, 143, 147–50, 152–3
Cassius Longinus, Q. (Tr. 49 BC), 27, 48, 50, 102
Celtiberians, 51

Cilicia, 58–9, 121–2, 124–5, 147–8, 150
Civil War, First (91–70 BC), 3–4, 7–8, 19, 23, 27, 44, 50, 52, 55, 58, 105, 115, 132, 134, 148, 151
Civil War, Second (63–62 BC), 145
Claudia, 149
Claudius Marcellus, M. (Cos. 51 BC), 134–5
Claudius Marcellus Aeserninus, M. (Cos. 22 BC), 27, 48
Claudius Pulcher, Ap. (Cos. 54 BC), 148
Cleopatra VII (Ptolemaic Pharaoh 51–30 BC), 16, 53, 63
Colline Gate, Battle of (82 BC), 115
Corcyra, 14, 24
Corduba, 64–7, 69–70, 95, 97, 101–103, 105, 113
Corduba, Battles of (48 BC), 27, 66–7
Corfinium, Battle of (49 BC), 6
Cornelius Cinna, L. (Cos. 87–84 BC), 23, 44, 148, 152
Cornelius Dolabella, P. (Cos. 44 BC), 11, 29, 127, 137, 143
Cornelius Scipio Aemilianus, P. (Cos. 147 & 134), 145
Cornelius Sulla, F., 22, 36, 43, 117
Cornelius Sulla, L. (Cos. 88 & 80, Dict. 82–81 BC), 3, 23, 115, 132, 134, 138, 141–2, 144–5, 148–9, 151
Cornificius, Q. (Pr. 45 BC), 25, 59–60
Cydnus, River, 147, 150
Cyrene, 14, 16, 20–1, 24

Didius, C., 49, 62, 65, 105–106, 108–109, 112, 118
Domitius Ahenobarbus, L. (Cos. 54 BC), 6, 19
Domitius Calvinus, Cn. (Cos. 53 & 40 BC), 138
Duumvirate (Pompeius & Crassus), 41
Duumvirate (Brutus & Cassius), 149
Dyrrhachium, 7, 12, 14, 16, 153–4
Dyrrhachium, Battle of (48 BC), 12–13, 32, 35–6, 45, 47, 54, 61, 71, 80, 90, 97

Eastern War (74–62 BC), 55, 120
Epidius Marcellus, C. (Tr. 44 BC), 139–40, 142
Epirus, 11–12, 30–1

Fabius Maximus, Q. (Cos. 45 BC), 52–3, 64–5, 69, 100–11, 136–7
Fufius Calenus, Q. (Cos. 47 BC), 26

Gabinius, A. (Cos. 58 BC), 25, 154
Gades, 106–107, 109
Gaul, Cisalpine, 3, 10, 53, 144, 149
Gaul, Narbonensis, 143
Gaul, Transalpine, 10
Getae, 153

Hadrumetum, Battle of (46 BC), 30–2
Harmodius, 150
Helvius Cinna, C. (Tr. 44 BC), 140
Herod (Judean King 37–4 BC), 124
Hispalis, 103–104, 107, 109, 112

Ilerda, Battle of (49 BC), 9, 42, 152
Illyria, 5–7, 10–11, 19, 21, 23–5, 27–8, 31, 153–5
Iulia, 132
Iulius Caesar, C. (Cos 59, 48, 46–44 BC), 3–37, 41–93, 95–8, 101–27, 131–55
Iulius Caesar, L., 135
Iulius Caesar, Sex., 60, 121
Iunia, 149
Iunius Brutus Albinus, D. (Pr. 45 BC), 133, 144, 149–51
Iunius Brutus, L. (Cos. 509 BC), 148
Iunius Brutus, M (Pr. 44 BC), 20, 53, 108, 125, 133, 135, 143, 147–54

Juba I (Numidian King c.85–46 BC), 8, 21–2, 32, 35–6, 41–3, 46–7, 50, 117–18
Judea, 60, 121, 124

Labienus, T. (Pr.?), 22, 32–7, 45–6, 48, 50–1, 60, 62, 64, 66, 70–1, 74, 76–8, 80, 82–4, 87–91, 93, 95, 101–102, 113, 119, 121, 146
Labienus, Q., 132
Licinius Crassus, L. (Cos. 95 BC), 132
Licinius Crassus, M. (Cos. 70 & 55 BC), 3–4, 20, 33, 41, 60, 123, 127, 131, 142, 147, 151
Licinius Lucullus, L. (Cos. 74 BC), 123
Ligarius, Q., 151
Lusitanians, 73, 103–104, 106, 108–109, 112

Macedonia, 12–13, 26, 56, 153
Magius Cilo, P., 134–5
Marcius, Crispus, Q. (Pr. 46 BC), 69, 123, 125–6
Marius, C. (Cos. 107, 105–100, 87 BC), 3, 5, 21, 23, 41–2, 58, 131–3, 144, 151
Marius, C. (Cos. 82 BC), 132
Marius, C., 132–4
Marius, M., 132
Marius Gratidianus, M. (Pr. 85–84 BC), 132
Masinissa, 117–18
Massilia, 9–10, 27, 49, 149
Mauri, 21, 26–7, 36, 48, 81, 83, 87–8, 117–18
Megara, 26
Mesopotamia, 4, 58, 148
Minucius Basilus, L. (Pr. 45 BC), 150–1
Mithridates, 57, 132
Mithridates VI (Pontic Emperor 120–63 BC), 24
Munatius Flaccus, L., 72–4
Munda, 76–80, 84, 90, 92, 96–7, 101, 103–104, 109–11
Munda, Battle of (45 BC), 4–5, 81, 83, 88, 91, 102, 111, 116–19, 122, 127, 131, 134, 137–8, 151
Mytilene, 135

Nasidius, L., 28
Naulochus, Battle of (36 BC), 127, 155
New Carthage, 50, 115–16, 119
Northern War (113–101 BC), 132
Numidia, 7–8, 10, 21–2, 26–7, 31–6, 41–2, 44–7, 61, 76, 81, 83, 117–18, 136, 142

Octavius, C. (Cos. 43, 33, 31–23 BC), 63–4, 113, 133–4, 138, 152
Octavius, M., 21, 24–6
Oricum, 125
Orodes II (Parthian Emperor 57–37 BC), 60, 124

Pacorus, 123–5, 127
Parthian Empire, 62, 105, 118, 120–1, 124–7, 132, 135, 151, 153
Pedius, Q. (Cos. 43 BC), 52–3, 64–5, 69, 133, 136

Peloponnese, 14, 19, 24, 26
Petreius, M. (Pr. c.64 BC), 8–9, 22, 32, 34, 42, 45
Pharnaces II (Bosporan King c. 97–47 BC), 15, 18, 23–4, 55, 59
Pharsalus, Battle of (48 BC), 4, 9, 13–16, 19–20, 23–6, 28, 31–3, 35, 42–8, 51, 54–5, 60–1, 77–8, 83, 92, 95, 101, 105, 120, 131, 135, 142–3, 147–9, 151
Philippi, Battles of (42 BC), 127
Pompeius, Sex., 22, 36, 47–8, 66, 95, 108, 112–19, 126–7, 144, 152, 155
Pompeius Magnus, Cn., 4, 22, 35–6, 43–55, 62–91, 95, 98, 101–102, 104–109, 111–12, 132–4
Pompeius Magnus, Cn. (Cos. 70, 55, 52 BC), 3–24, 26, 33, 36, 41–2, 54–6, 61, 64, 77–8, 90, 101, 103, 105, 108, 113, 120, 123, 127, 131, 133, 135, 139, 141, 143–5, 147–8, 151–3
Pompeius Strabo, Cn. (Cos. 89 BC), 55
Pontic Empire, 59
Pontius Aquila, 151
Porcia, 149–50
Porcius Cato, M. (Pr. 54 BC), 7, 21–2, 30, 36, 42–5, 54–5, 57, 97, 102, 136, 142, 144–5, 149
Praeneste, 132
Ptolemaic Empire, 16, 18, 41, 55, 60, 120
Ptolemy XII (Ptolemaic Pharaoh c.80–58 BC), 16
Ptolemy XIII (Ptolemaic Pharaoh 51–47 BC), 16, 23
Ptolemy XV (Caesarion) (Ptolemaic Pharaoh 44–30 BC), 53, 63, 133

Quintius Scapula, T., 49, 61, 101–102

Rhone, River, 41
Romano-Gallic War (58–50 BC), 45, 77, 149
Romano-Parthian War, First (55–50 BC), 23–4, 54, 56, 59–60, 117, 120–1, 125, 127, 135, 142, 147, 151–2
Romano-Pontic War, Fourth (48–47 BC), 18, 41, 55, 59, 120, 148
Rubicon, 3, 6, 32, 45, 116, 171
Rubrius Ruga, M., 151

Ruspina, Battle of (46 BC), 32–4, 36, 46, 61–2

Saburra, 118
Sacriportus, Battle of (82 BC), 132
Salonae, 154
Salsum, River, 68, 70–2
Sardinia, 7, 28, 32, 52
Scribonius Curio, C., 8
Seleucid Empire, 55, 121
Sempronius Gracchus, Ti. (Tr. 133 BC), 145
Sertorius, Q. (Pr. 83 BC), 44, 50, 58
Servilius Casca, C., 151
Servilius Isauricus, P. (Cos. 48 & 41 BC), 60, 122, 125
Sextius Naso, P., 151, 165
Sicily, 6–7, 11, 15, 28, 30, 32, 36, 47
Sittius, P., 56, 117–18
Soricaria, Battle of (45 BC), 75–6, 83
Spain, 4–5, 7–11, 21, 23, 25–9, 32, 36–7, 42–6, 48–9, 52–5, 58, 61, 63–5, 67, 70, 73, 76–8, 81–2, 90, 95–6, 102–106, 108–109, 111–19, 121–2, 125–7, 131–3, 135–6, 138, 143–6, 152–4
Spurius, M., 151
Staius Murcus, L. (Pr. 45 BC), 123, 125–7
Sulpicius Galba, Ser. (Pr. 54 BC), 125, 150
Syria, 53–61, 63, 105, 117–18, 120–7, 135, 138, 143, 147–8, 152

Tarquinius Superbus, L. (King 534–509 BC), 148
Thapsus, Battle of (46 BC), 4, 18, 34–6, 42–4, 46–9, 51–2, 54, 56, 58, 82–3, 92, 95, 101, 105, 117, 121, 131, 142, 151

Thessalonica, 6, 14
Three Hundred, 22, 30, 75, 142
Tillius Cimber, L. (Pr. 45), 125, 150–1
Trebonius, C. (Cos. 45 BC), 27, 48–52, 69, 81, 102, 137, 145–6, 149–51
Triumvirate (Pompeius, Crassus, Caesar), 126
Triumvirate (Scipio, Cato, Varus), 22, 44–5, 47, 82, 95
Triumvirate (Antonius, Lepidus, Caesar), 127
Tullius Cicero, M. (Cos. 63 BC), 20, 59, 124, 132, 134–5, 139, 144, 146–7, 150, 154
Tyre, 56–57

Ucubi, 68, 74–6
Ulia, 65–6
Ursao, 76, 111–12
Utica, 7, 30, 32, 36
Utica, Battle of (49 BC), 8
Uzitta, 34, 84

Vatinius, P. (Cos. 47 BC), 25–7, 153–4
Ventidius Bassus, P. (Pr. & Cos. 43 BC), 127
Via Egnatia, 12
Vibius Paciaecus, L., 66
Vibius Pansa Caetronianus, C. (Cos. 43 BC), 60
Vipsanius Agrippa, M. (Cos. 37, 28 & 27 BC), 62, 155
Volcatius Tullus, L. (Cos. 33 BC), 124–5

Zela, Battle of (47 BC), 41, 59, 120, 152

Dear Reader,

We hope you have enjoyed this book, but why not share your views on social media? You can also follow our pages to see more about our other products: facebook.com/penandswordbooks or follow us on X @penswordbooks

You can also view our products at www.pen-and-sword.co.uk (UK and ROW) or www.penandswordbooks.com (North America).

To keep up to date with our latest releases and online catalogues, please sign up to our newsletter at: www.pen-and-sword.co.uk/newsletter

If you would like a printed catalogue with our latest books, then please email: enquiries@pen-and-sword.co.uk or telephone: 01226 734555 (UK and ROW) or email: uspen-and-sword@casematepublishers.com or telephone: (610) 853-9131 (North America).

We respect your privacy and we will only use personal information to send you information about our products.

Thank you!